# STUDY GUIDE

David VanHoose
*University of Alabama*

Brenda Abbott
*Northern Alberta Institute of Technology*

Sam Fefferman
*Northern Alberta Institute of Technology*

# Economics Today:
# The Micro View

Second Canadian Edition

Roger LeRoy Miller
*Institute for University Studies, Arlington, Texas*

Brenda Abbott
*Northern Alberta Institute of Technology*

Sam Fefferman
*Northern Alberta Institute of Technology*

Ronald K. Kessler
*British Columbia Institute of Technology*

Terrence Sulyma
*Northern Alberta Institute of Technology*

Addison
Wesley
Longman

Toronto

ISBN 0-201-71689-5

Acquisitions Editor: Dave Ward
Developmental Editor: Laurie Goebel
Production Editor: Marisa D'Andrea
Production Coordinator: Janette Lush

6 7 8 9 DPC 07 06 05 04

Printed and bound in Canada.

# CONTENTS

# PREFACE

## TO THE STUDENT

This study guide is designed to help you understand, review, and apply the theory, the issues, and the policies presented in the text *Economics Today: The Micro View*, Second Canadian Edition. In each study guide chapter, you are encouraged to:

- begin by getting an overview of where you are in the course and where you are going next.
- familiarize yourself with the economics jargon and concepts in the chapter before proceeding to more comprehensive problems.
- concentrate on applying the theory in the chapter to real-world applications after completing the comprehensive problems.

## THE CONTENTS OF THE STUDY GUIDE

Both the sequencing and content of each study guide section provide you with thorough coverage of economic theory, policy, and applications covered in your text.

1. *Putting This Chapter Into Perspective*
   This section shows you where the particular chapter fits into the big picture.
2. *Learning Objectives*
   This list contains approximately ten things you will be able to do after you have completed the chapter.
3. *Chapter Outline*
   This section presents a sentence outline for the chapter. It provides you with a quick overview of the contents of each chapter.
4. *Key Terms and Concepts*
   This section provides a list of the most important terms and theoretical constructs used in the text chapter; these terms are crucial to your understanding and each is defined in the Glossary at the end of the Study Guide.
5. *Completion Questions*
   This set of short answer fill-in-the-blank questions is intended to test your knowledge of key terms and concepts and facts.
6. *True-False Questions*
   This section is another objective test to help you understand the chapter concepts in more depth. We explain what is wrong with each false statement in the answers section at the end of the Study Guide chapter.
7. *Multiple Choice Questions*
   The numerous multiple choice questions in each Study Guide chapter will help you identify areas that you may need to spend more time and effort on. Again, you will

find that in the answers section of the Study Guide chapter, the student is provided with a brief explanation of each multiple choice answer.

8. *Matching Questions*

The matching questions are intended to review and sharpen your understanding of the concepts that you have already read about and worked with in the text and the related Study Guide chapter. Once you have mastered the questions in this section you should be ready to tackle the more comprehensive questions and applications that will follow.

9. *Working with Graphs*

Because many students find working with graphs difficult, we have devoted an entire section in each of the chapters utilizing this very important tool of analysis. Many of the graphs presented in the Study Guide have numerical labels on the $x$ and $y$ axis, so as to make it easier for you to relate the graphic analysis to the economic concepts being explained and applied.

10. *Problems*

This section focuses on comprehensive problems that typically consist of utilizing and applying more than one chapter concept. As you work with these problems, you will gain a greater appreciation and deeper understanding of the economic theory.

11. *Business Section*

In this section, the economic theory in the text chapter is related or applied to a practical business problem. You will find that each business problem is classified according to the relevant functional area or field of business—marketing, accounting, finance, management, or small business. This section is consistent with the text's strong emphasis on applying economic theory to real-world applications.

12. *Answers*

We have placed the answers at the end of each Study Guide chapter, and not at the end of the Study Guide book. We believe that you will find this approach more convenient. Suggested answers to the text's *For Critical Analysis* questions in Example, International Example, Policy Example, and International Policy Example boxes also appear in the Study Guide answer section.

13. *Glossary*

Knowing the language of economics is crucial to understanding the economic theory and application in each chapter. We hope that by having all the key terms and concepts defined in one convenient place, such as at the end of the Study Guide, you will be reminded to check your understanding of the language if you are encountering difficulties with a question.

## HOW TO USE THIS STUDY GUIDE

As you begin to examine a new chapter in your text, we suggest you consider the following strategy:

1. Before reading the new chapter in your text, read the sections in the related Study Guide entitled *Putting This Chapter Into Perspective, Learning Objectives*, and *Chapter Outline*.
2. Read the *Chapter Summary* located at the end of your text chapter.
3. At this point, we suggest that you start on the first page of the text chapter and read the entire chapter. As you are reading, take note of the definitions provided in the margin of the text. Highlight the *Concepts in Brief* sections in your text chapter as you encounter them. Make sure that you read the brief real-world examples provided in the text, even if you do not fully understand how they relate to the theory in the chapter. Remember, these examples could be on your next exam.
4. After reading the text chapter once through, go back to the Study Guide. Take a quick look at the *Key Terms and Concepts*. Sharpen your pencil and start working on the Study Guide questions. Complete the questions in the order in which they are presented in the Study Guide. Remember to consult the *Glossary* at the end of the Study Guide if you are having problems with any terminology.
5. After you have checked your answer to the *Business Section* problems, we suggest that you return to the *For Critical Analysis* questions presented in the Example, International Example, Policy Example, and International Policy Example boxes in your text and see if you can now answer them. If you are having difficulties, take a look at the suggested solutions displayed in the Study Guide's *Answers to Example Questions for Critical Analysis*.

## HOW TO PREPARE FOR QUIZZES, TESTS, AND EXAMS

In studying for quizzes, tests, and exams, review the Study Guide and text as follows:
1. Review your course outline and compare it to the Table of Contents in your text.
2. In your text:
   a. Review those chapters covered in your course outline.
   b. Re-read the chapter openers.
   c. Review the *Concepts in Brief* found at the end of each section in the chapter.
   d. Re-read the *Chapter Summary* at the end of the chapter.
   e. Try the *Chapter Problems* at the end of the chapter. The answers for odd-numbered Problems are at the back of the text. The complete set of Problem answers (both odd- and even-numbered) appears in the *Instructor's Manual*.
3. In your Study Guide:
   a. Read the first three sections in your Study Guide—*Putting This Chapter Into Perspective, Learning Objectives*, and *Chapter Outline*.
   b. Review the key terms and concepts for each chapter assigned.
   c. Re-do the *Multiple Choice* sections of each assigned Study Guide chapter.
   d. Re-do the more comprehensive problems located in the *Working with Graphs* section, the *Problems* section, and the *Business Section*.

# CHAPTER 1

# THE NATURE OF ECONOMICS

## PUTTING THIS CHAPTER INTO PERSPECTIVE

The aim of Chapter 1 is to help you begin to get a feel for what economics is all about. The chapter defines economics and introduces the theory of economic behavior. Economists are concerned with how people actually behave in the economic arena *and not* with how they themselves describe their actions, motivations, and beliefs. We contend that people act in ways that promote their own (sometimes broadly defined) self-interest, and that they respond predictably to economic incentives.

By combining this theory of human behavior with the concept of marginal analysis and the "other things constant" assumption, economists are able to (1) generate numerous insights and testable theories about behavior, (2) explain widely disparate social phenomena, and (3) predict how people are likely to behave under numerous circumstances.

Although an understanding of Chapter 1 cannot possibly turn you into an economist, it can certainly begin to give you a feel for "the economic way of thinking." It is a good idea to re-read this chapter every three or four weeks, just to reinforce the important perspective that it provides.

## LEARNING OBJECTIVES

After you have read this chapter you should be able to

1. define economics.

2. define resource and wants.

3. distinguish between microeconomics and macroeconomics.

4. recognize the rationality assumption.

5. recognize the importance of marginal benefits and marginal costs in the process of making rational decisions.

6. recognize that economics is ultimately concerned with human behaviour.

7. recognize elements of an economic model, or theory.

8. distinguish between positive economics and normative economics, and be able to classify specific statements under each category.

9. define the major socio-economic goals.

10. recognize that theories can be used to understand how policies can relate to socio-economic goals

## CHAPTER OUTLINE

1. **Economics** is a social science that studies how people allocate limited **resources** to satisfy unlimited **wants**.
   a. Wants are the goods and services that people would consume if they had unlimited income.
   b. Because wants are unlimited and people cannot satisfy all their wants, individuals are forced to make choices about how to spend their income and how to allocate their time.

2. Economics is broadly divided into microeconomics and macroeconomics.
   a. **Microeconomics** studies decision making undertaken by individuals (or households) and by firms.
   b. **Macroeconomics** studies the behaviour of the economy as a whole; it deals with **aggregate** behaviour such as unemployment, the price level, and national income.

3. Economists assume that individuals are motivated by self-interest and respond predictably to opportunities for gain.
   a. The **rationality assumption** is that individuals act as if they were rational and hence will not undertake any action that would leave them worse off. This assumption implies that individuals will respond to **incentives**.
   b. In making rational choices, individuals compare marginal benefits with marginal costs.
   c. Self-interest often means a desire for material well being, but it can also be defined broadly enough to incorporate goals relating to love, friendship, prestige, power, and other human characteristics of human nature.
   d. By assuming that people act in a rational, self-interested way, economists can generate testable theories concerning human behaviour.

4. Economics is a Social Science.
   a. Economists develop **models**, or **theories**, which are simplified representations of the real world.
   b. Such models help economists to understand and predict economic phenomena in the real world. Models can be used to evaluate and formulate policies that can improve our individual or societal well being.
   c. Like other social scientists, economists usually do not perform laboratory experiments; instead, they typically examine what already has occurred in order to test their theories.
   d. Economic theories, like all scientific theories, are simplifications—and in that sense they are "unrealistic."
   e. Economists, like all scientists, employ assumptions; one important economic assumption is **ceteris paribus** or "all other things being equal."
   f. Models or theories are evaluated on their ability to predict, and not on the realism of the assumptions employed.
   g. Economic models relate to behaviour, not thought processes.

5. Economists maintain that the unit of analysis is the individual; members of a group are assumed to pursue their own goals rather than those of the group.

6. **Positive economics** is objective and scientific in nature, and deals with testable "if this, then that" hypotheses.

7. **Normative economics** is subjective and deals with value judgments, or with what "ought to be."

8. Commonly accepted socio-economic goals are: full employment, efficiency, economic growth, price stability and equitable distribution of income.

9. Economic models can be used to evaluate and formulate policies aimed at promoting socio-economic goals.

## KEY TERMS AND CONCEPTS

| | | |
|---|---|---|
| Economics | Aggregates | Positive economics |
| Resources | Rationality assumption | Normative economics |
| Wants | Incentives | Empirical |
| Microeconomics | Models, or theories | |
| Macroeconomics | Ceteris paribus assumption | |

## COMPLETION QUESTIONS
Fill in the blank or circle the correct term.

1. Economics studies how people allocate _____
   to satisfy _____.

2. Economics is a (natural, social) science.

3. Microeconomics deals with (individual units, the whole economy).

4. A nation's unemployment level is analyzed in (microeconomics, macroeconomics).

5. (Macroeconomics, Microeconomics) studies the causes and effects of inflation.

6. In economics we assume that people (do, do not) intentionally make decisions that will leave them worse off.

7. The rationality assumption is that individuals (believe, act as if) they are rational.

8. It is rational to choose a course of action when the marginal benefit of the action (is less than, exceeds) the marginal cost of the action.

9. Economists maintain that incentives (are, are not) important to decision making.

10. Economists define self-interest (narrowly, broadly).

11. Economists take the (individual, group) as the unit of analysis.

12. Economic models are (simplified, realistic) representations of the real world.

13. The *ceteris paribus* assumption enables economists to consider (one thing at a time, everything at once).

14. Economic statements that are testable by facts and are of an "if/then" nature are (positive, normative).

15. A superior economic policy promotes as many socio-economic goals as possible with (maximum, minimum) goal conflict.


## TRUE-FALSE QUESTIONS
Circle **T** if the statement is true, **F** if it is false. Explain to yourself why a statement is false.

T F   1. Economics is the study of how people allocate unlimited resources to satisfy limited wants.

T F   2.   Decisions regarding marriage, and the number of children to have, are outside the scope of economics as none of these decisions affect the use of one's resources.

T F   3.   Macroeconomics deals with aggregates, or totals, of economic variables.

T F   4.   When economists attempt to predict the number of workers a firm will employ, they are involved in macroeconomics.

T F   5.   The economist's definition of self-interest includes only the pursuit of one's own material well being.

T F   6.   Economists maintain that people respond in a predictable way to economic incentives.

T F   7.   The rationality assumption is that individuals attempt, quite consciously, to make rational economic decisions, and will admit to it.

T F   8.   Economists would argue that resources should continue to be allocated to activities that reduce criminal activity until all crime has been eliminated.

T F   9.   A model's usefulness depends crucially on the realism of the assumptions used in the model.

T F  10.   The statement "every working person should earn the same amount of income" is a positive statement.

T F  11.   The statement "if every working person receives a tax decrease, Canada's inflation rate will increase" is a positive statement.

T F  12.   One socio-economic goal is full employment.

**MULTIPLE CHOICE QUESTIONS**
Circle the letter that corresponds with the best answer.

1.   Economics is
   a.  a natural science.
   b.  nonscientific.
   c.  a social science.
   d.  usually studied through lab experiments.

2.    Economics focuses on
    a.  how unlimited resources are allocated to satisfy unlimited wants.
    b.  how unlimited resources are allocated to satisfy limited wants.
    c.  how limited resources are allocated to satisfy limited wants.
    d.  how limited resources are allocated to satisfy unlimited wants.

3.    Which of the following is not related to resources:
    a.  resources include labour, land, and machinery.
    b.  resources include goods and services that people consume.
    c.  resources refer to items that are used to produce goods and services.
    d.  resources are limited.

4.    Which of the following areas of study is concerned, primarily, with microeconomics?
    a.  the steel industry
    b.  inflation
    c.  the national unemployment rate
    d.  national income determination

5.    Macroeconomic analysis deals with
    a.  the steel industry.
    b.  how individuals respond to an increase in the price of gasoline.
    c.  inflation.
    d.  how a change in the price of energy affects a family.

6.    Economists maintain that Mr. Smith will usually make decisions that promote the interests of
    a.  his colleagues at work.
    b.  himself.
    c.  his class.
    d.  his race.

7.    The concept of making decisions *at the margin* means that
    a.  it is rational for one to choose an alternative as long it has some benefit.
    b.  it is rational for one to choose the lowest cost alternative.
    c.  it is rational to choose an alternative when its extra benefit exceeds its extra cost.
    d.  it is rational to choose an alternative when its extra cost exceeds its extra benefit.

8.    Ceteris paribus
    a.  refers to changing many variables at the same time.
    b.  is seldom practiced in laboratory research.
    c.  refers to the practice of examining how one variable relates to another variable, holding all other factors constant.
    d.  is another term for pursuing one's own self interest.

9.  An economic model is justifiably criticized if
    a.  its assumptions are unrealistic.
    b.  it cannot be tested in a controlled, laboratory experiment.
    c.  it fails to predict.
    d.  all of the above

10. Which of the following is a normative statement?
    a.  If price rises, people will buy less.
    b.  If price rises, people will buy more.
    c.  If price rises the poor will be less well off; therefore price should not be permitted to rise.
    d.  If price rises people will buy less; therefore we would expect to observe that quantity demanded falls.

11. Which of the following is a positive statement?
    a.  Full employment policies should be pursued.
    b.  If minimum wage rates rise, then unemployment will rise.
    c.  We should take from the rich and give to the poor.
    d.  The government should help the homeless.

12. Normative economics statements
    a.  are testable hypotheses.
    b.  are value-free.
    c.  are subjective, value judgments.
    d.  can be scientifically established.

13. Which of the following is **NOT** a commonly accepted socio-economic goal?
    a.  efficiency
    b.  equal distribution of income
    c.  economic growth
    d.  price stability

14. Suppose the government implements a policy that is aimed at increasing the number of skilled university and college graduates available to industry. This policy is most likely to promote the socio-economic goal of
    a.  efficiency
    b.  distribution of capital
    c.  economic growth
    d.  price stability

## MATCHING

Choose the numbered item in Column (2) that best matches the term or concept in Column (1).

| (1) | (2) |
|---|---|
| a.  microeconomics | 1.  nonscientific value judgments |
| b.  macroeconomics | 2.  objective, scientific hypotheses |
| c.  self-interest | 3.  study of individual behavior |
| d.  positive economics | 4.  study of economic aggregates |
| e.  normative economics | 5.  are the bases of policy |
| f.  socio-economic goals | 6.  rational behavior |
| | 7.  ceteris paribus |
| | 8.  limited resources |

## BUSINESS SECTION

### Finance: Fundamental Stock Investment Analysis

How might you go about determining whether to buy or sell a specific company stock? Obviously if you could predict the stock price, you would buy the stock if the price is predicted to increase in the near future, and possibly sell if the price is expected to fall. According to what is often called *fundamental stock analysis*, the single most important factor affecting a stock price is the expected profitability of the company that originally issued the stock. According to fundamental stock analysis, a company's stock price will increase if investors expect that the annual profit of this firm will increase significantly in the near future.

According to the fundamental analysis approach, the expected profit of any corporation will be affected by both *macroeconomic* and *microeconomic* factors. Macroeconomic factors would include broad global and national events and trends. In formulating profit expectations investors will also closely monitor microeconomic measures and trends at the specific industry and company level.

### Business Application Problem

For each event and hypothetical company listed below, determine whether the event
i. is a macroeconomic or microeconomic event
ii. will tend to increase or decrease the company's stock price. (Hint: predict how the event will affect the expected profit of the firm in question.)

   a.  *Event:* Due to the declining Canadian dollar (exchange rate) Canadian companies which export products to the U.S. experience a major increase in annual sales. Company: Timber Corp, a Canadian lumber company that exports 80% of their products.

b.   *Event:* Special taxes are imposed on Canadian firms manufacturing cigarettes.
Company: The Smoke Factory, a Canadian cigarette manufacturer.

c.   *Event:* With global inflation escalating out of control, investors lose confidence in
paper currency. As a result there is a worldwide trend towards the purchase of
items that investors feel will retain their value over time.
Company: Bre-Y Mining Corp, a large multinational gold mining firm.

d.   *Event:* As a result of new management, a department store is able to achieve the
same annual sales as the previous year at a much lower level of operating costs.
Company: Wardwoods, a Canadian clothing department store.

e.   *Event*: Due to an upward trend in Canadian interest rates, investors sell stocks in
all the major Canadian industries in order to purchase Canadian bonds.
Company: Morgan Mutual Fund, a corporation that manages investor funds by
buying blue chip stocks in a wide range of Canadian industries (on behalf of
investors).

### ANSWERS TO CHAPTER 1

**COMPLETION QUESTIONS**

1.   limited resources; unlimited wants
2.   social
3.   individual units
4.   macroeconomics
5.   macroeconomics
6.   do not
7.   act as if
8.   exceeds
9.   are
10.  broadly
11.  individual
12.  simplified
13.  one thing at a time
14.  positive
15.  minimum

**TRUE AND FALSE QUESTIONS**

1.   F   Economics is the study of how people allocate limited resources to satisfy unlimited wants.
2.   F   Marriage, and the decision to have children, is within the scope of economics as these decisions
do affect how one allocates his or her limited resources.

3.  T
4.  F   Microeconomics focuses on the individual firm, consumer, or industry.
5.  F   Economists define self-interest more broadly to include power, desire to help others, friendship, love, and so on.
6.  T
7.  F   That assumption is merely that people act as if they are rational, even if they do so unconsciously.
8.  F   Economists would argue that resources should continue to be allocated to criminal reducing activities only as long as the marginal benefit exceeds the marginal cost.
9.  F   All models employ simplified and somewhat unrealistic assumptions; what matters is how well they predict.
10. F   This is a normative statement as it is a value judgement and the validity of this statement cannot be tested with facts.
11. T
12. T

## MULTIPLE CHOICE QUESTIONS

1.  c; Economics is a social science concerned with studying human behaviour.
2.  d; Economics is a social science that studies how people allocate limited resources to satisfy unlimited wants.
3.  b; Resources are items used to produce goods and services; they are not the goods and services themselves.
4.  a; Microeconomics focuses on the individual consumer, firm, or industry.
5.  c; Macroeconomics studies the behavior of the economy as a whole. Inflation measures the increase in the prices of all goods and services in the economy.
6.  b; Individuals are motivated by self-interest.
7.  c; Making decisions at the margin means choosing an alternative when the marginal (extra) benefit exceeds the marginal (extra) cost.
8.  c; Ceteris paribus is a common practice in all types of scientific research. It refers to the practice of examining how one variable relates to another variable, holding all other factors constant.
9.  c; A good model should yield usable predictions and implications for the real world.
10. c; This statement contains the value judgement that the poor should never be made less well off. *TIP:* Normative economics involves value judgements.
11. b; This statement is value free, and can be tested by factual evidence.
12. c; Normative statements are based on what one prefers, likes, or desires.
13. b; Equitable or "fair" distribution of income is a socio-economic goal. Many people would not consider an equal distribution of income to be equitable or fair, if some work harder than others.
14. c; Economic growth, which means an economy with the ability to increase its rate of production in the future, due to a more skilled workforce.

## MATCHING

a and 3;  b and 4;  c and 6;  d and 2;  e and 1;  f and 5.

## BUSINESS SECTION

a.  i.  Macroeconomic event, as the decline in the Canadian dollar is a broad national trend.
    ii. Increase the stock price, as Timber Corp's sales will increase which will result in an increased profit.
b.  i.  Microeconomic event as the tax focuses on a specific industry – cigarette manufacturing.
    ii. Decrease the price of the stock. A tax increase will raise the costs of production and reduce the annual profit.

    c.   i.    Macroeconomic event, as the inflation is a broad global factor.
          ii.   Increase the stock price. When inflation is out of control, investors often
                purchase gold, as it has historically been popular in times of economic crisis.
                As gold prices rise, the profits of gold mines increase.
    d.   i.    Microeconomic event as this is a factor that affects the specific firm in
                question.
          ii.   Increase the stock price. When sales stay the same but operating costs
                decrease, the annual profit will increase.
    e.   i.    Macroeconomic event as interest rate trends tend to be a nationwide
                phenomenon.
          ii.   Decrease the stock price. Since investors are selling stocks across all
                industries, this reduces stock  prices, which, in turn, reduces the profit of
                Morgan Mutual Fund.

## ANSWERS TO EXAMPLE QUESTIONS FOR CRITICAL ANALYSIS

I.   **EXAMPLE 1-1: The Brain Drain: It Works Both Ways** (p. 4)
Nurses from other countries who typically earn less than nurses in the United Kingdom, acting in their own self interest, will likely fill the void resulting from the brain drain.

II.  **INTERNATIONAL POLICY EXAMPLE 1-1: Chinese Smuggling** (p. 5)
Any actions that reduce the benefits or increase the costs incurred from smuggling cigarettes and diesel oil into China, will reduce the incentives to smuggle. There are a number of policies that would reduce the benefits derived from smuggling. If the Chinese government lowered the domestic taxes on cigarettes manufactured in China, this would reduce the profit derived from exporting the cigarettes and then smuggling them back into China. Similarly, if the price of domestically produced diesel oil is lowered, this would reduce the profit resulting from smuggling foreign produced diesel oil into the country. One way the government could increase the costs of smuggling is to significantly increase the criminal penalty attached to the act of smuggling goods into China.

III  **EXAMPLE 1-2: What Does a Year at College Really Cost?** (p. 6)
Jane did not correctly determine the cost related to the decision to enroll in college full-time for eight months. She should only add the *extra* or *marginal* costs which would be the tuition, books, college fees and the income she sacrifices from not working full-time for eight months. This implies that the total costs of going to college would be \$2,580 + (8 months) x (\$1,100 per month) = \$11,380 for the eight months spent at college.

IV  **EXAMPLE 1-3: Giving Charity to Oneself?** (p. 7)
The evidence that low-income households contribute a higher portion of their income to charity than those with higher incomes can be explained in terms of rational cost-benefit behaviour. When compared to a high income household, the total extra (marginal) benefits that the low income household derives over his or her lifetime is much more likely to exceed the extra costs incurred from contributing to these charities.

V.  **INTERNATIONAL EXAMPLE 1-1: Incentives Work for Pigeons and Rats, Too**
(p. 9)
The series of experiments with pigeons and rats illustrate how scientifically controlled experiments involve the application of the *ceteris paribus* concept. That is, in order to identify precise relationships between two variables, scientists must try to hold the effects of other related variables constant. In this case, the relationship between the "price" and "purchasing" behaviour is being precisely observed by holding constant the "income" or number of lever pushes per day. Therefore, the animals were responding to the "price" incentive factor when they changed their "purchasing" behaviour. The simple model one can formulate based on this experiment is that when the price of a good  is decreased, the animals will tend to increase their purchases of the good.

# CHAPTER 2

# SCARCITY AND THE WORLD OF TRADE-OFFS

## PUTTING THIS CHAPTER INTO PERSPECTIVE

Chapter 1 defined wants and stressed that none of us can satisfy all our wants. Chapter 2 starts with this notion and builds upon it.  We all want more things—both material and nonmaterial (such as love, friendship, and affection)—than our individual and collective resources permit.  Because we cannot have everything that we want, scarcity forces us to make choices.  We are all faced with trade-offs; if we want more of good A, we must give up other goods. The concept of opportunity cost helps us identify and quantify the trade-offs that result from choices. As this chapter shows, the opportunity cost concept helps to decide which resource combinations are efficient, and which are not.

Chapter 2 uses the production possibilities curve to illustrate concepts that arise from scarcity, such as trade-offs, opportunity costs, efficiency, and economic growth.

## LEARNING OBJECTIVES

After you have studied this chapter you should be able to

1. define scarcity, production, resources, land, labour, human and physical capital, entrepreneurship, goods, economic goods, services, opportunity costs, production possibilities curve, technology, productive efficiency, productively inefficient point, allocative efficiency, law of increasing relative costs, specialization, absolute advantage, comparative advantage, and division of labour.

2. distinguish between a free good and an economic good.

3. determine the opportunity cost of an activity, when given sufficient information.

4. draw production possibilities curves under varying assumptions, and recognize efficient and inefficient points relating to such curves.

5.  distinguish between productive efficiency and allocative efficiency.

6.  recognise the trade-off between current consumption goods and capital goods, and the implication for the economy's rate of economic growth.

7.  understand the difference between absolute advantage and comparative advantage.


**CHAPTER OUTLINE**

1.  Because individuals or communities do not have the resources to satisfy all their wants, **scarcity** exists.
    a.  If society can get all that it wants of good A when the price of good A is zero, good A is not scarce.
    b.  If the price of good B is zero, and society cannot get all that it wants of good B, then good B is scarce.
    c.  Because resources, or factors of production, are scarce, the outputs they produce are scarce.
        i.    **Land**, the natural resource, includes all the gifts of nature.
        ii.   **Labour**, the human resource, includes all productive contributions made by individuals who work.
        iii.  **Physical capital**, the resource manufactured by society, includes the machines, buildings, and tools used to produce other goods and services.
        iv.   **Human capital** encompasses the education and training of workers.
        v.    **Entrepreneurship** includes the functions of organizing, managing, assembling, and risk-taking that are necessary for business ventures.
    d.  Goods include anything from which people derive satisfaction, or happiness.
        i.    Economic goods are scarce.
        ii.   Non-economic goods are not scarce.
        iii.  **Services** are intangible goods.
    e.  Economists distinguish between wants and needs; the latter are objectively indefinable.

2.  Because of **scarcity**, choice and **opportunity costs** arise.
    a.  Due to **scarcity**, people trade off options.
    b.  The **production possibilities curve** (PPC) is a graph of the trade-offs inherent in a decision.
        i.    When the marginal cost of additional units of a resource or good remains constant, the PPC curve is a straight line.
        ii.   When the **Law of Increasing Relative Costs** applies, the PPC curve is bowed outward.

iii.    Any point on a PPC assumes a fixed level of **technology** and resources, where the resources are fully and efficiently employed.
iv.    Points inside a PPC reflect unemployment or productive inefficiency; points outside the PPC are unattainable by definition.
v.    If a nation is producing that mix of goods (point on the PPC) most valued by its consumers, **allocative efficiency** is achieved.

3.  Economic growth can be depicted through PPCs.
    a.  There is a trade-off between present consumption and future consumption.
    b.  If a nation produces fewer consumer **goods** and more capital **goods** now, then it can consume more goods in the future than would otherwise be the case. This would result in a higher rate of economic growth or a greater outward shift in the nation's PPC.

4.  a.  When nations specialize according to **comparative advantage** (not **absolute advantage**), this results in an increase in productivity.
    b.  **Division of labour** permits greater specialization and therefore increases output.

## KEY TERMS AND CONCEPTS

Production            Services                         Law of increasing relative costs
Land                  Scarcity                         Goods
Labour                Opportunity cost                 Consumption
Physical capital      Production possibilities curve   Specialization
Human capital         Technology                       Absolute advantage
Entrepreneurship      Productive efficiency            Comparative advantage
Economic goods        Allocative efficiency            Division of labour
Inefficient point

## COMPLETION QUESTIONS

Fill in the blank or circle the correct term.

1.  The factors of production include _____, _____, _____, _____, and _____.

2.  If at a zero price, quantity demanded exceeds quantity supplied for a good, that good is a(n) _____; if at a zero price quantity supplied exceeds quantity demanded for a good, that good is a(n) _____.

3.  The _____ of good A is the highest-valued alternative that must be sacrificed to attain it.

4.  If the cost of additional units of a good remains constant, the production possibilities curve will be (linear, bowed outward); if the cost of additional units of a good rises, the production possibilities curve will be (linear, bowed outward).

5.  Because specialized resources are more suited to specific tasks, the cost of producing additional units of a specific good will (rise, fall).

6.  If an economy is productively inefficient, its actual output combination will lie (inside, outside) the production possibilities curve.

7.  (Productive efficiency, Allocative efficiency) is concerned with producing the mix of goods and services most valued by consumers.

8.  (Consumer goods, Capital goods) contribute to economic growth.

9.  Productivity is enhanced when individuals, regions, and nations specialize in those activities for which they have a(n) (comparative, absolute) advantage.

10. When an autoworker specializes in the production of bumpers and another autoworker specializes in car doors, this is an example of the _____ .


**TRUE-FALSE QUESTIONS**

Circle **T** if the statement is true, **F** if it is false. Explain to yourself why a statement is false.

T  F  1.  Most people's wants are limited.

T  F  2.  Scarcity arises due to unlimited wants and limited resources.

T  F  3.  If the price to a specific user is zero, the good must be a non-economic good.

T  F  4.  Most activities have no opportunity cost.

T  F  5.  The cost to society of lowering the speed limit is zero.

T  F  6.  If a production possibilities curve is linear, the cost of producing additional units of a good rises.

T  F  7.  At any given moment in time, it is impossible for an economy to be inside its production possibilities curve.

T  F  8.  Economic growth shifts the production possibilities curve outward.

T  F    9.    People have little incentive to specialize in jobs for which they have a comparative advantage.

## MULTIPLE CHOICE QUESTIONS
Circle the letter that corresponds with the best answer.

1.    Because of scarcity
       a.  people are forced to make choices.
       b.  opportunity costs exist.
       c.  people face trade-offs.
       d.  all of the above.

2.    Which of the following is NOT considered to be "land"?
       a.  bodies of water
       b.  fertility of soil
       c.  sawmill
       d.  climate

3.    Which of the following words does NOT belong with the others?
       a.  opportunity cost
       b.  non-economic good
       c.  scarcity
       d.  economic good

4.    Which statement concerning a production possibilities curve is NOT true?
       a.  A trade-off exists along such a curve.
       b.  It is usually linear.
       c.  Points inside it indicate productive inefficiency.
       d.  A point outside it is currently impossible to attain.

5.    The production possibilities curve is bowed outward because
       a.  the relative cost of producing a good rises as more of it is produced.
       b.  of the law of decreasing relative costs.
       c.  all resources are equally suited to the production of any good.
       d.  all of the above.

6.    When a nation expands its capital stock, it is usually true that
       a.  it must forego output of some consumer goods in the present.
       b.  the human capital stock must decline.
       c.  fewer consumer goods will be available in the future.
       d.  no opportunity cost exists for doing so.

7. When nations and individuals specialize
   a. overall living standards rise.
   b. trade and exchange increases.
   c. people become more vulnerable to changes in tastes and technology.
   d. all of the above

8. Ms. Boulware is the best lawyer and the best secretary in town.
   a. She has a comparative advantage in both jobs.
   b. She has an absolute advantage in both jobs.
   c. She has a comparative advantage in being a secretary.
   d. all of the above

## MATCHING

Choose the numbered item in Column (2) that best matches the term or concept in Column (1).

| (1) | (2) |
|---|---|
| a. manufactured resource | 1. production possibilities curve |
| b. economic good | 2. specialization |
| c. opportunity cost | 3. capital |
| d. trade-offs | 4. ability to produce at a lower unit cost |
| e. productive inefficiency | 5. specializing in one's comparative advantage |
| f. absolute advantage | 6. society cannot get all it wants at a zero price |
| g. productivity increase | 7. highest-valued foregone alternative |
| h. comparative advantage | 8. inside the PPC |
| | 9. entrepreneur |
| | 10. labour |

## WORKING WITH GRAPHS

1. Given the following information, graph the production possibilities curve in the space provided and then use the graph to answer the questions that follow.

| Combination (points) | Autos (100,000 per year) | Wheat (100,000 tons per year) |
|---|---|---|
| A | 16 | 0 |
| B | 14 | 4 |
| C | 12 | 7 |
| D | 9 | 10 |
| E | 5 | 12 |
| F | 0 | 13 |

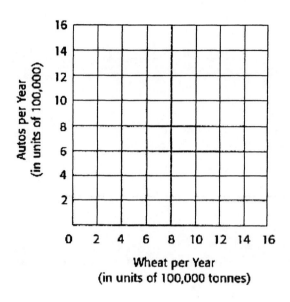

a.  If the economy is currently operating at point C, what is the opportunity cost of moving to point D? to point B?

b.  Suppose that the economy is currently producing 1,200,000 autos and 200,000 tons of wheat per year. Label this point in your graph with the letter G. At point G, the economy would be suffering from what? At point G we can see that it is possible to produce more wheat without giving up any auto production, or produce more autos without giving up any wheat production, or produce more of both. Label this region in your graph. This region appears to contradict the definition of a production possibilities curve. What is the explanation for this result?

c.  Suppose a new fertilizer compound is developed that will allow the economy to produce an additional 150,000 tons of wheat per year if no autos are produced. Sketch in a likely representation of the effect of this discovery, assuming all else remains constant.

d.  What sort of impact (overall) will this discovery have on the opportunity cost of more wheat production at an arbitrary point on the new production possibilities curve, as compared to a point representing the same level of output of wheat on the original curve?

2.  Consider the graphs below, then answer the questions that follow.

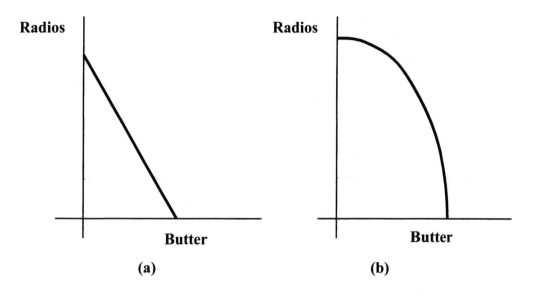

(a)                              (b)

a.  Which graph, (a) or (b), shows constant relative costs of producing additional units of butter?  Why?

b.  Which graph, (a) or (b), shows increasing relative costs of producing additional units of butter?  Why?

c.  Which graph seems more realistic, (a) or (b)?  Why?

3.      As an elected government official, you are particularly concerned with how your nation's limited resources are allocated in the production of various capital and consumer goods. The graph below describes alternate production possibilities for the next budget year (year 2003) for your country.

Production Possibility Curve for the Year 2003

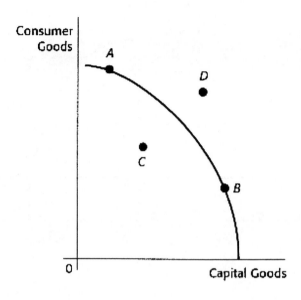

a.  Provide examples of consumer goods.

b.  Provide examples of capital goods.

c.  Which of the production combinations labeled above would be considered a productively inefficient point?

d.  Which of the production combinations labeled above is unattainable in the year 2003? What makes this point unattainable?

e.  Which production combination - **A** or **B** - will result in a higher rate of economic growth in future years?

f.  Which production combination would you feel more comfortable borrowing funds for (i.e. running a deficit)—combination **A** or **B**? Briefly explain.

g.  In general, what is the opportunity cost of choosing a production combination that will result in a very high rate of economic growth? Explain.

4.  Graph the probable relationship between
   a.  Income and the amount of money spent on housing.
   b.  Annual rainfall in Vancouver and the annual value of ice cream sales in Montreal.
   c.  Number of vegetarians per 10,000 people and meat sales per 10,000 people.

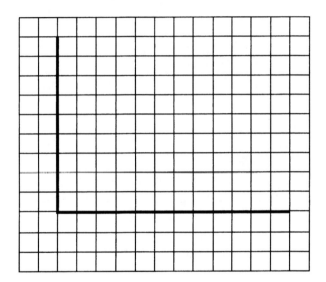

**PROBLEMS**

1.  If a *nation* wants to increase its future consumption it must forego some present consumption because it must allocate some resources to the production of capital goods.  Suppose *you* want to increase your future consumption, given a fixed lifetime income, what can you do?

2.  Suppose you have a friend currently working as a salesperson in a local computer store.  She is thinking about going back to school full-time to finish her computer science degree.  Your friend explains that she earns $15,000 (after taxes) per year in her current job, and that she estimates tuition will cost $1,600 per year.  In addition, she estimates fees, supplies, books, and miscellaneous expenses associated with attending school will run $800 per year.  She wants to attend a university that is located directly across the street from the store where she currently works.  She claims that she pays $350 per month for rent and utilities and that she spends about $200 per month on food.

Using what you have learned, calculate and explain to your friend the opportunity cost to her of another year back at school.

3.    Assume that Ms. Gentile values her time at $50 per hour because she has the opportunity to do consulting, and that Joe College values his time at $2 per hour. Assume that it costs $400 to fly from their hometown to Vancouver, and that the flight takes 6 hours.  Assume that it costs $200 to take a bus, and that the bus trip takes 24 hours.

   a.  What is the cheaper way for Ms. Gentile to get to Vancouver?  Why?

   b.  Which transportation is cheaper for Joe College?  Why?

4.    The Hughes family consists of Mr. Hughes, Mrs. Hughes, and their son, Scotty. Assume that Mr. Hughes can earn $30 per hour (after taxes) any time he chooses, Mrs. Hughes can earns $5 per hour, and the family values homemaker activities at $6 per hour.

   a.  Because the family requires income to purchase goods and services, who will probably work in the marketplace?

   b.  Who will probably do the housework?

   c.  If the family must pay $3 per hour to have its lawn mowed, who will be assigned that work?

   d.  If Scotty can now earn $4 per hour on a job, who now might mow the grass?

   e.  If wage rates in the marketplace for Mrs. Hughes rise to $7 per hour, what is the family likely to do?

## BUSINESS SECTION

### Finance: Is Deficit Financing Always Undesirable?

Deficit financing refers to the practice of having to incur a new debt when purchasing a good. Understanding the difference between *consumer* and *capital goods* may shed some light on whether or not deficit financing is appropriate. In general, economists are more likely to suggest financing capital goods on a deficit basis than consumption goods. Since most of the benefits of a capital good accrue in future periods, it is rational to borrow funds and then gradually pay back the loan in the future when the benefits of the investment good accrue. This holds true in the case of both private and public sector goods as the following problem will illustrate.

### Business Application Problem

For each pair of goods listed below, indicate which good is better suited to deficit financing.

a.   Spending $20,000 on a "fully loaded" sportscar vs. spending $20,000 obtaining a Bachelor Of Commerce Degree

b.   Constructing a civic convention center vs. constructing community leisure pools with water slides.

c.   Constructing an exercise gym on the work site which is to be freely available to your employees vs. paying for free trips to Mexico on behalf of your employees.

d.   An insurance salesman purchases an annual seasons pass to a posh golf course vs. a college instructor purchases an annual seasons pass to a posh golf course.

e.   Constructing an expensive, beautifully designed city hall vs. subsidizing the city's major league sports team.

### ANSWERS TO CHAPTER 2

#### COMPLETION QUESTIONS

1.   land, labour, physical capital, human capital, entrepreneurship
2.   economic good; non-economic good
3.   opportunity cost
4.   linear; bowed outward
5.   rise

6.  inside
7.  Allocative efficiency
8.  Capital goods
9.  comparative
10. division of labour

## TRUE-FALSE QUESTIONS

1.  F    Wants are unlimited, regardless of a nation's standard of living.
2.  T
3.  F    If, at a price of zero, there exists an excess demand for the product, this is an economic good.
4   F    An opportunity cost exists for most activities due to the problem of scarcity.
5.  F    If people drive more slowly they suffer opportunity costs for the extra time spent on the road.
6.  F    A linear PPC implies a constant cost of additional production.
7.  F    Productive inefficiency or unemployment often causes an economy to be inside its  PPC.
8.  T
9.  F    People can earn more income in jobs for which they have a comparative advantage.

## MULTIPLE CHOICE QUESTIONS

1. d; Limited resources and unlimited wants will cause all three to be true.
2. c; A sawmill is capital, not land.
3. b; All the others relate to scarcity.
4. b; The law of increasing relative costs causes the curve to be bowed outward.
5. a; This is the law of increasing relative costs.
6.. a; If additional limited resources are allocated to capital goods, less resources are
        available for consumer goods.
7. d; If specialization increases, trade and exchange must also increase.
8. b; She produces both services at a lower cost.
    *TIP:* Absolute advantage is the ability to produce a good or service at an absolutely lower cost, while
    comparative advantage is the ability to produce at a lower opportunity cost compared to others.

## MATCHING

a and 3;   b and 6;   c and 7;   d and 1;   e and 8;   f and 4;   g and 5;   h and 2;

## WORKING WITH GRAPHS

1.    See the following graph.

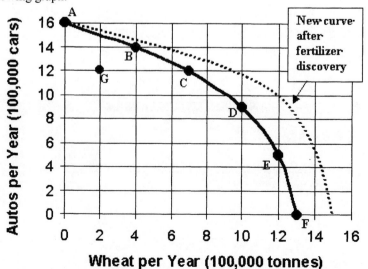

    a.    The move from C to D "costs" 300,000 autos—that is, the economy must give up 300,000 autos (1,200,000 - 900,000) to make such a move. The move from C to B "costs" 300,000 tons of wheat. Notice that in both cases there are gains (C to D involves 300,000 more tons of wheat and C to B means 200,000 more autos are produced), but we measure opportunity costs in terms of movements along a production possibilities curve and what has to be given up to make the choice reflected in the move.

    b.    See the preceding graph. Remember, the production possibilities curve shows all possible combinations of two goods that an economy can produce by the efficient use of all available resources in a specified period of time. Since point G is not on the production possibilities curve, the statement contained in this portion of the question does not contradict the definition of the curve. Point G is inside the curve, which implies available resources are not being used efficiently.

    c.    See the preceding graph.

    d.    It will lower the opportunity cost of additional wheat production.

2.    a.    Graph (a) shows constant relative costs because the PPC is linear.

    b.    Graph (b) shows increasing costs because the PPC is bowed outward.

    c.    Graph (b) is more realistic because it is likely that the production of radios and butter requires specialized resources.

3.    a.    vacations, automobiles for personal enjoyment, computer games, city swimming pools, dining at restaurants, visiting the local pub, watching videos etc.

    b.    new machinery, new equipment, new plant facilities, credit education, city convention centers, computer hardware and software used for business purposes ,etc.

    c.    **C**.

    d.    **D;**   due to the fixed level of resources and technology related to the year 2003.

    e.    **B**.

    f.    **B**. If one wisely borrows for capital goods, the resulting economic growth should more than pay for the principal and interest related to the borrowed funds.

    g.    lower consumption in the current year as illustrated when comparing combination **A** with **B**.

4.    a.    The graph should be upward sloping from left to right.

    b.    There should be no systematic relationship between these two variables.

    c.    The graph should be downward sloping from left to right.

## PROBLEMS

1.    If you want to increase your future consumption (for retirement, say) then you will have to save more out of your current income. The principal and interest that accrue will permit you to purchase more goods in the future than you otherwise would have been able to. Note that by doing so you must forego some present consumption in order to increase your future consumption. In that sense, what is true for the nation is also true for an individual.

2.    The opportunity cost of another year back at school for your friend is as follows:

| | |
|---|---|
| Foregone after-tax salary | $15,000 |
| Tuition costs | 1,600 |
| Expenses associated with school | 800 |
|     Total opportunity costs | $17,400 |

3.    a.    plane; flying costs her $400 plus 6 hours times $50 per hour, or $700, while taking a bus would cost her $200 plus 24 hours times $50 per hour, or $1400.

    b.    bus; taking the bus costs him a total of $248 while the total cost of flying is $412.

4.    a.    Mr. Hughes

    b.    Mrs. Hughes or Scotty

    c.    Scotty

    d.    The family (or perhaps Scotty) will hire someone to mow the lawn.

    e.    Mrs. Hughes may enter the labour force and the family may hire someone to do housework.

**BUSINESS SECTION**

    a.   A Bachelor of Commerce Degree is a capital good from an individual's view, to the extent that it increases the individual's future earning power.

    b.   A civic convention center would be considered to be a capital item from a city's viewpoint. One of the primary uses of this type of government resource is to generate revenues for the city in future years by bringing in visitors or convention delegates who will spend money on the city's hotels, restaurants, shops, and entertainment spots. Also, new business can be generated for firms in the cities who showcase their products and services through events like trade shows.

    c.   The exercise gym can be viewed as a capital item from the employer's view, to the extent it contributes towards a healthier, more productive employee who is rarely absent from work.

    d.   The seasons pass would more likely be a capital good for the insurance salesman to the extent that he meets potential clients on the golf course.

    e.   From a city's view, it would seem that a sports team would more likely enhance future revenues as opposed to a city hall. The sports team would bring in players and fans from outside the city. As a result, more money would be spent on the city's hotels, restaurants, shops, and entertainment spots.

**ANSWERS TO EXAMPLE QUESTIONS FOR CRITICAL ANALYSIS**

**I.   POLICY EXAMPLE 2-1: The Multi-Million Dollar Park** (p. 22)

One can use the concept of opportunity cost to estimate the minimum value of the protected wilderness area. In this case, the social value of the Muskwa Kechika land use area is at least equal to the hundreds of millions of dollars of oil that is being sacrificed, by protecting the wilderness area.

**II.   EXAMPLE 2-1: Teenagers Trade Off TV Time to Surf the Net** (p. 24)

If we are simply measuring the time spent on each activity (and not productivity or satisfaction derived from the two activities) the production possibilities curve for television and Internet use would be a downward sloping straight line indicating an opportunity cost of one hour of TV use for every additional hour of Internet use.

**III.   EXAMPLE 2-2: Economic Growth Due to Harder Working Workers** (p. 28)

In 1996, since labour productivity decreased by 0.1 percent, this factor alone would cause the production possibilities curves in Canada to shift inward, ceteris paribus. The increase in labour productivity in 1999 would cause the production possibilities curves in Canada to shift outward. However, in 1999, the unemployment problem would be described as points inside the expanded production possibilities curves.

**IV.   INTERNATIONAL EXAMPLE 2-1: Why the Light Turned Green Once the Trabi Was Parked** (p.31)

General Motors, Volkswagen, and Daimler-Chrysler gain from specialization, in many ways. First, as the article suggests, in many cases these auto manufacturers specialize in the assembly of the auto parts, rather than produce all the auto parts themselves. This way, these companies can become very proficient at the specific task of assembling new vehicles. As well, even in the assembly process, these auto manufacturers use assembly lines which encourage the specialization and division of labour. Thus, one team of workers might work on assembling bumpers, another team on installing brakes and so forth. This way each team becomes very efficient at completing its very specific or narrow task.

# CHAPTER 3

# ECONOMIES IN TRANSITION

## PUTTING THIS CHAPTER INTO PERSPECTIVE

This chapter studies how different economic systems answer the three fundamental questions facing all societies:  *what to produce, how to produce*, and *for whom goes the produce.*

Despite many years of central planning experience, command (communist) economies have not lived up to their economic promise; problems still abound in such economies. One major problem is the enormous administrative task involved in planning a modern economy; even sophisticated computers haven't been able to make a dent in the problem. Planners haven't been able to get around the problem of issuing specific orders or rules for production plans; enterprise directors and workers often find it advantageous to follow the letter, rather than the spirit, of the rules.  Finally, such economies have an enormous incentive problem; it is not easy to get people to be productive and innovative if they are not rewarded sufficiently.

It is not surprising, therefore, that communist economies have collapsed in the Soviet Union and in Eastern Europe.  While you are reading this chapter note how important property rights are; a successful economic system requires well-defined property rights.

Under capitalism private property rights to goods and services, including labour, are extended to individuals who make voluntary exchanges as buyers and sellers. Governments enforce such property rights. In Chapter 3, after examining the key features of capitalism, you will appreciate how this economic system answers the fundamental economic questions in a very decentralized manner.

Finally, you will sharpen your understanding of the relevant concepts presented in this chapter by studying the recent changes occurring in the Russian economy.

**LEARNING OBJECTIVES**

After you have studied this chapter you should be able to

1.  define economic system, resource allocation, command economy, capitalism, consumer sovereignty, laissez-faire, property rights, least-cost combination, mixed economy, and privatization.

2.  describe how market capitalism answers the three fundamental economic questions.

3.  recognize the least-cost combination of inputs.

4.  describe the four faces of capitalism.

5.  recognize the characteristics of the four stages of frontier capitalism.

6.  recognize the main elements of recent economic reforms in the Russian economic system.


**CHAPTER OUTLINE**

1.  One extreme type of economic system is the **command economy**; which has the following attributes:
    a.  Restricted private property rights with respect to the major factors of production.
    b.  Prices are (mostly) set by the state, not by the forces of supply and demand.
    c.  The mobility of labour and other resources is severely restricted; a centralized planning authority allocates resources.
    d.  "What", "how", and "for whom" are determined by the government.
    e.  Economic risk-taking is done by the state, not by individuals.
    f.  Taxation is used to redistribute income.

2.  In its theoretical form the  pure **capitalist economy** has the following attributes:
    a.  Private property rights are enforced by a judicial system.
    b.  Self interest governs decisions made by households and firms.
    c.  The economy is to serve the consumer- "consumer sovereignty".
    d.  A system of markets and prices guides the decisions of firms and resources.
    e.  Competition between sellers and buyers helps to ensure consumer sovereignty.
    f.  Limited government or "**laissez-faire**".

3.  Under capitalistic nations the price, or market, system answers the three economic questions.
    a.  The forces of supply and demand determine "What, and how much to produce"; market price must be sufficiently high to make a good profitable for producers to produce.

    b.  Profit maximization via the price system assures that the "How" question is answered so that the least-cost combination of resources will be used to produce outputs.

    c.  Under such a system "For Whom" is answered by the distribution of money income; those with high money incomes get more goods than those with low money incomes.

       i.   The quantity, quality, and type of the various human and non-human resources that a person owns determines his or her money income.

       ii.  A specific good or service is allocated to the highest bidders; hence the market rations each output to specific individuals.

    d.  Under capitalism voluntary exchanges in markets take place; as such, resources (inputs) are allocated to businesses, and goods and services (outputs) are allocated to households.

4.  Real-world economies are comprised of elements from both pure market capitalism and pure command socialism; they are **mixed economies**.  In the past many predicted that the two economic systems would converge, becoming more like the command economy; the collapse of the Soviet Union and Eastern-bloc economic systems changed this notion.  Today it appears that convergence will be toward the **mixed economy** model that exists in the United States.

5.  Because people respond to economic incentives, a successful economic system requires well-defined property rights that are enforced by the state; such a system encourages wealth creation.

6.  There are four faces of capitalism in existence:  consumer, producer, family, and frontier.

7.  When a centralized economy collapses, black markets arise, then small businesses emerge, followed by the development of financial markets; in the final stages of frontier capitalism foreign investments are attracted and **privatization** occurs.

8.  Russia, the most important part of the former Soviet Union, evolved into a system in which only a small elitist group lived well.

    a.  In its transition phase it is experiencing a crime wave.

    b.  As property rights emerge and a legal system develops, it is hoped that crime will abate.

## KEY TERMS AND CONCEPTS

| | |
|---|---|
| Economic system | Three P's |
| Resource allocation | Mixed economy |
| Pure command economy | Privatization |
| Pure capitalist economy | Laissez faire |

**COMPLETION QUESTIONS**
Fill in the blank or circle the correct term.

1.  Resource allocation involves answering the three basic questions of _____, _____, and _____ goods and services will be produced.

2.  Under a command economy, economic decisions were made by (a central authority, many individuals); the closer we go to a pure capitalist economy, the (less, more) political centralization there is.

3.  One of the important features of a command economy is that the non-labour means of production are owned by the _____.

4.  Central planning is important under a_____(capitalist, command) economy.

5.  The forces that determine relative rewards from production in a command economy are set by the (market, government).

6.  People respond to incentives, therefore property rights (are, are not) important.

7.  In its purest form, capitalism has the following attributes: _____ _____, _____, _____ and _____.

8.  Under _____ (capitalism, communism) individuals have vast, government-protected private property rights.

9.  Markets (reduce, increase) transaction costs.

10. Under (a command economy, a price system) resources will be more likely allocated such that the least-cost combination will be chosen by producers.

11. Under capitalism specific goods and services are allocated to the (highest bidders, rich).

12. Real world economies are _____ economies, because they have elements of both _____ and _____ economies.

13. The four types (faces) of capitalism are _____, _____, _____, and _____.

14. In recent years Russia has become (less, more) decentralized; individuals have gained (less, more) control over economic decisions.

15. In 1989-90 command economies (i.e. communism) were demonstrated to be an obvious economic (failure, success).

**TRUE-FALSE QUESTIONS**
Circle the **T** if the statement is true, the **F** if it is false.  Explain to yourself why a statement is false.

T  F  1.  In a command economic system (communism), producers follow the commands of many individuals, through the market.

T  F  2.  Under communism, all factors of production are owned by the state.

T  F  3.  In real world communist economies, no wage rate differentials existed.

T  F  4.  In command economies, economic risk-taking was undertaken mostly by individual enterprises.

T  F  5.  In the real world, economies are a mixture of capitalistic and command economies.

T  F  6.  In Russia, privatization has reduced criminal behaviour.

T  F  7.  Privatization is relatively painless for formerly command economies.


**MULTIPLE CHOICE QUESTIONS**
Circle the letter that corresponds to the best answer.

1.  Which of the following is **NOT** a key attribute of any actual command system?
    a.  The government owns the major productive resources.
    b.  A high degree of individual incentives motivates production.
    c.  Relative rewards for production are set by the state.
    d.  Production is guided by central planning.

2.  In command economies,
    a.  all factors of production were owned by the state.
    b.  no wage differentials existed.
    c.  an economic plan was developed by government decision makers.
    d.  households did not own durable goods.

3.  Under capitalism
    a.  income inequality is too extreme.
    b.  a price system allocates resources.
    c.  central planning plays a huge role.
    d.  what to produce is determined, in theory, by the government.

4.  For a capitalist economic system to be successful
    a.  a legal system must be developed.
    b.  property rights must be defined and enforced.

    c.  incentives must be provided to people.
    d.  All of the above

5.    In recent years the Russian economy is moving toward
    a.  less income inequality.
    b.  more privatization.
    c.  more government control of industry.
    d.  dramatic increases in private property rights.

6.    In the Russian economy recently there have been plans for
    a.  restructuring the economy.
    b.  reforming the price system.
    c.  increasing incentives by allowing more income inequality.
    d.  All of the above.

7.    As of the early 1990s, Russian economic reforms have
    a.  been extremely successful.
    b.  not been particularly successful.
    c.  transformed the Soviet economy into market capitalism.
    d.  None of the above

## MATCHING
Choose the numbered item in Column (2) that best matches the term or concept in Column (1).

| (1) | (2) |
| --- | --- |
| a.  what, how, for whom | 1.  transfer property rights from the government to the private sector |
| b.  command system | 2.  fundamental economic questions |
| c.  capitalist system | 3.  central planning |
| d.  least-cost combination | 4.  three P's |
| e.  privatization | 5.  allocative efficiency |
|  | 6.  productive efficiency |

## PROBLEMS

1.  The following questions illustrate how the three basic economic questions- *what, how,* and *for whom* – are all interrelated in a capitalist system.
    a.  Explain how *for whom* is affected if *what* changes, for example if tastes change in favor of figure skating and away from professional football.

b.  Explain how *for whom* is affected if *how* changes because unions increase wage rates relative to other factors of production.

c.  Explain how a change in *for whom* (taxing some and giving to others) might change *what* to produce.

2.  Assume that, given its resource base, an economy is able to produce output combinations A, B, C, and D.  Society values combination A at $10,000, combination B at $20,000, combination C at $30,000, and combination D at $15,000.
    a.  What is the opportunity cost of producing combination A?

    b.  What is the opportunity cost of producing combination B?

    c.  What is the opportunity cost of producing combination C?

    d.  What is the opportunity cost of producing combination D.

    e.  If the community wanted to maximize the value of its output, given its resource base, which combination should it produce?

    f.  If the community wanted to minimize the opportunity cost of its output, which combination would it choose?

**BUSINESS SECTION**
**Marketing: The Evolution of Marketing in a Capitalist System**

Economies in transition may find it instructive to examine how the concept or philosophy of successful marketing has changed as capitalist economies have matured.

Historically, the first concept of the marketing process was called the *production concept*. Here the firm focuses on the product itself rather than the customers needs. The prevailing view is that a quality or cheap product will sell itself.

As capitalism evolved, and competition increased, the *selling concept* became a popular view. Emphasis shifted to developing a strong sales force and aggressive promotional efforts to convince consumers to buy whatever the firm produces.

In mature capitalist economies the *marketing concept* has been adopted by many successful, well known companies. Firms who practice the marketing concept are successful in motivating all employees in the firm to understand the needs and wants of their target markets. After the target customer's wants and needs are identified, the firm proceeds to develop a profitable marketing mix – product, price , promotion and place – that responds to the target market.

**Business Application Problem**

Classify each of the following as  either the *production concept*, *selling concept*, or *marketing concept*.

a.  Harvey Gunn, a materials engineer, wants to start a new shoe manufacturing business to act out his dream of making shoes that never wear out.

b.  After studying the long distance phone call patterns of a customer, the phone company designs a long distance plan tailored to the phone customer's needs.

c.  After massive TV advertising, consumer purchases  of digital cameras skyrocket, even though the picture quality is inferior to the cheaper conventional cameras.

d.  A personal care products company convinces a large group of consumers to use body wash  products by aggressive promotions including free giveaway offers of body wash sponges. No conclusive evidence exists to suggest that the more expensive body wash products are an improvement over the conventional soap products.

e.  When a large university was investigating the reasons for low class enrollments, it was discovered that the mix of courses offered was solely based on the interests of the professors of the university.

f.  A large multinational restaurant chain offers a different menu in different countries based on extensive market research and ethnic and cultural diversity.

## ANSWERS TO CHAPTER 3

### COMPLETION QUESTIONS

1.  what, how, for whom
2.  a central authority; less
3.  state
4.  command
5.  government
6.  are
7.  private ownership of resources, self-interest, consumer sovereignty, markets and prices, competition, limited government.
8.  capitalism
9.  reduce
10. a price system
11. highest bidders
12. mixed, command, capitalist
13. consumer, producer, family, and frontier.
14. more, more
15. failure

### TRUE-FALSE QUESTIONS

1.  F  Commands are set by a centralized government.
2.  F  Labour is not completely owned by the state.
3.  F  They existed, and in some cases were quite large.
4.  F  It was assumed by the state.
5.  T
6.  F  Privatization without court enforced property rights has increased criminal behaviour.
7.  F  Prices and unemployment typically rise in the short run.

### MULTIPLE CHOICE QUESTIONS

1.  b;  There is a low degree of individual incentive to be productive as rewards are set by the state.
2.  c;  Centralized government committees determined production plans.
3.  b;  Under market capitalism a system of prices set by supply and demand factors in markets guides resource allocation decisions.
4.  d;  Individuals will only have the incentive to specialize in production and transfer private property rights to the extent that a legal system develops which protects private property rights and enforces contracts.
5.  b;  More resource allocation decisions are made by privately owned enterprises .
6.  d;  As Russia has taken on the face of frontier capitalism, all .of the above features apply to Russia.

7.  b; In the absence of well defined private property rights, Russia's transition towards capitalism has been accompanied by a significant amount of crime.

## MATCHING

a and 2;    b and 3;    c and 4;    d and 6;    e and 1

## PROBLEMS

1.  a.  The incomes of football players will fall; incomes of figure skaters will rise.  Thus a change in tastes (*what*) redistributes income from one group to another, and so *for whom* changes.

    b.  If wage rates rise relative to the price of capital and land, then producers will increase their demand for non-labour resources; non-labour resources will be substituted for labour.  Income will be redistributed from some newly laid-off labourers to people who own property or are skillful at designing and producing capital.  Thus a change in *how* leads to changes in *for whom*.

    c.  To the extent that people with low incomes have tastes different than people with high incomes, then "taxing the rich to give to the poor" will affect *what* is produced .

2.  a.  $30,000          c.  $20,000          e.  C
    b.  $30,000          d.  $30,000          f.  C

## BUSINESS SECTION

a.  production concept    b.  marketing concept    c.    selling concept
d.  selling concept       e.  production concept    f.    marketing concept

## ANSWERS TO EXAMPLE QUESTIONS FOR CRITICAL ANALYSIS

I.  **INTERNATIONAL POLICY EXAMPLE 3-1: A Booming Business in Facelifts by Russian Plastic Surgeons (p. 61)**

A Canadian planning to have a facelift in Russia would have the obvious cost of transportation to that country, along with the costs of staying there. These costs plus the cost of a facelift in Russia should be compared to the cost of a facelift in Canada. In addition, a facelift is a surgical procedure that could disfigure or seriously injure a person. A Canadian contemplating a facelift in Russia should be aware that there is no recourse in the Russian courts for malpractice. Therefore, he or she may have to have the procedure done again at his or her own expense. Thus, the consumer would have to incur search costs to find a reputable plastic surgeon.

# CHAPTER 4

# DEMAND AND SUPPLY

## PUTTING THIS CHAPTER INTO PERSPECTIVE

This chapter is one of the most important chapters in the text. To students who take the time to study it, the returns are exceptionally high. Chapter 4 analyzes the economist's most indispensable tools: demand and supply. Specifically, in this chapter you will study (a) demand and supply, (b) how demand and supply determine equilibrium (or market-clearing) price, (c) how periods of surpluses or shortages result if price is not at the equilibrium level, and (d) how the equilibrium level can change in response to changes in non-own-price factors.

It is important that you master the material in this chapter, because you will be applying and reapplying these same tools and principles to many different situations. When presented with a problem, the economist will first try to express the problem in terms of the concepts of demand and supply and then proceed to economic analysis proper. It is with this thought in mind that an anonymous writer once noted: "You can make even a parrot into a learned economist—all it must learn are the two words *supply* and *demand*."

Mastering Chapter 4, however, will require some time. Many pitfalls to understanding economics can be avoided if you learn and understand the key definitions in this chapter. You must understand *exactly* what demand and supply mean; *exactly* what quantity demanded and quantity supplied mean; *exactly* what a change in demand and a change in supply mean; *exactly* what a surplus and a shortage mean. A universal confusion exists for students and others about the distinction between a change in demand (or supply) and a change in quantity demanded (or quantity supplied). Similarly, unless you know exactly what a shortage or a surplus is, you will be continually misinterpreting economic events.

## LEARNING OBJECTIVES

After you have studied this chapter you should be able to

1.  define demand schedule, quantity demanded, supply schedule, quantity supplied, equilibrium, shortage, and surplus.

2.  state the law of demand and state two reasons why we observe the law of demand.

3.   graph a demand curve from a demand schedule.

4.   enumerate five non-own-price determinants of demand.

5.   predict the effects of a change in the price of one good on the demand for (a) a substitute good, and (b) a complementary good.

6.   predict the effects of an increase in income on the demand for (a) a normal good, and (b) an inferior good.

7.   recognize, from graphs, the difference between a change in demand and a change in quantity demanded.

8.   graph a supply curve from a supply schedule.

9.   enumerate five non-own-price determinants of supply

10.  recognize, from graphs, the difference between a change in supply and a change in quantity supplied.

11.  determine from a supply curve (schedule) and a demand curve (schedule) what the equilibrium price and the equilibrium quantity will be.

12.  explain how markets eliminate surpluses and shortages.

13.  predict what happens to equilibrium price and equilibrium quantity when supply increases or decreases relative to demand, and when demand increases or decreases relative to supply.


**CHAPTER OUTLINE**

1.  The **law of demand** states that at higher prices a lower quantity will be demanded than at lower prices, other things being equal.
    a.  For simplicity, things other than the price of the good itself are held constant.
    b.  Buyers respond to changes in **relative prices**, not absolute, prices.

2.  The demand schedule for a good is a set of pairs of numbers showing various possible prices and the quantity demanded at each price, for some time period.
    a.  **Demand** must be conceived of as being measured in constant-quality units.
    b.  A **demand curve** is a graphic representation of the demand schedule and it is negatively sloped, reflecting the law of demand.
    c.  A **market demand** curve for a particular good or service is derived by summing all the individual demand curves for that product at each price.

3. The determinants of **demand** include all factors (other than the good's own price) that influence the amount purchased.
   a. When deriving a **demand curve**, other determinants of demand are held constant. When such non-price determinants do change, the original demand curve shifts to the left (decrease in demand) or to the right (increase in demand).
   b. The major determinants of demand are consumers' income, tastes and preferences, changes in their expectations about future relative prices, the price of **substitutes** and **complements** for the good in question, population, and age composition of the population.
   c. A **normal good** is one in which consumer income is directly related to the demand for the good. An **inferior good** is one in which consumer income is inversely related to the demand for the good.
   d. If the price of good B is directly related to the demand for Good A, then A and B are substitutes. If the price of good B is inversely related to the demand for Good A, then A and B are complements.
   e. A change in demand is a shift in the demand curve, whereas a change in quantity demanded is a movement along a given demand curve.

4. **Supply** is the relationship between price and the quantity supplied, other things being equal.
   a. The **law of supply** states that a direct or positive relationship between price and quantity supplied exists, other things being equal.
      i. As the **relative price** of a good rises, producers have an incentive to produce more of it.
      ii. As a firm produces greater quantities in the short run, a firm often requires a higher relative price before it will increase output.
   b. A supply schedule is a set of numbers showing prices and the quantity supplied at those various prices.
   c. A **supply curve** is the graphic representation of the supply schedule; it is positively sloped.
   d. By summing individual supply curves for a particular good or service, at each price, we derive that good or service's market supply curve.
   e. The major determinants of supply are the prices of resources (inputs) used to produce the product, technology, taxes and **subsidies**, price expectations of producers, and the number of firms in an industry.
   f. Any change in the determinants of supply (listed in part e) causes a change in supply and therefore leads to a shift in the supply curve.
   g. A change in price, holding the determinants of supply constant, causes a movement along—but not a shift in—the supply curve.

5. By graphing demand and supply on the same coordinate system, **equilibrium** can be found at the intersection of the two curves.
   a. **Equilibrium** is a situation in which the plans of buyers and of sellers exactly coincide, so that there is neither excess quantity supplied or excess quantity demanded; at the **equilibrium price**, quantity supplied equals quantity demanded.
   b. At a price below the equilibrium price, quantity demanded exceeds quantity

supplied, and excess demand, or a **shortage**, exists.

   c.  At a price above the equilibrium price, quantity supplied exceeds quantity demanded, and an excess **supply**, or a **surplus**, exists.

   d.  Seller competition forces price down, and eliminates a surplus.

   e.  Buyer competition forces price up, and eliminates a shortage.

6.  Changes in **demand** and/or **supply** lead to changes in the **equilibrium price** and the equilibrium quantity.

   a.  If the demand curve shifts to the right (left), given supply, then the equilibrium price rises (falls) and the equilibrium quantity rises (falls).

   b.  If the supply curve shifts to the right (left), given demand, then the equilibrium price falls (rises) and the equilibrium quantity rises (falls).

   c.  When both supply and demand change, it is not always possible to predict the effects on the equilibrium price and the equilibrium quantity.

## KEY TERMS AND CONCEPTS

| | | |
|---|---|---|
| Law of demand | Substitutes | Market clearing, or equilibrium price |
| Relative price | Complements | Subsidy |
| Demand | Money Price | Surplus |
| Demand curve | Market | Shortage |
| Market demand | Law of supply | Equilibrium |
| Normal goods | Supply | |
| Inferior goods | Supply curve | |

## COMPLETION QUESTIONS
Fill in the blank or circle the correct term.

1.  The law of demand is that, other things being equal, more is bought at a (lower, higher) price and less is bought at a _____ price.

2.  A _____ relates various possible prices to the quantities demanded at each price,.

3.  There is a(n) (direct, inverse) relationship between price and quantity demanded, and demand curves will be (positively, negatively) sloped.

4.  By convention, economists plot (price, quantity) on the vertical axis and (price, quantity) on the horizontal axis.

5.  A change in quantity demanded is a (movement along, shift in) the demand curve; and a change in demand is a _____ the demand curve.

6.   When the other determinants of demand change, the entire demand curve shifts; the five major non-own-price determinants of demand are _____, _____, _____, _____, and _____.

7.   Videocassettes and videocassette players are (substitutes, complements); if the price of videocassette players rises, then the demand for videocassettes will _____.

8.   When the price of peaches rises, the demand for pears rises; peaches and pears are (substitutes, complements).

9.   A rise in demand causes the demand curve to shift to the (left, right); an increase in quantity demanded occurs when there is a movement (up, down) the demand curve.

10.   Without a used CD market the quantity demanded for new CDs at a given price would be (smaller, larger).

11.   The law of supply relates prices to quantities supplied; in general, as price rises, quantity supplied (rises, falls). Therefore a(n) (direct, inverse) relationship exists, and the supply curve is (positively, negatively) sloped.

12.   A _____ relates various prices to the quantities supplied at each price.

13.   The supply curve is positively sloped because as price rises, producers have an incentive to produce (less, more).

14.   When the non-price determinants of supply change, the entire supply curve will shift; five major non-price determinants of supply are _____, _____, _____, _____, and _____.

15.   At the intersection of the supply and demand curves, the quantity supplied equals the quantity demanded, and at that price a(n) _____ exists; at a price above that intersection, quantity supplied exceeds quantity demanded and a(n) _____ exists; at a price below that intersection, quantity demanded exceeds quantity supplied, and a(n) _____ exists.

16.   *Analogy:*   An excess quantity supplied is to a surplus as a(n) _____ is to a shortage.

17.   If the demand for pizza rises, given the supply, then the equilibrium price of pizza will (rise, fall) and the equilibrium quantity will (rise, fall).

18.   If demand shifts to the left, given supply, then the equilibrium price will (rise, fall) and the equilibrium quantity will (rise, fall).

19.    If supply shifts to the right, given demand, then the equilibrium price will (rise, fall) and the equilibrium quantity will (rise, fall).

20.    If both demand and supply shift to the right then the equilibrium price (will rise, will fall, is indeterminate) and the equilibrium quantity (will rise, will fall, is indeterminate).

21.    If, at the same time, there is an increase in demand and a decrease in supply, then the equilibrium price (will rise, will fall, is indeterminate), and the equilibrium quantity (will rise, will fall, is indeterminate).

## TRUE-FALSE QUESTIONS
Circle the **T** if the statement is true, the **F** if it is false.  Explain to yourself why a statement is false.

T  F    1.    Buyers are concerned with absolute, not relative prices.

T  F    2.    A demand schedule relates quantity demanded to quantity supplied, other things being constant.

T  F    3.    A graphical representation of a demand curve is called a demand schedule.

T  F    4.    A change in the quantity demanded of cigarettes results from a change in the price of cigarettes.

T  F    5.    The existence of a used CD market decreases the demand for new CDs.

T  F    6.    If the price of tennis racquets rises, the demand for tennis balls will tend to rise also.

T  F    7.    If the price of butter rises, the demand for margarine will rise.

T  F    8.    As producers increase output in the short run, the cost of additional units of output tends to rise.

T  F    9.    An increase in price leads to a leftward shift in demand and a rightward shift in supply.

T  F   10.    If price is below the equilibrium price, a shortage exists.

T  F   11.    If supply shifts to the left, given demand, then the equilibrium price and the equilibrium quantity will rise.

T  F   12.   If demand shifts to the left, given supply, then the equilibrium price and the equilibrium quantity will fall.

T  F   13.   If both supply and demand shift to the right, then equilibrium price and equilibrium quantity are indeterminate

T  F   14.   If the supply of good A increases relative to its demand, then good A is now more scarce, and its relative price will rise.

T  F   15.   If the published price is constant, but it takes consumers longer to wait in lines, there is a shortage.


## MULTIPLE CHOICE QUESTIONS
Circle the letter that corresponds to the best answer.

1.   A demand schedule
     a.   relates price to quantity supplied.
     b.   when graphed, is a demand curve.
     c.   cannot change.
     d.   shows a direct relationship between price and quantity demanded.

2.   If the price of milk rises, other things being constant,
     a.   there is a decrease in demand.
     b.   buyers will substitute milk for other beverages.
     c.   there is a decrease in quantity demanded.
     d.   the demand for cola drinks will fall.

3.   Which of the following will not occur if the price of hamburger meat falls, other things being constant?
     a.   The demand for hamburger buns will increase.
     b.   People will substitute hamburgers for hot dogs.
     c.   The demand for hot dogs will rise.
     d.   The quantity of hamburgers demanded will increase.

4.   If the price of good A rises and the demand for good B rises, then A and B are
     a.   substitutes.
     b.   complements.
     c.   not related goods.
     d.   not scarce goods.

5.   If income falls and the demand for steak falls, then steak is a(n)
     a.   substitute good.
     b.   complement good.
     c.   normal good.
     d.   inferior good.

6.   If the supply of gasoline rises, with a given demand, then
     a.   the relative price of gasoline will rise.
     b.   the equilibrium price of gasoline will rise.
     c.   the equilibrium quantity of gasoline will increase.
     d.   the equilibrium price and equilibrium quantity of gasoline will increase.

7.   Which of the following probably will **NOT** lead to a fall in the demand for
     hamburgers?
     a.   a decrease in income
     b.   an expectation that the price of hamburgers will rise in the future
     c.   a decrease in the price of hot dogs
     d.   a change in tastes away from hamburgers

8.   When a demand curve for good A is derived,
     a.   the price of A changes.
     b.   the price good B, a substitute, changes.
     c.   money income changes.
     d.   consumer tastes change.

9.   Which of the following will lead to an increase in supply?
     a.   an increase in the price of the good in question
     b.   a technological improvement in the production of the good in question
     c.   an increase in the price of labour used to produce the good in question
     d.   All of the above

10.  Several years ago some cities in North America passed a law that limited showers
     to 4 minutes, with a possible 30-day jail sentence for violators.  Which of the
     following statements is probably true for those cities?
     a.   A surplus of water existed.
     b.   The price of water was too high.
     c.   A shortage of water would exist regardless of how high its price got.
     d.   The price of water was below the equilibrium price.

Consider the graph below when answering questions 11 and 12.

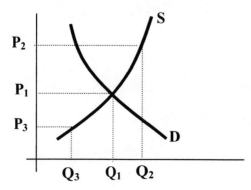

11. Given the figure above,
    a. the equilibrium price is $P_1$, the equilibrium quantity is $P_2$.
    b. the equilibrium quantity is $P_1$.
    c. the equilibrium price is $P_3$, the equilibrium quantity is $Q_1$.
    d. the equilibrium quantity is $Q_1$, the equilibrium price is $P_1$.

12. Which of the following is *not* true?
    a. A shortage exists at $P_2$.
    b. The equilibrium price is $P_1$.
    c. An excess quantity demanded exists at $P_3$.
    d. The market-clearing price is $P_1$.

13. If a surplus exists at some price, then
    a. sellers have an incentive to raise the price.
    b. buyers have an incentive to offer a higher price.
    c. sellers cannot sell all they wish to at that price.
    d. seller inventories are falling.

14. If a shortage exists at some price, then
    a. sellers can sell all they desire to sell at that price.
    b. sellers have an incentive to raise the price.
    c. buyers cannot get all they want at that price.
    d. All of the above.

15. If the demand for hamburgers rises, with a given supply, then
    a. the supply of hamburgers will rise because price rises.
    b. the equilibrium price of hamburgers will fall and the equilibrium quantity will rise.
    c. the equilibrium quantity and the equilibrium price of hamburgers will rise.
    d. the quantity supplied of hamburgers will decrease.

16. If demand shifts to the right (given supply), then equilibrium
    a. price will rise.
    b. price is indeterminate.
    c. price and equilibrium quantity are indeterminate.
    d. price will fall.

17. If supply shifts to the right (given demand), then equilibrium
    a. quantity will increase.
    b. price will rise.
    c. price and equilibrium quantity will fall.
    d. price and equilibrium quantity rises.

18.   If both supply and demand shift to the left, then equilibrium
      a.   price is indeterminate and equilibrium quantity rises.
      b.   price is indeterminate and equilibrium quantity falls.
      c.   price falls and equilibrium quantity falls.
      d.   price falls and equilibrium quantity is indeterminate.

19.   If the demand for good A falls relative to its supply, then
      a.   good A is now relatively more scarce.
      b.   good A is now relatively less scarce.
      c.   the relative price of good A will rise.
      d.   the actual price of good A will rise, even if A is not price flexible.

20.   If the demand for good B rises relative to it supply, then
      a.   good B is now relatively more scarce.
      b.   the relative price of good B will rise.
      c.   the actual price of good B will rise, even if good B is price inflexible.
      d.   All of the above

21.   If the demand for good A rises relative to its supply, and markets are price-flexible, then
      a.   no shortage of A can exist in the long run.
      b.   no shortage of A can exist in the short run.
      c.   the published price of A remains constant, but its actual price falls.
      d.   the published price of A remains constant, but its actual price rises.

22.   If the demand for good A rises relative to its supply, and markets are price-inflexible, then
      a.   a shortage can exist in the short run.
      b.   a shortage can exist in the long run.
      c.   the published price of A might remain constant, but its actual price rises.
      d.   All of the above

23.   If the demand for economists falls relative to their supply, then
      a.   more college students will major in economics.
      b.   some economists will change professions.
      c.   a shortage of economists will result, in the long run.
      d.   All of the above

## MATCHING
Choose the numbered item in Column (2) that best matches the term or concept in Column (1).

|              (1)                | (2) |
|---|---|

a.  demand schedule  
b.  bread and butter  
c.  eyeglasses and contact lenses  
d.  demand shifts to the left  
e.  supply curve  
f.  supply shifts to the left  
g.  equilibrium price  
h.  excess quantity demanded  
i.  excess quantity supplied  
j.  equilibrium price rises  

1.  law of supply  
2.  relation between price, quantity demanded  
3.  population increases  
4.  raw material prices rise  
5.  income falls and normal good  
6.  market clearing price  
7.  surplus  
8.  complements  
9.  substitutes  
10. shortage  
11. increase in supply  

## WORKING WITH GRAPHS

1.  Consider the two graphs below, in panels (**a**) and (**b**).

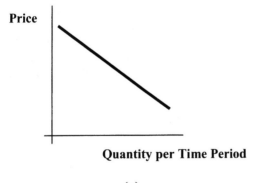

(a)

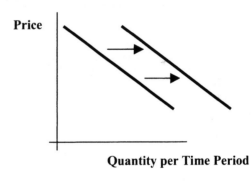

(b)

Which panel shows an increase in quantity demanded?  Which shows an increase in demand?

2.  Distinguish between a decrease in supply and a decrease in quantity supplied, graphically, using the space below.  Use two panels.

| Decrease in Supply | Decrease in Quantity Supplied |
| --- | --- |
| | |

3.  Use the demand schedule below to plot the demand curve on the following coordinate grid.  Be sure to label each axis correctly.

| Price per Bottle of Shampoo | Quantity of Bottles Demanded per Week (thousands) |
| --- | --- |
| $6 | 8 |
| $5 | 10 |
| $4 | 12 |
| $3 | 14 |
| $2 | 16 |
| $1 | 18 |

4. Use the supply schedule below to plot the supply curve on the coordinate grid in problem 3.

| Price per Bottle of Shampoo | Quantity of Bottles Supplied per Week (thousands) |
|:---:|:---:|
| $6 | 18 |
| $5 | 15 |
| $4 | 12 |
| $3 | 9 |
| $2 | 6 |
| $1 | 3 |

5. Using the graphs from problems 3 and 4, indicate on the graph the equilibrium price and the equilibrium quantity for bottles of shampoo. What is the equilibrium price? the equilibrium quantity?

6. Continuing with the previous example, assume that the government puts a price ceiling at $3 per bottle of shampoo. What is the quantity demanded at that price? the quantity supplied? Does a surplus or a shortage exist at that price?

7. Consider the graphs below in panel **(a)**. Then show, in panel **(b)**, the new equilibrium price (label it $P_1$) and the new equilibrium quantity (label it $Q_1$) that results due to a change in tastes in favor of the good in question.

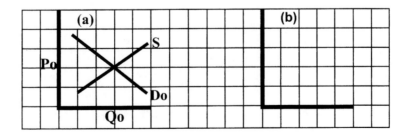

**PROBLEMS**

1. List the non-price determinants of demand that will lead to a decrease in demand. Be specific.

2.  List the non-price (other) determinants of supply that will lead to an increase in supply.  Be specific.

3.  Concerning apples, indicate whether each event leads to (i) a rightward shift in demand, (ii) a leftward shift in demand, (iii) an increase in quantity  demanded, (iv) a decrease in quantity demanded, (v) a rightward shift in supply, (vi) a leftward shift in supply, (vii) an increase in quantity supplied, (viii) a decrease in quantity supplied.

    (Note:  some events may lead to more than one of the above.)
    _____    a)    An early frost in Ontario destroys some apple orchards.
    _____    b)    Apple pickers organize a union which raises wage rates.
    _____    c)    The price of  apples rises.
    _____    d)    The price of  apples falls.
    _____    e)    The Federal government lowers the price of apples below equilibrium and freezes the price at the lower level.
    _____    f)    Apple growers leave the industry.
    _____    g)    Pears (but not apples) are demonstrated to cause cancer in lab rats.
    _____    h)    The government subsidizes apple growers at 3 cents per apple.
    _____    i)    News is released that the government forecast is for a poor apple crop next year.
    _____    j)    The price of pears rises (assume now that apple growers can also grow pears).

4.  For each of the statements (a) through (j) in the previous question, decide whether the market clearing *(equilibrium)* price for apples will rise, fall, or be unaffected.

    a)  _____          f)  _____
    b)  _____          g)  _____
    c)  _____          h)  _____
    d)  _____          i)  _____
    e)  _____          j)  _____

## BUSINESS SECTION

### Marketing: Market Segmentation - The Aging Population

A typical first year text in economics tends to focus on a market at the product (or resource) level. However, in order to gain a better understanding of consumer demand, the marketing staff of a company  will often segment (subdivide) a product market in order to identify a potentially profitable target market or market niche. In short, a market segment (target market) consists of a group of consumers who respond in a similar way to a given set of marketing efforts.

A very useful basis of market segmentation in the 1990's has been the age related demographic trends inherent in the Canadian population . David Foot, in his book "Boom,Bust & Echo", illustrates that during the current period (1991-2001) the age group between 15 –34 years of age will experience zero to  negative growth. The baby boom generation aged between 35 and 54 is now considered to be the consumers with the highest level of buying power. Within this group those between 45-54 are experiencing the fastest growth rates. As well, the population 65 years and over, the "grey population" is also experiencing significant positive growth rates. Source: David Foot, *Boom, Bust & Echo*, , page 84 (Macfarlane Walter & Ross, 1996).

## Business Application Problem

Contrast the effect that the aging population will have upon the demand for each of the following sets of items.

a.  Tennis vs. golf

b.  Diet Coke vs. Pepsi

c.  Urban condominiums vs. suburban homes

d.  Minivans vs. recreational vehicles

e.  Red meat vs chicken

## ANSWERS TO CHAPTER 4

**COMPLETION QUESTIONS**

1.  lower; higher
2.  demand curve or schedule
3.  inverse; negatively
4.  price; quantity
5.  movement along; shift in
6.  income, tastes and preferences, prices of related goods, expectations about future relative prices, population
7.  complements; fall
8.  substitutes

9.    right; down
10.   smaller
11.   rises; direct; positively
12.   supply curve or schedule
13.   more
14.   prices of inputs, technology, taxes and subsidies, price expectations,
      number of firms in industry
15.   equilibrium; surplus; shortage
16.   excess quantity demanded
17.   rise; rise
18.   fall, fall
19.   fall, rise
20.   indeterminate, will rise
21.   rise, indeterminate

## TRUE AND FALSE

1.    F    Buyers respond to changes in relative prices.
2.    F    A demand schedule relates quantity demanded to price.
3.    F    A graphical representation of a demand schedule is a demand curve.
4.    T
5.    F    It increases the demand for new CDs.
6.    F    The demand for tennis balls will tend to *fall*, because they are complements.
7.    T
8.    T
9.    F    An increase in price leads to a decrease in quantity demanded and an increase in quantity
           supplied – movement along the curves occurs.
10.   T
11.   F    The equilibrium quantity falls.
12.   T
13.   F    Equilibrium quantity rises.
14.   F    Good A is now less scarce, and its relative price will fall.
15.   T

## MULTIPLE CHOICE QUESTIONS

1.b;    Graphing the quantity demanded against the product's own price displays a
        negatively sloped demand curve.
2.c;    If the price of milk rises, there will be a decrease in quantity demanded, not a
        decrease in demand, and a movement along the demand curve will occur.
        *TIP*: If the price of milk rises, this will result in a movement along the milk's
        demand curve, not a shift in the milk's demand curve.
3.c;    Since hamburgers and hot dogs are substitutes, the demand for hot dogs will fall,
        not increase.
4.a;    If A and B are substitutes, then when the price of A rises, consumers will buy less
        of A and more of B. As a result, this will cause the demand for B to increase or
        the demand curve for B to shift rightward.
5.c;    A normal good is one in which there is a direct relation between income and
        demand.
6.c;    If the supply of gasoline rises, this will display as a rightward shift in the supply
        curve. As a result, there will be an increase in the equilibrium quantity of
        gasoline.
7.b;    If consumers expect the price of hamburgers to rise in the future, they are likely to
        increase their demand for hamburgers in the current period.
8.a;    When a demand curve is derived, all other non-own price factors are assumed to
        remain to stay the same.

9.b;    A technological improvement in the production of a good will make the good
        more profitable to sell at each possible price. Graphically this implies a rightward
        shift in the supply curve or what we term an increase in supply.
        *TIP*: An increase in quantity supplied is caused by a change in the product's own
        price; an increase in supply is caused by a change in non-own price factors.

10.d;   The price of water was below equilibrium, which resulted in a shortage situation.
        Instead of letting the price rise to its equilibrium level, the government reacted to
        the shortage by passing a law limiting showers to 4 minute episodes.

11.d;   Equilibrium occurs at the point at which the supply and demand curves meet.

12.a;   Since $P_2$ is a price above the equilibrium price, there will be as surplus, not a
        shortage.

13.c;   If a surplus exists at some price, this means that the quantity demanded by
        consumers is less than the quantity supplied by sellers.
        *TIP:* If a surplus occurs, sellers have an incentive to lower the price to eliminate
        the surplus.

14.d;   If a shortage exists at some price, then buyers cannot get all they want at that
        price. As a result, sellers have an incentive to raise the price as the sellers will be
        able to sell all that they desire to sell at the new price.

15.c;   If the demand for hamburgers rises, there will be a rightward shift in the demand
        curve for hamburgers. If the supply curve remains unchanged the equilibrium
        price and quantity for hamburgers will both increase. As price increases, the
        quantity supplied will rise but there will not be a rise in supply.

16.a;   If demand shifts right, this reflects an increase in demand. An increase in demand
        will eventually cause the equilibrium price to rise.
        *TIP*: Sketch an original demand and supply curve. Then, draw a new demand curve to the right of
        the original demand curve. At the new intersection between demand and supply what has
        happened to price  (on the vertical axis)?

17.a;   If supply shifts rightward, this reflects an increase in supply. This increase in
        supply will temporarily cause a surplus which, in turn, will cause the new
        equilibrium price to be lower. At the lower price consumers will be encouraged to
        purchase more and therefore the higher level of output will be maintained.
        *TIP*: Sketch an original demand and supply curve. Then, draw a new supply curve
        to the right of the original supply curve. At the new intersection between demand
        and supply what has happened to quantity (on the horizontal axis)?

18.b;   *TIP:* One way to solve this is to analyze one shift at a time. A shift left in demand
        (decrease in demand) will cause the equilibrium <u>price to fall</u> and equilibrium
        <u>quantity to fall</u>. A shift left in supply (decrease in supply) will cause the equilibrium <u>price to rise</u>
        and equilibrium <u>quantity to fall</u>. From the results in the previous two sentences we can see that we
        can only predict that the quantity will fall.

19.b;   Since good A is now relatively less scarce, the equilibrium price will fall.
        *TIP:*You can analyze this change by using a graph to sketch a decrease in demand
        (shift left in demand) while holding the supply curve constant. You will see that
        the new equilibrium price will be lower. The lower price implies that good A is
        now  relatively less scarce.

20.d;   The equilibrium price will increase, as good B is relatively more scarce.
        *TIP*: You can analyze this change by using a graph to sketch an increase in demand
        (shift right in demand) while holding the supply curve constant.

21.a;   If the demand for Good A rises there will be a shortage in the short run causing the price  of  good
        A to rise. As the price rises, this will lead to an increase in quantity supplied  which  will  eliminate
        the shortage in the long run.

22.d;   If the price does not increase, in the short run, then the quantity supplied will not
        increase in the long run. The shortage will therefore remain in the long run.

23.b;   *TIP:* You can analyze this change by simply assuming a decrease in demand with
        supply remaining constant. At the original wage (price) there will now be a surplus of economists.
        This will cause the equilibrium wage (price) to decline. As the wages of economists decline, the
        surplus will be eliminated by having some economists switch into other professions.

**MATCHING**

a and 2;   b and 8;   c and 9;   d and 5;   e and 1;   f and 4;   g and 6;   h and 10;   i and 7;   j and 3;

**WORKING WITH GRAPHS**

1.    Panel (a); Panel (b)

2.

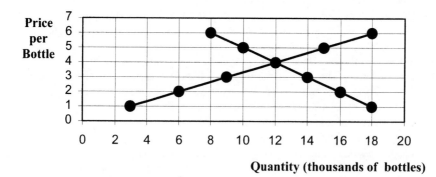

3.    See graph below in 4.
4.    See graph below.

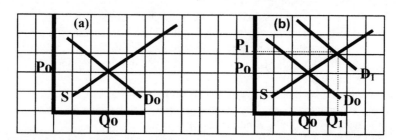

Quantity (thousands of bottles)

5.    $4; 12 thousand bottles (see graph above)
6.    14 thousand bottles; 9 thousand bottles; shortage of 5 thousand bottles.
7.

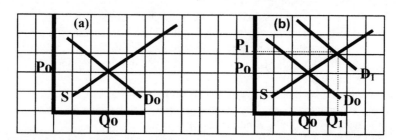

**PROBLEMS**

1.    Income falls for a normal good; change in tastes occurs away from the good; price of a substitute falls
      or price of a complement rises; expectations exist that the good's future relative price will fall;
      decrease in population occurs.

2.    Reduction in the price of inputs; decrease in a sales tax on the good or increase in the (per unit)
      subsidy of the good; expectation that the future relative price will fall; increase in the number of firms
      in the industry.

| 3. | a. | vi and iv | f. | vi and iv |
|----|----|-----------|----|-----------|
|    | b. | vi and iv | g. | i and vii |
|    | c. | iv and vii | h. | v and iii |
|    | d. | iii and viii | i. | i |
|    | e. | iii and viii | j. | i and vi |
| 4. | a. | rise | f. | rise |
|    | b. | rise | g. | rise |
|    | c. | be unaffected | h. | fall |
|    | d. | be unaffected | i. | rise |
|    | e. | be unaffected | j. | rise |

## BUSINESS SECTION

a. Decrease in demand for tennis, increase in demand for golf (less strenuous).
b. Increase in demand for Diet Coke (healthier), decrease in demand for Pepsi (younger generation image).
c. Increase in demand for urban condominiums, decrease in demand for suburban homes.
d. Decrease in demand for minivans, increase in demand for recreational vehicles (for retirement).
e. Decrease in demand for red meat, increase in demand for chicken (healthier).

## ANSWERS TO EXAMPLE QUESTIONS FOR CRITICAL ANALYSIS

**I  INTERNATIONAL EXAMPLE 4-1: Garth Brooks, Used CDs, and the Law of Demand** (p. 75)

The existence of a secondary used-book market means that to people who choose to resell their recently acquired books, the net cost of any new book will be reduced. According to the law of demand, if the net cost of a new book is reduced, the quantity demanded will increase. The law of demand, in this case, will tend to eliminate the fears of publishers and authors that used books are "killing them". However, just as was the case with used CD's, used books also serve as a cheaper substitute to the purchase of new books for many consumers. If this "cheap substitute effect" is less of a factor than the law of demand, authors and publishers will have nothing to fear from the used book market.

**II  EXAMPLE 4-1: Is Dental Care Becoming an Inferior Good?** (p. 77)

Cosmetic dentistry is more likely to be a normal good. That is, as aggregate Canadian income levels continue to increase, many more Canadians can now afford the luxury of making their teeth appear more beautiful. Therefore, more dentists are responding to the increased demand for this normal good by specializing in cosmetic dentistry.

**III  EXAMPLE 4-2: Getting Your Degree Via the Internet** (p. 78)

As this example notes, online learning resources are both substitutes and complements of the services provided by college professors. To the extent that these learning resources are used more as substitutes (and not as complements) this will likely reduce the demand for college professors in the next decade, thus shifting the demand curve for professors leftward. However, if in the next decade, the online teaching resources strongly complement the services of college professors, it is conceivable that the demand curve for college professors could shift right, reflecting an increase in demand. Since effective online courses require substantial "up front" preparation, many college instructors will be needed to develop and maintain high quality online learning resources. Thus one may find that some of the college instructors who traditionally taught in the classroom will now switch to online course development and maintenance. Also, the convenience of online resources may well bring in additional consumer demand for college and university education, which again may increase the demand for college professors.

**IV  INTERNATIONAL EXAMPLE 4-2: Caviar Poaching is Making a Pricey
Delicacy Even Pricier** (p. 85)
If the policies banning caviar poaching are successful, this should increase the market
supply of caviar. In turn, the market price will not increase as much as currently predicted.

**V  EXAMPLE 4-3: Why Babysitters Are Earning More** (p. 90)
If a significant number of retiring baby boomers offer to baby-sit, this will increase
the supply of baby sitting services. The increase in supply will reduce the equilibrium
price or fee paid to babysitters.

# CHAPTER 5

# ELASTICITY

## PUTTING THIS CHAPTER INTO PERSPECTIVE

In the previous chapter you studied principles of demand and supply that focus on predicting the *direction* of price and quantity in a typical product or resource market. In Chapter 5 you will sharpen your understanding of demand and supply by examining the concept of elasticity. Elasticity of demand and supply will yield more precise predictions in terms of the *magnitude* by which the quantity or price will change in a given product or resource market.

The law of demand posits an inverse relationship between price and quantity demanded, other things being constant. Knowing that quantity demanded will rise if price falls and that quantity demanded will fall if price rises, other things being constant, is useful information—to be sure. However, the concept of price elasticity of demand goes one step further; it is concerned with how responsive quantity demanded is to changes in price. If price rises, will quantity demanded fall by a little or a lot? If price falls, will quantity demanded rise by just a little bit, or by a great amount?

Price elasticity of demand is defined as the percentage change in quantity demanded divided by the percentage change in price. Because of the law of demand, the price elasticity of demand coefficient (number) will always be negative. By convention, therefore, economists ignore the sign; and if the coefficient is greater than one, less than one, or equal to one, we refer to a good (in the relevant price range) as being elastic, inelastic, or unit elastic, respectively.

Price elasticity of demand is a very useful concept. If you are in business and you know the price elasticity of demand coefficient for your good, you can raise your total revenues (and perhaps profits) by raising or lowering your sales price, depending on whether the elasticity coefficient is less than or greater than one. If you are in charge of raising revenues for a government, you would be well advised to tax only those goods for which at current prices the price elasticity of demand coefficient is quite low. Many other issues, in this chapter and throughout the remainder of this text, will involve understanding the concept of elasticity.

In Chapter 5 we analyze how price elasticity of demand coefficients can be measured; we also analyze the cross elasticity of demand, income elasticity of demand, and price elasticity of supply.

There are several pitfalls that you should be careful to avoid.  Many students think in terms of whether a *good* is price elastic or inelastic; instead you should realize that for each good (given a linear demand curve) there are ranges of price elasticity and price inelasticity.  For that reason you should always be careful to specify the *price range* when analyzing elasticity of demand.  Finally, many students believe that a business can increase its profits by raising selling price; but as the text indicates, if a firm raises price when the demand is highly price elastic at the current price, its total revenues will fall dramatically; so too, probably, will its profits.

## LEARNING OBJECTIVES

After you have studied this chapter you should be able to

1.    define price elasticity of demand, elastic demand, unit elastic demand, inelastic demand, perfectly inelastic demand, perfectly elastic demand, cross elasticity of demand, income elasticity of demand, price elasticity of supply, perfectly elastic supply, and perfectly inelastic supply.

2.    calculate price elasticity of demand in two ways, given the relevant information.

3.    classify an elasticity coefficient as indicating whether demand is elastic, unit elastic, or inelastic, in the relevant price range.

4.    recognize from a graph whether the demand for a good is perfectly elastic or perfectly inelastic in the specified price range.

5.    predict what will happen to a firm's total revenues if the firm changes price, given price elasticity of demand.

6.    identify the determinants of price elasticity of demand.

7.    calculate the cross elasticity of demand coefficient, and determine from the sign of that coefficient whether or not the goods in question are substitutes or complements.

8.    calculate income elasticity of demand from relevant information and distinguish price elasticity of demand from income elasticity of demand.

9.  calculate price elasticity of supply, identify the determinants of price elasticity of supply, and recognize a graph of a perfectly elastic supply curve and of a perfectly inelastic supply curve.

## CHAPTER OUTLINE

1.  Elasticity measures quantity responsiveness to price changes.
    a.  **Price elasticity of demand** is defined as the percentage change in quantity demanded divided by the percentage change in price.
        i.  Because of the law of demand, the price elasticity of demand is always negative; by convention, the sign is ignored.
        ii. Price elasticity of demand relates percentage changes, not absolute changes.
    b.  There are two ways to calculate the price elasticity of demand.
        i.  Price elasticity of demand may be calculated by dividing the change in quantity demanded over the original quantity demanded by the change in price over the original price; this method yields a different elasticity over the same range of the demand curve, depending on whether price rises or falls.
        ii. In order to get consistent results over the same range of a demand curve, it is possible to calculate price elasticity by using average values for base price and base quantity.

2.  If the calculated price elasticity of demand for a good is greater than one, the demand is called elastic; if it is equal to one, the demand is called **unit elastic**; if it is less than one, the demand is called inelastic.

3.  There are two extreme price elasticities of demand.
    a.  **Perfectly inelastic demand** indicates no change in quantity demanded as price changes; such a demand curve is vertical at the given quantity.
    b.  **Perfectly elastic demand** indicates that even a slight increase in price will lead to a zero quantity demanded; such a demand curve is horizontal at the given price.

4.  Elasticity is related to a firm's total revenues.
    a.  In the range of elastic demand, if a firm lowers price its total revenues will rise; if it raises price its total revenues will fall.
    b.  In the range of unit elastic demand, small changes in price leave the firm's total revenues unaltered.
    c.  In the range of inelastic demand, if a firm lowers price its total revenues will fall; if it raises price its total revenues will rise.
    d.  Along a linear demand curve (which has a constant slope, by definition), a good has an elastic, a unit elastic, and an inelastic range.

5.  There are three major determinants of the price elasticity of demand.
    a.  The closer the substitutes for a particular good, and the more available they are, the greater will be its price elasticity of demand.
    b.  The higher the proportion of total expenditures that people allocate to a good, the higher will be that good's price elasticity of demand.
    c.  The longer any price change persists, the greater the price elasticity of demand; the distinction between the short-run and long-run consumer adjustment period varies with the good in question.

6.  **Cross elasticity of demand** is defined as the percentage change in the quantity demanded of one good (holding its price constant) divided by the percentage change in the price of a related good.
    a.  If the sign of the cross elasticity of demand is positive, the two goods are substitutes.
    b.  If the sign of the cross elasticity of demand is negative, the two goods are complements.

7.  **Income elasticity of demand** is defined as the percentage change in the quantity demanded for a good (holding its price constant) divided by the percentage change in money income.

8.  **Price elasticity of supply** is defined as the percentage change in quantity supplied divided by the percentage change in price.
    a.  One extreme is **perfectly elastic supply**, where a slight decrease in price leads to a zero quantity supplied; such a supply curve is horizontal at the given price.
    b.  Another extreme is **perfectly inelastic supply**, where quantity supplied is constant, regardless of what happens to price; such a supply curve is vertical at the given quantity.
    c.  The longer the time for adjustment, the more price elastic is the supply curve.
    d.  Empirical evidence indicates that short-run elasticities for goods are considerably smaller than long-run elasticities.

9.  Governments tax products that are considered demand inelastic; however, the long-run demand elasticities are higher because buyers can find alternative sources for such goods.

## KEY TERMS AND CONCEPTS

Price elasticity of demand
Elastic demand
Unit elasticity of demand
Inelastic demand
Perfectly inelastic demand
Perfectly elastic demand

Cross elasticity of demand
Income elasticity of demand
Price elasticity of supply
Perfectly elastic supply
Perfectly inelastic supply

## COMPLETION QUESTIONS
Fill in the blank or circle the correct term.

1. Price elasticity of demand is a measure of (buyer, seller) responsiveness to price changes.

2. Price elasticity of demand is defined as the percentage change in _____ divided by the percentage change in _____;  the problem with this measure is that we get (the same, a different) numerical value when we move up, as opposed to down, the same range of the demand curve.

3. In order to correct for the problem in question 2 above, the _____ value method of calculating the price elasticity of demand can be used.

4. Assume a 1 percent change in price.  If quantity demanded changes by less than 1 percent then we say that in that range the demand for the good is _____; if quantity demanded changes by 1 percent then in that range demand is _____; if quantity demanded changes by more than 1 percent then in that range demand is _____.

5. A demand curve that exhibits zero responsiveness to price changes is _____; such a demand curve is (horizontal, vertical) at the given quantity; a demand curve in which even the slightest increase in price will lead to a zero quantity demanded is _____; such a demand curve is (horizontal, vertical) at the given price.

6. If price falls and total revenues rise, then in that range demand  was price _____; if price falls and total revenues remain constant, then in that range demand was price _____; if price falls and total revenues fall, then in that range demand was price _____.

7. If price rises and total revenues fall, then demand was price _____; if total revenues rise, then demand was price _____; if total revenues remain constant, then demand was _____.

8. The determinants of price elasticity of demand are _____, _____, and _____.

9. Cross elasticity of demand is defined as the percentage change in the _____ for one good, holding its _____ constant, divided by the percentage change in the _____ of another good.

10. If the cross elasticity of demand is positive, then the two goods are _____; if it is negative, the two goods are _____.

11.    The income elasticity of demand is defined as the percentage change in _____ for a good, holding its _____ constant, divided by the percentage change in _____.

12.    The price elasticity of supply measures the responsiveness of the _____ of a good to a change in its price; a supply curve in which a slight decrease in price leads to a zero quantity supplied is _____; if quantity supplied remains constant no matter what happens to price, the supply curve is _____.


## TRUE-FALSE QUESTIONS

Circle the **T** if the statement is true, the **F** if it is false.  Explain to yourself why a statement is false.

T  F    1.    Price elasticity of demand measures the responsiveness of price to changes in quantity demanded.

T  F    2.    Because of the law of demand, price elasticity of demand will always (implicitly) be a negative number.

T  F    3.    Price elasticity of demand deals with absolute, not relative values.

T  F    4.    When price elasticity of demand is computed by the average-value approach, price elasticity is the same whether price rises or falls over a given demand curve range.

T  F    5.    If the price elasticity of demand is 3, then over the relevant price range, demand is inelastic.

T  F    6.    If the demand for good A is perfectly elastic, its demand curve is horizontal at that price.

T  F    7.    If the demand for good A is perfectly inelastic over *all* prices, consumers would buy the same amount no matter how high the price.

T  F    8.    If price falls and total revenues rise, then over that price range demand is inelastic.

T  F    9.    If a firm discovers that at current prices the price elasticity of demand is 0.50, the firm may want to lower prices to increase profits.

T  F    10.    The price elasticity of demand for McDonald's hamburgers is less than the price elasticity of demand for hamburgers.

T  F    11.  The less time people have to respond to a price change, the higher is the price elasticity.

T  F    12.  If the cross elasticity of demand for goods A and B is negative, A and B are complements.

T  F    13.  Suppose that as incomes increase five percent, the demand for good A increases by ten percent. In this case demand is income elastic.

T  F    14.  If supply is perfectly inelastic, the curve will be horizontal.


## MULTIPLE CHOICE QUESTIONS
Circle the letter that corresponds to the best answer.

1.  Price elasticity of demand measures responsiveness of
    a.  quantity demanded to changes in price.
    b.  quantity demanded to changes in income.
    c.  price to changes in quantity demanded.
    d.  price to changes in demand.

2.  Which of the following is **NOT** true concerning the price elasticity of demand?
    a.  Its sign is always negative, due to the law of demand.
    b.  It is a unitless, dimensionless number.
    c.  It equals the percentage change in price divided by the percentage change in quantity demanded.
    d.  It measures the responsiveness of quantity demanded to changes in price.

3.  If price elasticity of demand is calculated using the original price and quantity, then over a given range in the demand curve, price elasticity of demand
    a.  differs depending on whether price rises or falls.
    b.  is the same, regardless of whether price rises or falls.
    c.  is equal to 1.
    d.  rises as price falls.

4.  If the price elasticity of demand is 1/3, then
    a.  demand is unitary elastic.
    b.  demand is inelastic over that price range.
    c.  demand is elastic.
    d.  demand is elastic over that price range.

5.  If price falls by 1 percent and quantity demanded rises by 2 percent, then the price elasticity of demand
    a.  is inelastic over that range.
    b.  is 1/2.

    c.  is elastic over that range.
    d.  cannot be calculated from this information.

6.    If the demand for good A is perfectly inelastic at all prices,
    a.  quantity demanded does not change as price changes.
    b.  the law of demand is violated.
    c.  the demand curve is vertical at the given quantity.
    d.  All of the above

7.    If the demand for good A is perfectly elastic,
    a.  quantity demanded does not vary with price.
    b.  the demand curve is horizontal.
    c.  the demand curve is vertical.
    d.  the demand curve is positively sloped.

8.    If price rises and total revenue rises, then the price elasticity of demand over that range is
    a.  elastic.
    b.  inelastic.
    c.  unitary elastic.
    d.  equal to 1.

9.    If price falls and over that price range demand is inelastic, total revenues will
    a.  remain constant.
    b.  fall.
    c.  rise.
    d.  fall, then rise.

10.    Which of the following is **NOT** a determinant of the price elasticity of demand?
    a.  existence and closeness of substitutes
    b.  proportion of the good to the consumer's budget
    c.  price elasticity of supply
    d.  length of time allowed for adjustment to a price change

11.    At current prices for salt, salt is highly price
    a.  elastic.
    b.  inelastic.
    c.  cross elastic.
    d.  unitary elastic.

12.    If the cross elasticity of demand between good A and good B is positive, the goods are
    a.  substitutes.
    b.  complements.
    c.  unrelated.
    d.  necessities.

13.  If the cross elasticity between good A and good B is -10, then A and B are
     a.  close substitutes.
     b.  near substitutes.
     c.  strongly complementary.
     d.  mildly complementary.

14.  Baseballs and baseball bats are
     a.  substitutes.
     b.  complements.
     c.  not related goods.
     d.  necessities.

15.  When the income elasticity of demand for good A is calculated,
     a.  the price of good A varies.
     b.  it is based on the degree to which the demand curve shifts when income changes.
     c.  a movement along the demand curve for good A is measured.
     d.  All of the above

16.  *Analogy*:  A movement along a demand curve is to price elasticity of demand as a shift in the demand curve is to
     a.  an increase in demand.
     b.  changes in taxes or subsidies.
     c.  income elasticity of demand.
     d.  substitutes and complements.

17.  Which of the following goods is probably the most highly income elastic?
     a.  salt
     b.  food
     c.  alcoholic beverages
     d.  private education

18.  A perfectly inelastic supply curve
     a.  shows great quantity supplied responsiveness to price changes.
     b.  is horizontal at the given price.
     c.  indicates zero quantity supplied responsiveness to price changes.
     d.  is a normal situation.

19.  If the supply of good B is perfectly elastic and price falls, quantity supplied will
     a.  remain unchanged.
     b.  rise.
     c.  fall.
     d.  fall to zero.

20.  If price rises, the quantity supplied will be greater the
     a.  longer the time that elapses.
     b.  more income elastic is the good.
     c.  higher the price elasticity of demand for the good.
     d.  All of the above

## MATCHING

Choose the numbered item in Column (2) that best matches the term or concept in Column (1).

| (1) | (2) |
|---|---|
| a.  perfectly inelastic demand | 1.  elasticity coefficient less than 1 |
| b.  inelastic | 2.  horizontal supply curve |
| c.  perfectly elastic demand | 3.  complements or substitute goods |
| d.  determinant of price elasticity | 4.  quality of substitutes |
| e.  cross-price elasticity of demand | 5.  horizontal demand curve |
| f.  perfectly elastic supply | 6.  vertical demand curve |
| g.  perfectly inelastic supply | 7.  vertical supply curve |
| | 8.  elasticity coefficient equals 1 |
| | 9.  elasticity coefficient exceeds 1 |

## WORKING WITH GRAPHS

1.  Recently, the majority of apple growers in the Ciderview Valley area voted to form a marketing board. Instead of selling the typical 100,000 kgs of delicious apples per week, they are contemplating a "supply restriction policy" where the market supply would be   restricted to 95,000 kgs per week. The marketing board estimates that the market demand curve for delicious apples is as follows.

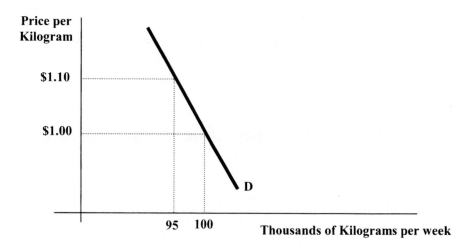

a. Calculate the price elasticity of demand in the $1.00 to $1.10 price range.

b. According to the calculation in question a. above, is it possible for the apple growers to increase their total revenue by restricting quantity sold below 100,000 kgs per week (i.e., to 95,000 kgs per week)? Explain.

c. Verify your answer to question b above by calculating the change in total revenue received by selling 95,000 kgs per week as opposed to 100,000 kgs per week.

d. Can you think of other products or services where the "supply restriction policy" would effectively increase the income of the suppliers involved?

## PROBLEMS

1. Suppose you are given the following data on the market demand and supply for CDs in a small record store. (Use the average elasticity measure.)

| Price | Quantity demanded (per week) | Quantity supplied (per week) |
|---|---|---|
| $4.00 | 50 | 10 |
| 4.50 | 45 | 15 |
| 5.00 | 40 | 25 |
| 5.50 | 35 | 35 |
| 6.00 | 30 | 45 |

a. What is the equilibrium price for CDs?

b. What is the price elasticity of demand over the price range $4.50 to $5? Over the range $5.50 to $6?

   c.   What is the price elasticity of supply over the same two ranges of price?

   d.   Now suppose that most students in the area are working for the minimum wage and that the minimum wage has gone up.  As a result, at each price, two more CD's per week are demanded.  Calculate the price elasticity of demand over the same ranges as in part (b).

   e.   After comparing your answers from parts (b) and (d), what can you conclude about the price elasticity of demand as the demand curve shifts to the right?

2.   Suppose we have the following information for a low-income family:

|  | Income per month | Quantity of hamburger demanded per month | Quantity of steak demanded per month |
|---|---|---|---|
| Period 1 | $750 | 8 kgs. | 2 kgs. |
| Period 2 | 950 | 5 kgs. | 4 kgs. |

   a.   What is the income elasticity of demand for hamburger?

   b.   What is the income elasticity of demand for steak?

   c.   From our study of demand in an earlier chapter, we know _____ is a normal good, whereas _____ is an inferior good.

   d.   In general, when income elasticity of demand is positive, this indicates a (normal, inferior) good. When income elasticity of demand is negative, this indicates a (normal, inferior) good.

3. Suppose the price of color print film has recently risen by 10 percent due to an increase in the cost of the silver that is used to make film. As a result, less film is being sold in the camera store where you work. You do some checking and find that camera sales (number of cameras) are down by 4 percent. What is the cross-price elasticity of cameras and film? Are these two goods complements or substitutes?

## BUSINESS SECTION
## Marketing: Segmented Pricing

A company may charge different prices for the same product to different market segments due to differences in elasticity. In marketing terms this practice is often called "segmented pricing". In general, in order to increase total revenue and total profit, the company will charge higher prices in the inelastic market segments and lower prices in the elastic segments.

As an example, let us use the concept of price elasticity of demand to explain why "Saturday night stay-over flights" are cheaper than "weekday flights" for the same plane seat and the same destination.

The business traveler, who travels by necessity, typically travels during weekdays. Since this tends to be an inelastic demand market segment, the airlines can enhance revenues by charging higher weekday airfares. On weekends, to fill the same flights, the airlines will often lower fares to attract the more elastic leisure traveler market segment.

## Business Application Problem

Use the concept of price elasticity of demand to explain how companies can profit from segmented pricing in each of the following situations.

    a.  Airline fares charged to those who book flights months in advance vs. those who book just days before the flight.

    b.  Prices charged to view a movie just after it has been released vs. the same movie viewed months later.

    c.  Prices charged by a supermarket which has a monopoly in a suburban area vs. the prices charged by the same supermarket for the same goods in an urban center where the firm faces a lot of competition.

d.  Prices charged on a brand name golf shirt  distributed in the pro shop of a posh golf club vs. the same golf shirt sold through a store located in a suburban mall.

e.  The profit margin (based on the price charged) associated with alcoholic drinks and gambling activities provided in a pub vs. the profit margin associated with food served in the same pub.

**ANSWERS TO CHAPTER 5**

**COMPLETION QUESTIONS**

1.  buyer
2.  quantity demanded; price; a different
3.  average
4.  inelastic; unit elastic; elastic
5.  perfectly inelastic; vertical; perfectly elastic; horizontal
6.  elastic; unit elastic; inelastic
7.  elastic; inelastic; unit elastic
8.  closeness of available substitutes; proportion of the good in consumer budgets; length of time to respond
9.  quantity demanded; price; price
10. substitutes; complements
11. quantity demanded; price; money income
12. quantity supplied; perfectly elastic; perfectly inelastic

**TRUE-FALSE QUESTIONS**

1.  F   It measures the responsiveness of quantity demanded to price changes.
2.  T
3.  F   It deals with percentage changes which are relative values.
4.  T
5.  F   It is price elastic because the coefficient exceeds 1.
6.  T
7.  T
8.  F   It must have been elastic. If the price falls by say ten percent and quantity increases by more than ten percent, you can see that total revenue will increase.
9.  F   In this case elasticity is price inelastic. When it is inelastic, the firm would want to increase prices to increase total revenue and profit.
10. F   It is greater, because there are more substitutes for *McDonald's* hamburgers than for hamburgers.
11. F   Elasticity increases over time because substitutes become more readily available over time.
12. T
13. T
14. F   It will be vertical, at the given quantity.

**MULTIPLE CHOICE QUESTIONS**

1. a;  Price elasticity of demand equals the percentage change in quantity demanded divided by the percentage change in price.
2. c;  It equals the percentage change in quantity divided by the percentage change in price.
3. a;  Because of this inconsistency, economists prefer to use average values for the base price and base quantity.
4. b;  Since the price elasticity is less than one it is inelastic.
5. c;  The price elasticity of demand is two. Since it exceeds one. it is elastic.
6. d;  If demand is perfectly inelastic, quantity demanded will remain fixed, no matter how the price changes. Graphically, this implies a vertical demand curve.
7. b;  If the demand for good A is perfectly elastic, the slightest price increase will drive the quantity demanded to zero. This implies a horizontal demand curve.
8. b;  In order for total revenue to increase as the price increases, the percentage change in quantity must be less than the percentage change in price. This is an inelastic situation.
9. b;  If demand is inelastic, the percentage change in quantity demanded is less than the percentage change in price.. Therefore, if, say, the price were to fall by 10%, the quantity would only increase by 5%, causing total revenue to fall.
10. c;  Price elasticity of supply reflects the behaviour of sellers (and not buyers) and therefore supply elasticity has its own  set of determinants.
11. b;  Since ones salt expenditure comprises such a low portion of ones monthly income, its demand is very inelastic.
12. a;  If the cross elasticity of demand between good A and good B is positive, this implies that an increase in the price of good B will increase the demand for good A. Therefore, goods A and B must be substitutes.
13. c  If the cross elasticity between good A and good B is negative, this implies that the two good are complement goods. A relatively high numeric value implies a strong relation between the two goods.
14. b;  Baseballs and baseball bats are consumed together and therefore are complements.
15. b;  The responsiveness of demand to changes in income, holding relative price constant. *TIP*: Recall that a change in income causes a shift in the demand curve (and not a movement along the curve).
16. c;  Income is a determinant of demand and when it changes it will cause a shift in demand.
17. d;  Private education is considered to be an expensive luxury item, while the other goods are necessities which tend to be inelastic.
18. c;  If supply is perfectly inelastic, the quantity supplied will stay the same, no matter how much the price changes. This implies zero responsiveness on the part of quantity supplied.
19. d;  Recall that a perfectly elastic supply curve is a horizontal curve that implies that the slightest decrease in price will drive quantity supplied to zero.
20. a;  If price rises, over the longer run, the supplier can vary both variable inputs, such as labour, and fixed inputs such as plant size.

**MATCHING**

a and 6;   b and 1;   c and 5;   d and 4;   e and 3;   f and 2;   g and 7

**WORKING WITH GRAPHS**

1. a.  P.E.D.= -.54
   b.  Yes, as a lower quantity will increase the price. When the price increases, and demand is inelastic, total revenue will increase.

c.  Total revenue increases by $4,500
d.  Generally, this could relate to any product or service where the demand is inelastic such as other food products, medical services, limited edition vehicles appealing to the very rich.

## PROBLEMS

1.  a.  $5.50
    b.  1.12; 1.77
    c.  4.75; 2.88
    d.  1.07; 1.67
    e.  As the demand curve shifts to the right, for any price range, demand becomes less elastic—or, alternatively stated, more inelastic.
2.  a.  -1.96
    b.  2.83
    c.  steak; hamburger
    d.  normal, inferior
3.  -0.40; complements as the cross elasticity is negative.

## BUSINESS SECTION

a.  The airlines can profit by charging higher fares on those who book just days before, because these people are booking out of necessity and thus represent an inelastic market segment.
b.  Profit can be enhanced by charging higher prices for "just released movies" as the market segment for these movies is inelastic.
c.  Profit can be increased by charging higher prices in the monopoly (inelastic) situation. In a monopoly situation, there are no close substitutes.
d.  The manufacturer of the golf shirt can enhance its profit by charging higher prices for the golf shirt sold through the pro shop. This is an inelastic market segment due to the prevalence of the affluent consumer.
e.  Since alcoholic drinks and gambling can be addictive in nature, they tend to be inelastic. Therefore relative to cost, higher prices are charged for these items resulting in higher profit margins than for the food items sold in the pub.

## ANSWERS TO EXAMPLE QUESTIONS FOR CRITICAL ANALYSIS

**I    POLICY EXAMPLE 5-1: Increasing Taxes on Cigarettes** (p. 101)
The rise of cigarette smuggling suggests that the $E_p$ is actually less than 0.72. Official statistics show that adult smoking dropped by 43 percent. However, with smuggling, some of those adults are probably still smoking but are not officially counted. Therefore, the drop in the number of adult smokers would be less than officially noted, and the $E_p$ would be smaller as well.

**II   INTERNATIONAL EXAMPLE 5-1:The Price Elasticity of Demand for Newspapers** (p.103)
If the formula for average elasticity had not been used, then
$E_p$ = [Change in Quantity/ Original Quantity]/ [Change in Price/ Original Price]
= [(1,050,000-590,000)/590,000]/[(25 pence -10 pence)/ 25 pence] = 1.30
Note that the average value calculation yields an inelastic estimate, while the original values estimate yields an elastic estimate. Since the total revenue actually declined, when the price declined, it seems that the average estimate is the best estimate.

**III  INTERNATIONAL POLICY EXAMPLE 5-1: To Cut Drug Abuse, Make the Price of a "High" Higher** (p. 104)

According to the evidence provided in this example, a legal crackdown policy will be more effective in reducing teen abuse than in reducing adult abuse. A legal crackdown will increase the expected price of consuming cocaine. Since the evidence suggests that the teen cocaine demand is less inelastic (almost unit elastic) than adult demand, the higher price will reduce the quantity of cocaine demanded by the teens more than the adults.

**IV  INTERNATIONAL EXAMPLE 5-2: A Pricing Decision at Disneyland Paris** (p. 108)

The weather may have been better. Advertising may have improved. Tastes and preferences may have moved in favour of Disneyland Paris.

**V   EXAMPLE 5-1: What Do Real World Price Elasticities of Demand Look Like?** (p. 111)

According to the data provided in this example, the demand for food is quite inelastic (0.12), while the demand for motor vehicles is elastic (1.14). The determinants that explain why food is relatively inelastic are *existence of substitutes*. Since food is a necessity item, the consumer is less able to substitute other items. One can explain the elastic nature of motor vehicles based on the determinants such as *existence of substitutes* and *share of total budget spent*.

**VI  POLICY EXAMPLE 5-2: Should Public Libraries Be Shut Down?** (p. 112)

The cost of using an on-line information service is basically the cost of the Internet provider and the value of the time used. To use an on-line service all one has to do is turn on the computer and access the Internet. Copies of desired materials can be downloaded and printed or simply saved in digital format, to be used when it is convenient. To use a library, one may have to pay a small annual fee. In addition, the use of a library involves physically going to the library and then doing a computerized search of the library catalogue. Then the books or periodicals must be located and either checked out or read in the library. The cost of using a library in terms of time is much greater than the cost of using an on-line service.

**VII EXAMPLE 5-2: Frequent Flyer Miles as Income** (p. 113)

If individuals have to pay additional taxes on flights paid for with frequent flyer miles, this will reduce the demand for flights, given the same level of money income. Therefore, this tax policy will reduce the income elasticity of demand.

# CHAPTER 6

# THE PUBLIC SECTOR

## PUTTING THIS CHAPTER INTO PERSPECTIVE

To date you have learned that scarcity is a human condition, that economists study how resources are allocated to satisfy wants, and that there are many potential determinants of how resources are rationed in specific situations.  In Chapter 6 we analyze how governments influence resource use—or more specifically, how individuals and groups use the institution of government to influence resource use.

It is important to master this chapter because our overall goal is to understand how resources are rationed in the Canadian economy.  The role of the government in our economy has grown tremendously since World War II; some maintain that it is nearly as important as the price system in determining resource use in Canada.

It is generally agreed that the price system is an efficient resource allocator.  Typically the value of output will be maximized (opportunity costs will be minimized) if the price system is permitted to allocate resources to satisfy wants.  Nevertheless, the resource allocation that results from a price system is not always efficient.  In this chapter you learn that if externalities exist, then the price system will transmit *incorrect* signals, and resource misallocation will result as the economy overproduces or underproduces specific goods and services.  Similarly, because of the "free rider" problem, the price system will underproduce public goods.  For these reasons the government has an *economic* function to perform; it can help to correct resource misallocation by providing the correct signals to economic agents.

The government has important *political* functions to perform also; it affects the output of merit and demerit goods and it redistributes income if the political process decides that the income distribution that results from the price system is unfair.

Chapter 6 provides a brief overview of the *Theory of Public Choice*, which focuses on how government decisions are made. In general, public choices are made through collective decision-making–actions of voters, politicians, political parties, interest groups, and bureaucrats.

In analyzing collective decision making it is important to note various similarities and differences between the private market sector and the public sector. Similarities include scarcity, competition, and similarity of individuals. Key differences between the private and public sectors are: government goods at zero price, possible use of force, and voting vs. spending. In a political system, *majority rule* prevails, whereas the market system is run by *proportional rule*.

Bureaucrats and special interest groups can have a disproportionate amount of power in terms of public sector decisions due to *rational ignorance* on the part of voters. Rational voters will often remain at some level of ignorance about government programs and policies because the additional cost of obtaining information outweighs the additional benefits to the typical voter. However for the special interest group(s) involved, the extra benefits of obtaining additional information may far exceed the extra costs.

It is impossible to analyze the public sector without understanding the role of taxes and government expenditures. In this chapter we distinguish between marginal and average tax rates and analyze the effects of raising tax revenues through various types of tax systems. The major types of government expenditures incurred at different levels of government is examined.

## LEARNING OBJECTIVES

After you have studied this chapter you should be able to

1. define anti-combines legislation, monopoly, spillover or externality, third parties, effluent fee, market failure, property rights, private goods, public goods, principle of rival consumption, exclusion principle, free-rider problem, merit good, demerit good, transfer payment, transfers in kind, marginal and average tax rates, proportional, progressive, and regressive taxation, capital gain, capital loss, retained earnings, tax incidence, collective decision making, bureaucrats, special interest groups, majority rule, proportional rule, rational ignorance.

2. predict whether a specific good will be overproduced, underproduced, or produced in just the right amount if resources are allocated by the price system.

3. identify which graphs take into account an externality and which do not.

4. list the two ways in which a government can correct for negative externalities.

5. identify the three ways in which a government can correct for positive externalities.

6. list four characteristics of public goods that distinguish them from private goods.

7. enumerate the five economic functions of government.

8.  enumerate the two political functions of government closely related to resource allocation.

9.  recognize differences and similarities between market and collective decision-making.

10. understand the consequences of *rational ignorance*.

11. appreciate how the incentive structure motivating bureaucrats affects public sector decisions.

12. distinguish between a marginal and an average tax rate.

13. distinguish between a proportional, progressive and regressive tax.

14. classify the major types of taxes in Canada as either proportional, progressive or regressive taxes.

15. identify the major types of taxes and government outlays of the Federal and provincial governments.

16. recognize the costs and benefits of a flat tax.


**CHAPTER OUTLINE**

1.  The government provides many economic functions that affect the way in which resources are allocated.
    a.  If a benefit or cost associated with an economic activity *spills over* to **third parties**, the price system will misallocate resources; and **market failure** in the form of externalities occurs. A proper role for government is to correct such **externalities** or spillovers.
        i.  If a negative externality exists, the price system will over-allocate resources to that industry; the government can correct this by taxing, charging **effluent fees**, or regulating such activities.
        ii. If a positive externality exists, the price system will under-allocate resources to that industry; the government can correct this by financing additional production, by providing special subsidies, or by regulation.
    b.  A legal system that defines and enforces **property rights** is crucial to the process of buyers and sellers engaging in contracts in markets.
    c.  Because a competitive price system transmits correct signals, an important role for government is to promote competition and prevent the occurrence of **monopoly. Anti-combines legislation** attempts to promote competition.
    d.  A price system will underallocate resources to the production of **public goods**.
    i.  Characteristics of public goods or **government goods** include:
        -They are usually indivisible.
        -They can be used by more people at no additional cost.

-Additional users of public goods do not deprive others of any of the services of the good.

    -It is difficult to charge individual users a fee based on how much they themselves consume of the public good.

   ii.  Because public goods must be consumed collectively, individuals have an incentive to take a **free ride** and not pay for them.

   iii.  Because the price system underproduces public goods, a proper role of government may be to ensure their production.

  e.  In recent years the government has taken on the economic role of ensuring economy-wide stability:  full employment, price stability, and economic growth.

2.  The government provides political functions that also affect resource allocation.

  a.  Governments subsidize the production of **merit goods** and tax or prohibit the production of **demerit goods**.

  b.  By combining a progressive tax structure with **transfer payments**, the government attempts to redistribute income from higher to lower income groups.  (Although many "loopholes" frustrate such a  policy.)

3.  In order to understand how resources are allocated by governments, economists have developed the **public choice model**, which analyses **collective decision making**, which involves the actions of voters, politicians, bureaucrats, political parties, and special interest groups.

4.  There are similarities and dissimilarities in how resources are allocated in the private sector vs. the public (government) sector.

  a.  As is true for private economy decision makers, all participants in the political marketplace follow the dictates of rational self-interest.

  b.  In the private marketplace firms  specialize in the production of private goods, while governments provide political goods at a zero price; in the private sector buyers can reveal the intensity of their wants via a **proportional rule** (dollar votes), whereas in the political sector an all or nothing **majority rule** is followed, hence the composition of output would be different under each system.

5.  **Bureaucrats** are non-elected governmental officials who organize special interest groups and defend the rights of such "clients."

  a.  Because performance in government is often measured by the number of clients served, bureaucrats have an incentive to expand the size of their clientele.

  b.  Bureaucratic rewards do not depend on profits (as would be the case in the private sector); therefore their rewards appear not so much in high salaries but in job perks which provide further incentives for **bureaucrats** to protect their jobs.

  c.  Due to rational ignorance on the part of voters, bureaucrats and special interest groups can disproportionately affect the allocation of resources.

6.    Governments tax in order to obtain revenues to finance expenditures.
   a.  The **marginal tax rate** is the change in the tax payment divided by the change in income.
   b.  The **average tax rate** equals the total tax payment divided by total income.

7.    There are three main types of taxation systems.
   a.  Under a **proportional taxation** system, as a person's income rises, the percentage of income paid (rate of taxation) in taxes remains constant.
   b.  Under a **progressive taxation** system, as a person's income rises, the percentage of income paid in taxes rises.
   c.  Under a **regressive taxation** system, as a person's income rises, the percentage of income paid in taxes falls.

8.    The federal government imposes income taxes on individuals and corporations, and it collects sales taxes and other taxes.
   a.  The most important tax in the Canadian economy is the personal income tax, where the level of taxation  paid is based on individual annual income.
   b.  The difference between the buying and selling price of an asset, such as a share of stock or a plot of land, is called a **capital gain** if a profit results, and a **capital loss** if it doesn't.

9.    The corporate income tax is a moderately important source of revenue for the various governments in the Canadian economy.
   a.  Corporate stockholders are taxed twice: once on corporate income and again when dividends are received or when the stock is sold.
   b.  The incidence of corporate taxes falls on people—consumers, workers, management, and stockholders—not on such inanimate objects as "corporations."

10.   An increasing percentage of federal tax receipts is accounted for each year by taxes (other than income) levied on payrolls, such as Canada Pension contributions  and Employment Insurance.

11.   Major sources of revenue for provincial and local governments are income, sales, excise and property taxes.

12.   Federal government outlays are made mostly for interest on the public debt; elderly benefits, transfers to provinces, Employment Insurance benefits; provincial and local government expenditures allocate more funds to health, education, and social services than to other categories.

13.   A value added tax assesses a tax on the difference between what the firm sells its final product for and the value of the goods that it bought and used to produce the final product.

14.  Alternatives to our current federal progressive income tax system are (1) a flat tax, (2) a national sales tax or a value-added tax, and (3) a consumption tax.

## KEY TERMS AND CONCEPTS

| | | |
|---|---|---|
| Market failure | Merit goods | Proportional tax |
| Externality | Demerit goods | Progressive tax |
| Effluent fee | Theory of public choice | Regressive tax |
| Third parties | Bureaucracy | Tax incidence |
| Property rights | Collective decision making | Capital gain |
| Private goods | Bureaucrats | Capital loss |
| Exclusion principle | Proportional rule | Tax bracket |
| Principle of rival consumption | Majority rule | Average tax rate |
| Free rider problem | Incentive structure | Retained earnings |
| Public good | Marginal tax rate | |
| Monopoly | Transfer payments | |
| Anti-combines legislation | Government, or political goods | |

## COMPLETION QUESTIONS
Fill in the blank or circle the correct term.

1.  Positive and negative externalities are examples of market _____.

2.  If externalities are an important result of an economic activity, then the price system is (inefficient, efficient).

3.  If Mr. Johnson buys an automobile from General Motors, then those people not directly involved in the transaction are considered _____.

4.  Pollution is an example of a (negative, positive) externality.

5.  When there are spillover costs, a price system will (under, over) allocate resources to the production of the good in question.

6.  If third parties benefit from a good, then (negative, positive) externalities exist, and the price system (under, over) allocate resources to the production of the good in question.

7.  A government can correct negative externalities by imposing (taxes, subsidies)

8.  A government can correct positive externalities by _____, _____, _____.

9.   Anti-combines legislation, in theory, is supposed to (decrease, promote) competition in the private sector.

10.  Public goods have four distinguishing characteristics.  They are usually (divisible, indivisible); they can be used by more people at _____ additional cost; additional users (do, do not) deprive others of the services of a public good; it is very (easy, difficult) to charge individuals based on how much they used the public good.

11.  A free rider has an incentive to (pay, not pay) for a public good.

12.  The five economic functions of federal government in our capitalistic system are _____, _____, _____, _____, _____.

13.  Demerit goods are goods for which society wants to (decrease, increase) production.

14.  Important political functions of government include (encouraging, discouraging) the production of demerit goods and _____ income from higher income to lower income groups.

15.  Many government, or political, goods are provided to consumers at a (zero, positive) price; but the opportunity cost to society of providing government goods is (zero, positive).

16.  The public choice model assumes that even though regulators and bureaucrats are (like, unlike) the rest of us, they face a (similar, different) incentive system.

17.  The public choice model assumes that politicians, bureaucrats, and regulators pursue (society's, their own) self-interest.

18.  Private sector buyers can reveal the intensity of their wants via (majority, proportional) rule through _____ votes; in the political sector the all or nothing (majority, proportional) rule is followed; we can conclude that the composition of output will (differ, be the same) under those two rules of supplying goods to customer/clients.

19.  Bureaucrats are (elected, non-elected) governmental officials whose clients are _____ groups; bureaucrats' rewards take the form of _____.

20. Because information to voters (is, is not) free and because voters will not be concerned with expenditure programs that affect them only slightly, voters often choose to be (rationally informed, rationally ignorant).

21. Fundamental to the theory of public choice is the idea that voters, bureaucrats, and politicians follow the dictates of rational _____, just as do private decision-makers.

22. If the price of an asset rises after its purchase, the owner receives a _____ gain; if the price falls, the owner suffers a _____ loss.

23. The marginal tax rate applies only to the (lowest, highest) tax bracket reached.

24. The corporate income tax is paid by one or more of the following groups: _____, _____, and _____.

25. A flat tax is a (proportional, regressive) tax.

26. A consumption tax (encourages, discourages) saving.


**TRUE-FALSE QUESTIONS**
Circle the **T** if the statement is true, the **F** if it is false.  Explain to yourself why a statement is false.

T  F    1.    In the Canadian economy the government plays only a minor role in resource allocation, because the country is capitalistic.

T  F    2.    If externalities, or spillovers, exist, then a price system misallocates resources, so that inefficiency exists.

T  F    3.    If a negative externality exists, buyers and sellers are not faced with the true opportunity costs of their actions.

T  F    4.    If a positive externality exists when good A is produced, a price system will underallocate resources into the production of good A.

T  F    5.    One way to help correct for a negative externality is to tax the good in question, because that will cause the price of the good to fall.

T  F    6.    A price system will tend to overallocate resources to the production of free goods, due to the free rider problem.

T  F    7.    If third parties are hurt by the production of good B and they are not compensated, then too many resources have been allocated to industry B.

T  F    8.    Governments provide a legal system, but this important function is not considered an economic function.

T  F    9.    One aim of anti-combines legislation is the promotion of competition.

T  F   10.   Deciding what is a merit good and what is a demerit good is easily done and does not require value judgements.

T  F   11.   Scarcity exists in the market sector, but not in the public sector.

T  F   12.   The public choice model assumes that regulators and bureaucrats are mostly concerned with their own—not the public's—self-interest.

T  F   13.   The public choice model indicates that households will be provided the same goods by elected representatives as they would by the private sector.

T  F   14.   It is often rational for voters to remain ignorant of political issues and of candidates.

T  F   15.   Bureaucrats can often exert great influence on matters that concern themselves.

T  F   16.   In the private marketplace dollar votes indicate majority, not proportional rule.

T  F   17.   In a progressive tax structure, the average tax rate is greater than the marginal tax rate.

T  F   18.   Positive economics confirms that a progressive taxation system is more equitable than a regressive taxation system.

T  F   19.   In Canada the tax system that yields the most revenue to all governments combined is the corporate income tax.

T  F   20.   When corporations are taxed, consumers and corporate employees are also affected.

T  F   21.   A flat tax is regressive.

**MULTIPLE CHOICE QUESTIONS**
Circle the letter that corresponds to the best answer.

1.  Market failure exists if
    a.  Mr. Smith cannot purchase watermelons in his town.
    b.  buyers and sellers must pay the true opportunity costs of their actions.
    c.  third parties are injured and are not compensated.
    d.  the government must provide merit goods.

2.  Which of the following will properly correct a negative externality that results from producing good B?
    a.  subsidizing the production of good B
    b.  letting the price system determine the price and output of good B
    c.  forcing sellers of good B to pay the true opportunity costs of their actions.
    d.  banning the production of good B

3.  Which of the following statements concerning externalities is true?
    a.  If a positive externality exists for good A, A will be overproduced by a price system.
    b.  If externalities exist, then resources will be allocated efficiently.
    c.  Efficiency may be improved if the government taxes goods for which a positive externality exists.
    d.  The output of goods for which a positive externality exists is too low, from society's point of view.

4.  Which of the following is not an economic function of government?
    a.  income redistribution
    b.  providing a legal system
    c.  ensuring economy-wide stability
    d.  promoting competition

5.  A price system will misallocate resources if
    a.  much income inequality exists.
    b.  demerit goods are produced.
    c.  externalities exist.
    d.  All of the above

6.  Which of the following does not belong with the others?
    a.  positive externality
    b.  negative externality
    c.  demerit good
    d.  public good

7.    The exclusion principle
   a.   does not work for public goods.
   b.   does not work for private goods.
   c.   causes positive externalities.
   d.   makes it easy to assess user fees on true public goods.

8.    Which of the following is **NOT** a characteristic of public goods?
   a.   indivisibility
   b.   high extra cost to additional users
   c.   exclusion principle does not work easily
   d.   difficult to determine how each individual benefits from public goods

9.    The free rider problem exists
   a.   for private goods.
   b.   for goods that must be consumed collectively.
   c.   only if people can be excluded from consumption.
   d.   All of the above

10.   If Mr. Ayres loves good A, he can convey the intensity of his wants if good A is
   a.   a private good.
   b.   a public good.
   c.   not subject to the exclusion principle.
   d.   expensive

11.   Merit and demerit goods
   a.   are examples of public goods.
   b.   are examples of externalities.
   c.   indicate market failure.
   d.   are not easily classified.

12.   If the government taxes group A and gives to group B, then economic incentives for
   a.   group A may be reduced.
   b.   group B may be reduced.
   c.   both may change so as to reduce output.
   d.   All of the above.

13.   Which of the following characterizes collective, but not market, decision making?
   a.   the legal use of force
   b.   a positive price usually is charged to users
   c.   intensity of wants is easily revealed
   d.   proportional rule

14. People who work in the public sector
    a. are more competent than other workers.
    b. are less competent than other workers.
    c. face a different incentive structure than many workers in the private sector.
    d. would behave in the same way if they worked for a small private business.

15. The public-choice theory assumes that voters, bureaucrats, and politicians usually
    a. attempt to pursue their self-interest.
    b. are concerned with society's interests.
    c. exhibit behaviour not subject to economic analysis.
    d. are indifferent to what voters want.

16. Voters often find it rational to remain ignorant of issues and candidates because
    a. ignorance is bliss.
    b. politicians don't care what voters want anyway.
    c. information is costly to obtain.
    d. they don't have to pay for expenditures anyway.

17. Voters tend to be
    a. very knowledgeable about the issues.
    b. ignorant of many political issues.
    c. very knowledgeable about a candidate's political platform.
    d. willing to spend much time and effort to become knowledgeable.

18. Bureaucrats
    a. often can exert great influence on matters concerning themselves.
    b. seldom can exert great influence on matters concerning themselves.
    c. cannot influence public demand; they only have political influence.
    d. refrain from exerting political influence because they are concerned with society's interests.

19. According to the public choice model, people enter politics mostly to
    a. maximize their income and wealth.
    b. do good for society.
    c. help the poor.
    d. eliminate economic rents.

20. In a progressive tax structure,
    a. the marginal tax rate exceeds the average tax rate.
    b. equity exists.
    c. the average tax rate falls as income falls.
    d. All of the above

21.   If Mr. Romano faces a 90 percent marginal tax rate,
      a.   the next dollar he earns nets him ninety cents.
      b.   his total tax payments equal 90 percent of his total income.
      c.   he has a strong incentive to not earn extra income.
      d.   his average tax rate must be falling.

22.   A proportional tax system
      a.   is unfair.
      b.   cannot be consistent with people's ability to pay such taxes.
      c.   means that upper income people pay smaller percentages of their income in taxes than do lower income people.
      d.   requires upper income people to pay more tax dollars than lower income people pay.

23.   Which of the following statements is true?
      a.   Under a regressive tax structure the average tax rate remains constant as income rises.
      b.   If upper-income people pay more taxes than lower income people, equity must exist.
      c.   The  Canadian federal personal income tax system is progressive.
      d.   Sales taxes tend to be progressive in nature.

24.   The tax incidence of the corporate income tax falls on
      a.   corporate stockholders.
      b.   corporate employees.
      c.   consumers of goods and services produced by corporations.
      d.   All of the above

25.   Which of the following statements about CPP premiums is **NOT** true?
      a.   Since it is a compulsory levy it is considered to be a tax.
      b.   The CPP premium rate is predicted to decrease due to demographic trends.
      c.   Both employees and employers pay CPP premiums.
      d.   It is a payroll tax.

26.   Which of the following is most unlike the others?
      a.   income tax
      b.   sales tax
      c.   consumption tax
      d.   value added tax

27.   A consumption tax
      a.   is placed on earnings.
      b.   is progressive.
      c.   encourages saving.
      d.   reduces the nation's growth rate.

## MATCHING

Choose the numbered item in Column (2) that best matches the term or concept in Column (1).

(1)                                           (2)

a.  spillover                                 1.  pollution
b.  positive externality                      2.  externality
c.  negative externality                      3.  national defence
d.  anti-combines legislation                 4.  alcohol
e.  government good                           5.  eliminate monopoly
f.  demerit good                              6.  flu shots
g.  public choice theory                      7.  proportional rule
h.  rational ignorance                        8   self-interested politicians
i.  intensity of wants revealed              9.  information is too costly to obtain
                                             10. progressive tax
                                             11. regressive tax

## WORKING WITH GRAPHS

1.    Consider the graph below, then answer the questions.   Assume S represents industry supply and S' includes pollution costs to society as well as industry private costs.

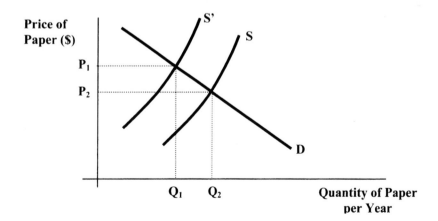

a.  If no governmental intervention takes place, what will be the market equilibrium price?  The market equilibrium quantity?

b.  At the market equilibrium quantity ($Q_2$), which are higher: private costs or social costs?

c.  From *society's* point of view, what is the price that reflects the true opportunity costs of paper?  From that same point of view, what is the optimal quantity of paper?

d.  Considering your answers in the above three questions, will a price system produce too little, or too much paper.

e.  Does a negative externality or a positive externality exist?

2.  Consider the graph below, then answer the questions that follow.  Assume that D represents private market demand and that D' represents benefits that accrue to third parties as well as private benefits.

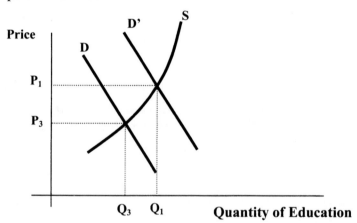

a.  If no government intervention occurs, what will be the market equilibrium price?  The market equilibrium quantity?

b.  At the market equilibrium quantity, which is greater, private benefits or social benefits?

c.  From *society's* point of view, what is the optimal price and the optimal quantity of education?

d.  In this example, does the price system provide too much, or too little education?

e. Is there a positive externality or a negative externality for this good?

3. Suppose you know the demand and supply of fertilizer locally, and you have graphed them as shown in the graphs that follows. The fertilizer plant that operates in your town is also producing pollution. This pollution is a constant amount per unit of output (proportional to output) at the plant. If the government decides to try to combat the pollution problem by imposing *a $20-per-ton tax on fertilizer produced*:

a. Show graphically, on the graph provided below, what will happen to the fertilizer market.

b. Will the level of pollution in your town be reduced? If so, by how much? If not, can you offer a solution to the pollution problem?

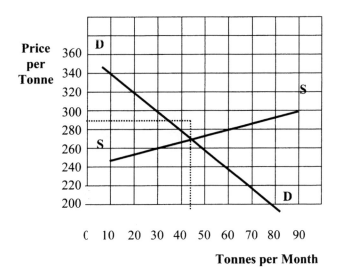

**PROBLEMS**

1.    In the text the following economic and political functions of government  were examined: *providing legal system, promoting competition, correcting externalities, providing public goods, stabilizing the economy, encouraging merit goods, discouraging demerit goods, redistribution.*    Match each of the following government activities to one (or more) of the functions listed above. Write in the matching function(s) in the blank space provided below.

      a)  Providing aid to welfare recipients          _____
      b)  Passing anti-combines laws                    _____
      c)  Subsidizing the arts                          _____
      d)  Prohibiting the sale and possession of drugs  _____
      e)  Providing national defense                    _____
      f)  Enforcing a progressive tax structure         _____
      g)  Enforcing contracts                           _____
      h)  Providing public education to children        _____
      i)  Prosecuting fraud                             _____
      j)  Providing funds for AIDS research             _____
      k)  Creating jobs to reduce unemployment          _____

2.    One important purely economic function of government is to promote competition, which presumably makes the price system more efficient.  During the 1970s the OPEC oil cartel was able to restrict output dramatically, which permitted the cartel to charge much higher prices and earn higher profits.  How did consumers, businesses, and other governments react to the higher relative price of oil?  Were such actions rational, from the point of view of the individuals involved?  Did such decisions lead to a misallocation of resources from *society's* point of view?  (Hint: the OPEC price was artificially high because the cartel reduced output and repressed competition.)

3. Complete the following table for three taxes and then indicate what type of tax each is.

| Income | Tax 1 | | Tax 2 | | Tax 3 | |
|---|---|---|---|---|---|---|
| | Tax paid | Average tax rate | Tax paid | Average tax rate | Tax paid | Average tax rate |
| $ 1,000 | $ 30 | _____ | $ 10 | _____ | $ 100 | _____ |
| 3,000 | 90 | _____ | 60 | _____ | 270 | _____ |
| 6,000 | 180 | _____ | 180 | _____ | 480 | _____ |
| 10,000 | 300 | _____ | 400 | _____ | 700 | _____ |
| 15,000 | 450 | _____ | 750 | _____ | 900 | _____ |
| 20,000 | 600 | _____ | 1200 | _____ | 1000 | _____ |
| 30,000 | 900 | _____ | 2100 | _____ | 1200 | _____ |

4. Suppose the above table had a fourth tax as shown below.  Find the average and marginal tax rates and explain what type of tax it would be.

| Income | Tax paid | Average tax rate | Marginal tax rate |
|---|---|---|---|
| $ 1,000 | $ 30 | _____ | _____ |
| 3,000 | 120 | _____ | _____ |
| 6,000 | 300 | _____ | _____ |
| 10,000 | 500 | _____ | _____ |
| 15,000 | 600 | _____ | _____ |
| 20,000 | 700 | _____ | _____ |
| 30,000 | 900 | _____ | _____ |

## BUSINESS SECTION

### Accounting: Personal Income Tax Planning Strategies

The *marginal tax rate (MTR)* relating to the highest tax bracket of an individual tax payer is frequently used to determine the tax savings that can be achieved by pursuing possible legal tax planning strategies. The following two formulae are frequently used:

*Formula 1:*    **Extra Dollar Tax Payable = MTR x Extra Income Earned**

*Formula 2:*    **Extra Dollar Tax Savings = MTR x Extra Deductions Claimed**

The table below compares the "top marginal tax rates" that apply to individuals earning an annual taxable income of $50,000 in the different Canadian provinces in 2000. The marginal tax rates that are displayed combine both the federal and provincial personal income tax rates for each province. (Source: *EY/Personal RRSP Calculator 2000,* Ernst and Young, Feb 28,2001. On-line. Internet. March 1, 2001. (Available: http://www.tax.ca/taxtools/tools/2000taxcalc.cfm?p=1&c=1)

|  | Top Marginal Tax Rates in Percent | | |
|---|---|---|---|
| Province | Dividends | Capital Gains | Other Income |
| British Columbia | 21.83% | 18.70% | 37.40% |
| Alberta | 21.63% | 18.25% | 36.50% |
| Saskatchewan | 25.68% | 20.94% | 41.88% |
| Manitoba | 27.02% | 20.61% | 41.22% |
| Ontario | 20.19% | 17.31% | 34.62% |
| Quebec | 26.76% | 21.69% | 43.38% |
| New Brunswick | 23.85% | 20.11% | 40.21% |
| Nova Scotia | 26.63% | 19.98% | 39.95% |
| P.E.I | 22.97% | 19.69% | 39.38% |
| Newfoundland | 24.17% | 20.72% | 41.43% |

The Other Income category in the table above would apply to forms of income such as employment income, interest income, and self-employment income. According to formula 1 and the table above, if a resident of BC and earns an extra $1,000 of employment or interest income then his/her extra tax payable would be:
$1000 x .3740 = $374

Some of the common tax planning strategies used to minimize an individual's personal income tax payable is described below. Make sure that you consult your General Tax Guide as well as Revenue Canada to ensure that these strategies apply to your province.

## Strategy 1: Earning income which is taxed at rates below the "Other Income" tax rate.

### Business Application Problem 1
At the start of 2000 Bill Dawson, a resident of Manitoba, transferred funds from his savings account to purchase stocks. As a result, Bill earned extra dividends in 2000 worth $10,000. How much did Bill save by earning $10,000 of dividend income instead of $10,000 of interest income.

### Business Application Problem 2
In 2000, Mona Bullock, a Nova Scotia resident decided to give up $8,000 worth of part time employment income in order to better manage her existing savings. In 2000, Mona managed to earn an extra $8,000 of capital gains by frequently buying and selling stock. How much did Mona save by earning $8,000 of capital gains income instead of $8,000 of employment income.

## Strategy 2: Deferring Income: Registered Retirement Savings Plan (RRSP)

### Business Application Problem 3
Rachel Manovickz, a resident of Ontario, used funds from her employment earnings in 2000 to deposit  $5,000 into a RRSP. By doing this, Rachel was able to claim an extra $5,000 deduction on her income tax return.  Calculate the extra tax savings that will accrue in 2000 due to this RRSP. Will Rachel ever have to pay tax on this $5,000 of employment income?

## Strategy 3: Claim the maximum allowable tax deductions and tax credits.

### Business Application Problem 4
On his 2000 Saskatchewan tax return Perry Cuomo decided to claim $3,000 worth of moving costs he incurred when moving between cities to start a new job. Calculate the extra tax savings resulting from this extra deduction.

### ANSWERS TO CHAPTER 6

COMPLETION QUESTIONS

1. failure
2. inefficient
3. third parties
4. negative
5. over
6. positive; under
7. taxes
8. subsidizing production, financing production, regulation
9. promote
10. indivisible; zero; do not; difficult
11. not pay
12. providing a legal system,  promoting competition, correcting externalities, providing public goods, ensuring economy-wide stability.
13. decrease
14. discouraging, redistributing
15. zero; positive
16. like; different
17. their own
18. proportional, dollar; majority; differ
19. non-elected; special interest; perks such as a large staff, pensions
20. is not; rationally ignorant
21. self interest

22. capital; capital
23. highest
24. stockholders, consumers, employees
25. proportional
26. encourages

## TRUE-FALSE QUESTIONS

1.  F    Even in capitalist countries the government plays a major role.
2.  T
3.  T
4.  T
5.  F    A tax will cause the price of the good to *rise*, which is a movement in the correct direction.
6.  F    The free rider problem deals with goods that are *scarce*, but for which the exclusion principle does not work well. The price system will under-allocate resources to public goods.
7.  T
8.  F    It is an economic function because by enforcing contracts government can promote incentives to buy and sell which makes markets operate effectively.
9.  T
10. F    Whether or not a good is a merit good requires value judgements about good or bad.
11. F    Scarcity exists in the public sector too; after all, the government uses and allocates scarce goods.
12. T
13. F    The goods will differ because proportional rule in the private sector can reveal intensity of wants, while majority rule cannot.
14. T
15. T
16. F    Dollar votes indicate a proportional rule system.
17. F    For average taxes to rise with income (a progressive tax) the marginal tax rate must exceed the average tax rate.
18. F    "Equitable" is a normative statement based on value judgements.
19. F    No, the personal income tax does so.
20. T
21. F    It is proportional.

## MULTIPLE CHOICE QUESTIONS

1. c;   When injured third parties are not compensated this results in overproduction of  the product in question, a symptom of market failure
2. c;   When buyers and sellers are forced to pay the full opportunity costs of their actions it is in their best interests to refrain from allocating too many resources to the production and consumption of the good in question
3. d;   In a positive externality situation, the producing firm is not compensated for the the benefits conferred on third parties. Therefore this product is underproduced from a social view.
4. a;   Income redistribution is a political function as it is normative in nature.
5. c;   When externalities exist the market system misallocates resources by either overallocating resources or underallocating resources in the market.
        *TIP*: The market overallocates resources to the production of a good which entails external costs. The market underallocates resources to the production of a good which entails external benefits.
6. c;   A demerit good is the only situation which relates to the political function.
7. a;   Since it is very difficult, if not impossible to exclude non payers from benefiting from a public good, the exclusion principle does not work in these cases.
8. b;   The principle of rival consumption does not apply to public goods. In other words,  if one individual  consumes some of the benefits from national security, this does not reduce the amount of benefit that is available to another consumer.

9. b;  If goods are consumed collectively, non payers can still benefit from the public good. This means that there is no incentive to pay for the provision of the good. *TIP:* Due to the free rider problem, the private sector would not produce a desirable public good. Because of this type of market failure, the government must provide the public good.

10. a;  If good A is a public good it is not subject to the exclusion principle. This means that Mr Ayres has no incentive to convey the intensity of his wants as it is impossible to deny him the benefits even if he does not pay for good A. *TIP: Principle of rival consumption* implies that if one consumer wants to consume more of a private good this means that less of the good will be available to other consumers. In order to obtain more of the private good the consumer will have to convey his/her intensity of wants by paying a higher price.

11. d;  These goods are not easily classified as it depends on whether the political system deems these goods desirable or undesirable. These classifications can change over time.

12. d;  If group A is taxed, the reduced after tax income may reduce A's incentives. If group B receives the proceeds of the taxes without earning them, this also may reduce incentives.

13. a;  All governments are able to engage in the legal use of force to ensure individuals adhere to collective decisions. As an example, governments can seize your assets if you refuse to pay your taxes.

14. c;  Due to the absence of the profit motive and competition, there is less of an incentive to be efficient in the public sector. Bureaucrats often have an incentive to expand the size of their department.

15. a;  The public choice theory assumes that voters, bureaucrats, and politicians attempt to pursue their self interest. As an example since bureaucrats are often rewarded based on the size of their clientele, they are motivated to increase the size of the government department.

16. c;  For many public issues, voters decide to remain at some level of ignorance as the extra benefits from obtaining more information may not be worth the extra cost.

17. b;  Voters tend to be ignorant of many issues, for rational reasons; the extra benefits from obtaining more information may not be worth the extra cost. *TIP: Rational ignorance* explains why voters often choose to be uninformed about a public issue as the extra benefits from obtaining more information may not be worth the extra cost. Rational ignorance can explain how a minority of politicians, bureaucrats and interest groups can have a disproportionate amount of political power.

18. a;  Due to rational ignorance, bureaucrats can organize and coach their clientele (interest groups) so as to  influence the amount of funding granted and the activities which they engage.

19. a.  Due to rational ignorance, people may be tempted to enter politics as a means to maximize income and wealth.

20. a;  With progressive taxes, since the marginal tax rate exceeds the average tax rate, the average tax rate increases as taxable income increases.

21. c;  A 90% marginal tax rate means that for each additional dollar of income earned, Mr Romano only can take home $.10. He would have a strong incentive not to earn additional income.

22. d.  An example of a proportional tax would be a 20% flat tax. This means that an individual earning $10,000 would pay $2,000 in taxes. A person earning $100,000 would  pay $20,000 in taxes.

23. c;  The personal income tax is progressive. As ones taxable income increases, the percentage of income paid in taxes also increases.

24. d;  To the extent that due to the corporate income tax, consumers pay higher prices, employees earn lower wages and shareholders receive a reduced profit. All these groups "pay" for this tax.

25. b;   The CPP premium rate is  predicted to increase due to the demographic trend
         of an ageing population.
26. a;   The income tax is unlike the other taxes as it is not based on the sale or
         consumption of goods. Rather it is based on ones income level.
27. c;   A tax on consumption encourages savings as this is  one way one can avoid the
         tax.

## MATCHING

a and 2;   b and 6;   c and 1; d and 5;   e and 3;   f and 4;   g and 8;   h and 9;
i and 7

## WORKING WITH GRAPHS

1.   a.   $P_2; Q_2$
     b.   social costs
     c.   $P_1; Q_1$
     d.   too much
     e.   negative
2.   a.   $P_3; Q_3$
     b.   social benefits
     c.   $P_1; Q_1$
     d.   too little
     e.   positive
3.   a.   The supply curve after the tax is imposed shifts to $S_1$—that is, upward by $20 at each quantity.
          This is shown in the graph below.

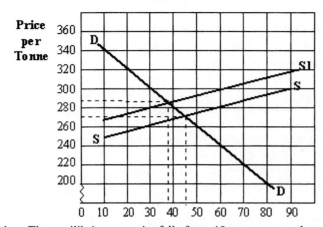

     b.   The equilibrium quantity falls from 45 tons per month to below 40 tons per
          month as a result.  Thus the quantity of fertilizer produced has declined by more
          than 10 percent.  This means that the output of pollution has declined by more
          than 10 percent, because the output of pollution is a constant per unit of output
          of fertilizer. The result of the analysis should not be extended in a general
          fashion without regard to other possible effects that a tax of this nature might
          have.  We might also wish to consider other factors before imposing a pollution
          tax.  Among these factors are the effects of the increased price of the fertilizer,
          the likely reduction in employment as a result of the reduced quantity of
          fertilizer produced, and the ability of alternative methods of pollution control to
          achieve the same results.

**PROBLEMS**

1.  a.  redistribution
    b.  promoting competition
    c.  providing merit goods
    d.  discouraging demerit goods
    e.  providing public goods
    f.  redistribution
    g.  providing legal system
    h.  correcting positive externality
    i.  providing legal system
    j.  correcting negative externality
    k.  stabilizing economy

2.  Consumers joined car pools, drove less often, bought smaller cars, and endured less comfortable temperatures at home; businesses invested in the production of such oil substitutes as solar energy, nuclear energy, shale oil, coal, etc.; governments subsidized the production of gasohol and shale oil, etc.  Such actions were rational because they were responses to a perceived increase in the relative price of oil and its  distillates.  From society's point of view, such actions led to a misallocation because the lack of competition caused the price system to transmit an incorrect signal.  The signal was that oil had become more scarce—but the signal was induced by an artificial restriction of supply.

3.  Tax 1:  3 percent; 3 percent; 3 percent; 3 percent; 3 percent; 3 percent; 3 percent; proportional
    Tax 2:  1 percent; 2 percent; 3 percent; 4 percent; 5 percent; 6 percent; 7 percent; progressive
    Tax 3:  10 percent; 9 percent; 8 percent; 7 percent; 6 percent; 5 percent; 4 percent; regressive

4.  ATR:  3 percent; 4 percent; 5 percent; 5 percent; 4 percent; 3.5 percent; 3 percent
    MTR:  3 percent; 4.5 percent; 6 percent; 5 percent; 2 percent; 2 percent; 2 percent

    The average tax rate for this tax initially rises and then falls, as does the marginal tax rate.  As a result, this tax is progressive up to an income of $6,000, proportional from there to $10,000, and regressive for levels of income above $10,000.  Thus this tax is a combination of all three types of taxes as income varies.  Can you graph the ATR and MTR for this tax?  What specific taxes might behave in this manner?

**BUSINESS SECTION**

1.  (.4122x$10,000) - (.2702x$10,000) = 4122 – 2702 = $1420 of savings
2.  (.3995x$8000) – (.1998x$8000) =3196 – 1598.40 = $1597.60 of savings
3.  (.3462x5000) = $1731 of savings in 2000. In later years, when Rachel withdraws the funds from her RRSP she may have to pay the related tax, depending on her income.
4.  (.4188x$3000) = $1256.40 savings

**ANSWERS TO EXAMPLE QUESTIONS FOR CRITICAL ANALYSIS**

**I    INTERNATIONAL POLICY EXAMPLE 6-1: Who Should Pay the High Cost of a Legal System?** (p. 127)
Other costs that society pays in the legal system include the following:
- Lost output that could have been produced by witnesses and litigants during the time spent in court.
- Salaries of other court officials such as court reporters.
- Lawyers fees passed on in the prices of goods and services.

**II    INTERNATIONAL EXAMPLE 6-1: Are Lighthouses a Public Good?** (p. 129)
1. Indivisible: If a lighthouse is built and operated, then any ship at sea can see the light. The light cannot be packaged and sold in discrete units.
2. Can be used by additional people at no additional cost: Once the lighthouse is built, its light can be seen by increasing numbers of mariners while the cost of the light remains the same.

3. Additional users do not deprive others of any of its services: A mariner viewing the light from the lighthouse does not "use up" any of the light. Thus any number of people can see the light and be warned by it.

III    **INTERNATIONAL POLICY EXAMPLE 6-2: Do Government-Funded Sports Stadiums Have a Net Positive Effect on Local Economies?** (p. 130)
Theoretically, the answer to this question is that government funded sports stadiums can provide external economies to the local community. From a direct benefit view, the sports stadium can attract people from other cities to the home city, such as players, player staff, player families, media staff, and the general public. Many of these visitors spend money in the local hotels, local restaurants and shops. From an indirect view, the fact that a city has a major league sports team can help to attract new resident firms and homeowners. However, "there has not been an independent study by an economist over the past thirty years, suggesting an overall net positive impact on the local community. According to this evidence, sports stadiums do fall in the category of merit goods.

IV    **EXAMPLE 6-1: Education Transfer Payments** (p. 131)
A tax deduction acts as an incentive to the taxpayer to undertake the activity which will earn the deduction. The positive externalities from increased participation in post-secondary education would be greater than any benefits flowing from home ownership.

V    **INTERNATIONAL POLICY EXAMPLE 6-3: Average and Marginal Tax Rates Around the World** (p. 137)
Theoretically, one would expect that ones marginal tax rate plays a bigger role in affecting ones incentive to work harder to earn additional income. This is because it is the marginal tax rate that applies to the additional income one is planning to earn.

# CHAPTER 7

# CONSUMER CHOICE

### PUTTING THIS CHAPTER INTO PERSPECTIVE

Chapter 7 analyzes consumer choice.  The body of this chapter is concerned with the traditional, or classical, theory of consumer behavior, which is referred to as utility analysis.  In the appendix to this chapter (which is analyzed separately immediately following this section), the more modern approach to the study of consumer behavior— indifference curve analysis—is presented.

Your understanding of Chapter 7 and its appendix will be aided immeasurably by your learning to distinguish between an ordinal measure and a cardinal measure.  (See footnote 1, in the text.)  In this chapter we deal with utility as something that can be measured cardinally.  The analysis in the appendix, however, requires only that utility be measured ordinally—a less stringent, and therefore more analytically powerful—requirement.

You are also well-advised to study carefully the distinction between total utility and marginal utility—and how they are related.  As long as marginal utility is positive, total utility will rise; if marginal utility is rising, total utility will rise at an *increasing* rate; if marginal utility is constant, total utility will rise at a constant rate (the total utility curve would be linear); if marginal utility falls, then total utility will rise at a *decreasing* rate. Learn how "marginal" and "total" are related now, because we shall return to these concepts often.

Equally important is the relationship between marginal utility and average utility (or "average" and "marginal" anything); marginal pulls and tugs average.  Thus, if marginal is above average, then average will rise; if marginal is below average, then average will fall; if marginal equals average, then average will remain constant.  The relationship between marginal and average is also a recurring thread in this text; learn it now, once and for all.

Another important (and recurring) topic is the concept "marginal utility per dollar's worth," which in equation form is MU/P, or marginal utility divided by price.  Play around with this ratio; convince yourself that given MU, changes in price lead to changes in marginal utility per dollar's worth of a good.  Also, learn exactly what the inequality $MU_1/P_1 > MU_2/P_2$ means, and *exactly* what the inequality $MU_1/P_1 < MU_2/P_2$ means, and learn what such an inequality implies about consumer optimization behavior.

Time spent now on the concepts stressed here will pay handsome dividends in the future. If you really master these concepts, then the analysis that lies ahead in later chapters will be much easier.

## LEARNING OBJECTIVES

After you have studied this chapter you should be able to

1.  define utility, util, marginal utility, marginal analysis, diminishing marginal utility, and consumer optimum.

2.  distinguish between total utility and marginal utility, and answer questions that require an understanding of how they are related.

3.  distinguish between marginal utility and average utility, and answer questions that require an understanding of how they are related.

4.  apply the concept of diminishing marginal utility to the law of demand.

5.  predict what happens to the marginal utility per dollar's worth of a good when (a) its price changes, other things being constant and (b) more or less is consumed, other things being constant.

6.  predict what a consumer will do if the marginal utility per dollar's worth of good A is greater (less) than the marginal utility per dollar's worth of good B.

7.  answer questions that require an understanding of how economists can explain the diamond-water paradox.

## CHAPTER OUTLINE

1.  **Utility analysis** is the study of consumer decision making based on utility maximization.
    a.  A **util** is an artificial unit by which **utility** is measured.
    b.  Total utility is the sum of all the **utils** derived from consumption; **marginal utility** is the change in total utility due to a one-unit change in the quantity of a good consumed.
    c.  Economists maintain that economic decisions are made by comparing the marginal benefit of an activity with its marginal cost.
    d.  When relative price changes, it is the marginal buyers who respond, not the average buyers.
    e.  As long as **marginal utility** is positive, total utility will rise.
    f.  If **marginal utility** becomes negative—the good becomes a nuisance— total utility will fall.

2.    The principle of **diminishing marginal utility** states that as more of any good or service is consumed, eventually its extra benefit declines.

3.    Consumers are assumed to optimize their consumption choices; the consumer attempts to maximize total utility subject to such constraints as income and relative prices.

4.    When relative price changes, the **consumer optimum** is affected and the consumer reacts consistently and predictably. A consumer is optimizing when she allocates all of her money income in such a way that the **marginal utility** per dollar's worth of goods and services purchased is equated.

5.    The "law" of **diminishing marginal utility** can account for the law of demand; because the marginal benefit falls to consumers as they consume more per unit of time, price must fall to induce them to purchase more.

6.    The *diamond-water paradox* is that diamonds are unessential to life and have a high relative price, while water is essential to life yet has a low relative price.
      a.    The total utility of water to humans far exceeds the total utility of diamonds to humans; but the **marginal utility** of water is relatively low and the **marginal utility** of diamonds is high.
      b.    The price of a good, therefore, reflects its value on the margin—not its total or average value.

## KEY TERMS AND CONCEPTS

Utility                           Marginal utility
Util                              Utility analysis
Consumer optimum          Diminishing marginal utility

## COMPLETION QUESTIONS

Fill in the blank or circle the correct term.

1.    The want-satisfying power that a good or service possesses is referred to as

      _____.

2.    The _____ is an artificial unit by which utility is measured.

3.    The change in total utility due to a one-unit change in quantity consumed is called
      _____; _____ analysis is the study of what happens when small changes take place relative to the status quo.

4.  When relative price changes, the (average, marginal) buyer responds; economists maintain that (average, marginal) analysis is the key to understanding human behaviour

5.  If marginal utility is positive, total utility must (fall, rise); if marginal utility is negative, total utility must (fall, rise); if marginal utility falls (but is positive) then total utility must (fall, rise) at a decreasing rate.

6.  Economists maintain that as more of a good or service is consumed, per unit of time, its marginal benefit (falls, rises); therefore before buyers will purchase more and more of a good, its price must (fall, rise).

7.  The consumer optimum exists when consumers (minimize, maximize) their total utility; in order to optimize, a consumer should allocate his income so that the marginal utility per dollar's worth of each good or service he purchases is (equal, not equal).

8.  Assume a consumer is in consumer optimum and then the price of good A rises, other things being constant.  It is now true that the marginal utility per dollar's worth of good A is (less, greater) than the marginal utility per dollar's worth of other goods; the consumer will now feel (richer, poorer) and probably spend (more, less) on good A.

9.  Although the (marginal, total) utility of water is greater than that of diamonds, the (marginal, total) utility of diamonds is higher; the price of a good reflects its (marginal, average, total) utility.


## TRUE-FALSE QUESTIONS

Circle the T if the statement is true, the F if it is false.  Explain to yourself why a statement is false.

T  F  1.  Economists today maintain that utility can be measured cardinally.

T  F  2.  Economists maintain that decisions are made on the margin; hence the concept of "margin" is usually more important than that of "average."

T  F  3.  Positive economics permits economists to say that person 1 gets more utility from ice cream than does person 2.

T  F  4.  If total utility rises at a decreasing rate, then marginal utility must be falling.

T  F  5.  If marginal utility is less than average utility, then average utility must rise.

T  F     6.    Economists typically assume that as a person consumes more of any good, that good's total utility must fall.

T  F     7.    If the MU of good X/price of good X exceeds the MU of good Y/price of good Y, the consumer can increase her total utility by substituting good X for good Y.

T  F     8.    The law of diminishing marginal utility implies the law of demand, assuming consumers wish to optimize.

T  F     9.    Because price reflects average utility rather than total utility, diamonds are more expensive than water.

## MULTIPLE CHOICE QUESTIONS

Circle the letter that corresponds to the best answer.

1.    If marginal utility is positive, but falling, then total utility
      a.  falls.
      b.  falls at a decreasing rate.
      c.  rises.
      d.  rises at a decreasing rate.

2.    Which of the following words is most unlike the others?
      a.  marginal
      b.  average
      c.  incremental
      d.  extra

3.    When the relative price of good A rises, the
      a.  average buyer is affected.
      b.  marginal buyer is affected.
      c.  total buyer is affected.
      d.  marginal utility of good A falls.

4.    As more of good A is consumed per week, over broad ranges
      a.  the marginal utility of good A falls.
      b.  the total utility of good A rises.
      c.  the total utility of good A rises at a decreasing rate.
      d.  All of the above

5.    If marginal utility is negative, then
      a.  total utility falls.
      b.  total utility rises at a decreasing rate.
      c.  total utility must be negative.
      d.  None of the above.

6.    Consumer optimizing requires that the consumer
      a.  maximize income.
      b.  maximize total utility, subject to an income constraint.
      c.  maximize marginal utility, subject to an income constraint.
      d.  maximize average utility, subject to an income constraint.

7.    If the price of good A rises, other things being constant, then
      a.  the marginal utility of good A falls.
      b.  the marginal utility of good A rises.
      c.  the marginal utility per dollar's worth of good A falls.
      d.  the relative price of good A falls.

8.    Diamonds have a higher price than water because
      a.  people are shallow and shortsighted.
      b.  price reflects total, not marginal, utility.
      c.  price reflects marginal, not total, utility.
      d.  the total utility of diamonds is greater, but the marginal utility of water is greater.

**WORKING WITH GRAPHS**

1.    Use the information given below to complete the table.

| Hamburgers consumed per month | Total utility (in utils) | Marginal utility (in utils) |
|---|---|---|
| 0 | 0 | _____ |
| 1 | 5 | _____ |
| 2 | 14 | _____ |
| 3 | 22 | _____ |
| 4 | 28 | _____ |
| 5 | 33 | _____ |
| 6 | 36 | _____ |
| 7 | 35 | _____ |
| 8 | 32 | _____ |

a)  Graph the total and marginal utility curves on the graph provided below.  (Plot the marginal utilities at the midpoint between quantities.)

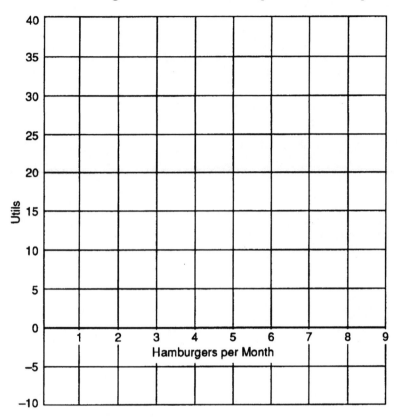

b)  At what quantity does diminishing marginal utility set in?

2.  Consider the graphs below, then answer the questions that follow.

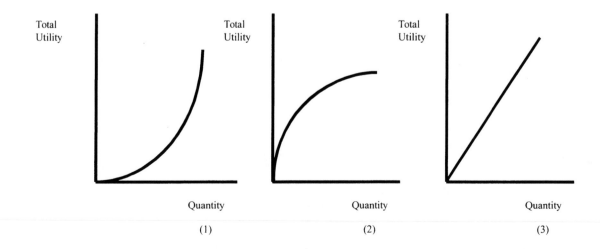

a.  Which panel indicates constant marginal utility?


b.  Which panel indicates increasing marginal utility?


c.  Which panel indicates decreasing marginal utility?


## PROBLEMS

1.  Consider the following information.

| Quantity Consumed per week | Candy Bars ($.25) | | | Apples ($.125) | | |
|---|---|---|---|---|---|---|
| | Total utility | Marginal utility | MU/P | Total utility | Marginal utility | MU/P |
| 0 | 0 | ___ | ___ | 0 | ___ | ___ |
| 1 | 10 | ___ | ___ | 15 | ___ | ___ |
| 2 | 18 | ___ | ___ | 24 | ___ | ___ |
| 3 | 25 | ___ | ___ | 30 | ___ | ___ |
| 4 | 29 | ___ | ___ | 32 | ___ | ___ |
| 5 | 30 | ___ | ___ | 29 | ___ | ___ |

a.  Complete the columns containing the marginal utilities of each good.


b.  With unlimited income, a consumer described by the above information would consume _____ candy bars and _____ apples.


c.  If candy bars cost 25 cents each and apples are two for a quarter (12.5 cents each) and the consumer has $1.50 to spend on candy and apples, what quantity of candy bars and apples will put the above consumer into an equilibrium situation? See the table above.


d.  Now suppose the consumer suffers a loss of income and has 20 cents to spend. In addition, the price of candy bars is now 10 cents and the price of apples is 2 cents. What quantities of each will put the consumer in equilibrium? See the table below.

| Quantity Consumed per week | Candy Bars ($.10) | | | Apples ($.02) | | |
|---|---|---|---|---|---|---|
| | Total utility | Marginal utility | MU/P | Total utility | Marginal utility | MU/P |
| 0 | 0 | ____ | ____ | 0 | ____ | ____ |
| 1 | 10 | ____ | ____ | 15 | ____ | ____ |
| 2 | 18 | ____ | ____ | 24 | ____ | ____ |
| 3 | 25 | ____ | ____ | 30 | ____ | ____ |
| 4 | 29 | ____ | ____ | 32 | ____ | ____ |
| 5 | 30 | ____ | ____ | 29 | ____ | ____ |

2.  Mr. Smith does not believe that economists are correct when they say that diminishing marginal utility is the rule for most goods.  He claims that *increasing* marginal utility is the rule:  as he consumes more and more of any good, his marginal utility rises.

    Assume that Mr. Smith spends his income one dollar at a time, and that he can purchase one dollar's worth of any good.  Assume further that he wishes to maximize his total utility. On what good does Mr. Smith spend his first dollar?  The second?  The third?

    What predictions can you make about his behavior?

    Do most people behave that way?  Does anyone?

**BUSINESS SECTION**
**Marketing: Four Types of Utility**

In order to offer a product or service that meets the needs of the target market, marketers find it useful to strive to respond to four types of utility that consumers consider important – form utility, place utility, information utility, ownership utility.

Form utility refers to the nature of the product or service including other important product related features (where relevant)  such as the packaging, safety features, after purchase support, and warranties. Place utility focuses on the need to have the product available when it is needed by the consumer at a convenient location. Information utility concerns the availability of knowledge about a product or service through various media such as the newspaper, radio, T.V, personal selling and the internet. Promotional incentives such as coupons and contests relate to informational utility. Ownership utility refers to facilitating the exchange process at the point of purchase. Affordable prices, discounts, credit terms, and lay-away plans assist the consumer in obtaining ownership or possession of the product.

## Business Application Problem

Specific strategies and activities undertaken by the Toronto Blue Jays organization during the 1990s are listed below. Match the activity/strategy below to one of the four types of utilities described above.

1.  a.  Each Blue Jays game gets good coverage by all the major national newspapers in Canada.

    b.  The SkyDome was deliberately built in the downtown area, which makes it very accessible using the existing public transit.

    c.  The Blue Jays players engage in lots of charity and community work in the Toronto area.

    d.  There are a lot of good restaurants situated right in the stadium so fans rarely have to wait in lines for concession products.

    e.  The price of a ticket is relatively low when compared to major U.S. stadiums.

    f.  The stadium dome is designed to provide open air viewing when the weather is cooperative and shelter when it is not.

    g.  The Toronto Blue Jays management has deliberately restricted the number of seasons tickets so as to allow the casual baseball fan access to ball games.

    h.  The stadium has been designed in a way that most of the seats have a good view of the play in progress.

    i.  Both players and fans are featured in regular radio spots.

    j.  Each game features a lot of giveaways.

### ANSWERS TO CHAPTER 7

**COMPLETION QUESTIONS**

1.  utility
2.  util
3.  marginal utility; marginal
4.  marginal; marginal

5. rise; fall; rise
6. falls; fall
7. maximize, income; equal
8. less; poorer, less
9. total, marginal; marginal

## TRUE-FALSE QUESTIONS

1.  F   They need only to assume that it can be measured ordinally.
2.  T
3.  F   Interpersonal utility comparisons require normative judgments.
4.  T
5.  F   If marginal is less than average, average will fall
6.  F   They assume that its *marginal utility* falls.
7.  T
8.  T
9.  F   Price reflects marginal utility.

## MULTIPLE CHOICE QUESTIONS

1. d;  Total utility is the sum of all utils derived from consumption.
2. b;  All the other terms would mean "additional".
3. b;  We compare additional benefits with additional costs.
4. d;  As extra satisfaction decreases, total satisfaction would still be increasing but at a slower rate.
5. a;  A rational consumer would stop purchasing at the point marginal utility becomes negative, therefore, total utility would decrease.
6. b;  Choose a set of goods and services that maximize satisfaction.
7. c;  If there is less satisfaction with good A, then, MU of good A is divided by price of good A.
8. c;  We get more satisfaction from one extra diamond.

## WORKING WITH GRAPHS

1.  a.   0; 5; 9; 8; 6; 5; 3; 1; -3

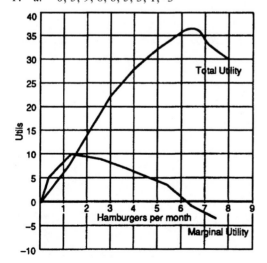

   b.  with the third hamburger consumed each month

2.  a.  3
    b.  1
    c.  2

## PROBLEMS

1.  a.  marginal utility of candy bars:  0, 10, 8, 7, 4,1 MU/P 0, 40, 32, 28, 16, 4; marginal utility of apples:  0, 15, 9, 6, 2, -3  MU/P 0, 120, 72, 48, 16, -24
    b.  5, 4
    c.  4 candy bars and 4 apples
    d.  marginal utility of candy bars:  0, 10, 8, 7, 4,1 MU/$ 0, 100, 80, 70, 40, 10; marginal utility of apples:  0, 15, 9, 6, 2, -3  MU/$ 0, 750, 450, 300, 100, -150 therefore equilibrium would be 1 candy bar and 4 apples.  Note that the consumer has 2 cents left over, cannot purchase another candy bar, and will not purchase another apple, since the additional apple has a negative marginal utility (total utility declines).
2.  Mr. Smith will spend every dollar of his income on the same good—that which gives him the highest marginal utility per dollar's worth of his first dollar spent.  Only drug addicts, perhaps, behave that way.

## BUSINESS SECTION

1.  a.  Information utility        b.   Place utility           c.   Information utility
    d.  Product utility           e.   Ownership utlity        f.   Product utility
    g.  Ownership utility         h.   Product utility         i.   Information utility
    j.  Product and/or information utility.

## ANSWERS TO EXAMPLE QUESTIONS FOR CRITICAL ANALYSIS

**I    EXAMPLE 7-1: Newspaper Vending Machines Versus Candy Vending Machines** (p. 154)
One situation would be where an important historic event such as the end or beginning of a war, or a landing on the moon has taken place. In this case, the front page which carries the headlines could have value in the future.

**II    INTERNATIONAL EXAMPLE 7-1: The World of Water in Saudi Arabia** (p. 159)
People in Saudi Arabia would use showers that use very little water compared to those in Canada. They might even turn off the shower while they soaped up, turning it back on to rinse. They would not shower as often. Water would not be used to grow lawns or to wash cars. Water-intensive appliances such as dishwashers would probably not be used.

## APPENDIX B

## MORE ADVANCED CONSUMER CHOICE THEORY

### PUTTING THIS APPENDIX INTO PERSPECTIVE

In Appendix B the more modern, but more difficult, theory of consumer demand is analyzed. Here we assume that utility *cannot* be measured cardinally; instead it can be measured only ordinally. In other words, people can only rank one combination of goods and services as being more preferable to, less preferable to, or equally preferable to another combination of goods. Another way to think of this is to realize that 30 utils is preferable to 15 utils, but 30 utils are not necessarily *twice* as preferable as 15 utils (as would be the case if utility were cardinally measurable).

In this appendix we introduce the indifference curve, explore its properties, and develop an indifference map. Then a budget line is constructed, and its properties are explored. By graphing an indifference map and a budget line, a more sophisticated analysis of the consumer optimum position is possible.

Then we turn to some of the fun topics. We show what happens to consumer optimum when income, and then price, changes; next we derive a price-consumption line; finally we derive a demand curve using the indifference curve-budget line model.

### LEARNING OBJECTIVES

After you have studied Appendix B you should be able to

1. define indifference curve, budget constraint, income-consumption curve, and price-consumption curve.

2. draw an indifference curve based on data presented in a table.

3. answer questions that require a proper interpretation of an indifference curve and of an indifference map.

4. recognize properties of indifference curves.

5. interpret the meaning of the slope of an indifference curve and the slope of a budget line.

6. recognize the consumer optimum combination of goods, given an indifference map and a budget line.

7. interpret and sketch an income-consumption curve and a price-consumption curve.

8.  predict what happens to a budget line when each price changes and when income changes.


## APPENDIX OUTLINE

1.  This appendix presents a more rigorous and more formal analysis of consumer behaviour.
    a.  An **indifference curve** is the set of consumption alternatives which yield the same total amount of satisfaction.
    b.  **Indifference curves** have important properties.
        i.  **Indifference curves** are negatively sloped.
        ii. **Indifference curves** are never linear; they are convex with respect to the origin.
    c.  The slope of an **indifference curve** is referred to as the marginal rate of substitution, which is the change in the quantity of one good that just offsets a one-unit change in the consumption of another good, so that total satisfaction remains constant.

2.  An indifference map is a set of **indifference curves**; higher **indifference curves** represent higher levels of satisfaction (because they permit more consumption of *both goods*), and lower **indifference curves** represent less preferred combinations of goods.

3.  A **budget constraint** represents the set of opportunities facing a decision maker.
    a.  The budget line is derived assuming a fixed money income and a given set of relative prices.
    b.  The slope of a budget line is (the negative of) the ratio of the prices of the relevant goods.
    c.  The position of a budget line depends on the level of nominal income; if nominal income changes, a parallel shift in the budget line results.

4.  Consumer optimum exists at that point (combination of goods and services) where the slope of the **indifference curve** equals the slope of the budget line; at that point the consumer is maximizing utility.

5.  If nominal and relative prices are held constant and income is increased, an **income-consumption curve** can be derived.

6.  A **price-consumption curve** is the set of consumer optimum combinations of two goods that results when the price of one good changes, holding money income and the price of the other good constant.

7.  A demand curve can be derived from the indifference map-budget line model; as the price of one good changes, other things being constant (the price of the other

good and money income), consumer optimum changes so as to indicate an inverse relationship between price and quantity demanded.

## KEY TERMS AND CONCEPTS

Indifference curve                          Price–consumption curve
Income–consumption curve               Budget constraint

## COMPLETION QUESTIONS
Fill in the blank or circle the correct term.

1. A curve that indicates combinations of goods and services that yield an equal level of satisfaction is called a(n) _____ curve; such a curve is (positively, negatively) sloped.

2. Ignoring its sign, the slope of an indifference curve (falls, rises) as we move down the curve; a set of indifference curves is called an indifference _____.

3. If indifference curve B lies below indifference curve A, it is (less, more) preferred; if indifference curve C lies above indifference curve A, indifference curve C permits a consumer to consume (less, more) of both goods.

4. A _____ line is derived holding relative (income, prices) constant and holding nominal (income, prices) constant; the slope of a budget constraint line is determined by relative (income, prices), and the position of such a line depends on (income, prices).

5. Consumer optimum exists where the budget constraint line is (parallel, tangent) to a(n) _____ curve; at such a point the (lowest, highest) indifference curve is achieved.

6. If income falls, other things being constant, the budget line shifts (inward, outward); generally a reduction in income will lead to a(n) (decrease, increase) in its quantity demanded.

7. If the price of one good changes, the slope of an indifference curve (remains constant, changes); if the price of one good changes, the slope of a budget constraint line (remains constant, changes); if nominal income changes, the slope of a budget constraint line (remains constant, changes).

8. Along a price-consumption curve, which relates the combinations of good A and good B that a consumer will purchase, the price of good A falls while the price of good B (rises, falls, remains constant) and nominal income (rises, falls, remains constant).

## TRUE-FALSE QUESTIONS
Circle the T if the statement is true, the F if it is false.  Explain to yourself why a statement is false.

T  F    1.  Along an indifference curve, a consumer has the same level of marginal utility.

T  F    2.  Indifference curves are negatively sloped.

T  F    3.  Indifference curves are usually linear.

T  F    4.  The slope of the budget constraint curve is referred to as the marginal rate of substitution.

T  F    5.  Points below a budget constraint line are not an attainable goods combination for a consumer.

T  F    6.  If indifference curve 3 lies above indifference curve 2, it is less preferable to the consumer.

T  F    7.  Indifference curves that lie entirely above a budget constraint line are unattainable for the consumer.

T  F    8.  If nominal income changes, then the slope of an indifference curve changes.

T  F    9.  If nominal income changes, then the slope of a budget constraint line changes.

T  F    10. If relative prices change, then the slope of a budget constraint line changes, but the slope of an indifference curve is unaltered.

T  F    11. Consumer optimum is attained where the budget constraint line is tangent to the highest possible indifference curve.

T  F    12. Along an income-consumption curve, prices remain constant.

T  F    13. Along a price-consumption curve, relative prices change, but money income is constant.

**MULTIPLE CHOICE QUESTIONS**

Circle the letter that corresponds to the best answer.

1.  Along an indifference curve,
    a.  total utility stays the same.
    b.  marginal utility stays the same.
    c.  average utility stays the same.
    d.  All of the above

2.  In indifference curve analysis, if combination A is preferred to combination B and combination B is preferred to combination C, then
    a.  A is on a higher indifference curve than B or C.
    b.  C is on a lower indifference curve than A or B.
    c.  A, B, and C are on different indifference curves.
    d.  All of the above

3.  Indifference curves
    a.  are upward sloping.
    b.  are linear.
    c.  are convex with respect to the origin.
    d.  indicate objective, not subjective, valuations of a consumer.

4.  As we move down an indifference curve, the marginal rate of substitution
    a.  remains constant.
    b.  remains constant, but total utility rises.
    c.  changes.
    d.  changes, but total utility rises.

5.  The negative of the slope of a(n) _____ is the marginal rate of substitution.
    a.  production possibilities curve
    b.  budget constraint line
    c.  income-consumption curve
    d.  indifference curve

6.  Where consumer optimum is reached,
    a.  the slope of the budget constraint line equals the slope of an indifference curve.
    b.  the ratio of relative prices equals the marginal rate of substitution.
    c.  the consumer attains the highest indifference curve, given the budget constraint line.
    d.  All of the above

7.  The slope of the budget constraint line
    a.  reflects the relative prices of the two goods in question.
    b.  reflects the consumer's income.
    c.  varies as nominal income varies.
    d.  always equals the slope of the indifference curve.

8.    If income rises, other things being constant, then
      a.   an indifference curve shifts outward.
      b.   a parallel, rightward shift in the budget constraint line occurs.
      c.   the slope of the budget constraint line falls.
      d.   the slope of the budget constraint line rises.

9.    When a price-consumption curve is derived,
      a.   the relative price of both goods changes.
      b.   the relative price of only one good changes.
      c.   money income changes.
      d.   consumer optimum is not attained.

10.   When an income-consumption curve is derived,
      a.   relative prices remain constant.
      b.   income changes.
      c.   consumer optimum exists at each point along such a curve.
      d.   All of the above

11.   When the price of good A rises, other things being constant,
      a.   the indifference map does not change.
      b.   the slope of the budget constraint line changes.
      c.   a new consumer optimum is reached, where less of good A is purchased.
      d.   All of the above

## WORKING WITH GRAPHS

1.    Suppose that a consumer is faced with the choice of only two goods:  food and
      entertainment.   After some consideration, the consumer provides the following
      information about various combinations of food and entertainment per month to
      which she is indifferent, given some particular level of satisfaction.

| Units of entertainment per month | Units of food per month |
|---|---|
| 35 | 7 |
| 20 | 11 |
| 10 | 15 |
| 5 | 20 |
| 3 | 30 |
| 2 | 45 |

      a.   Use this information and the following grid to plot this consumer's indifference
      curve for entertainment and food for a given level of satisfaction.  Label the curve I.

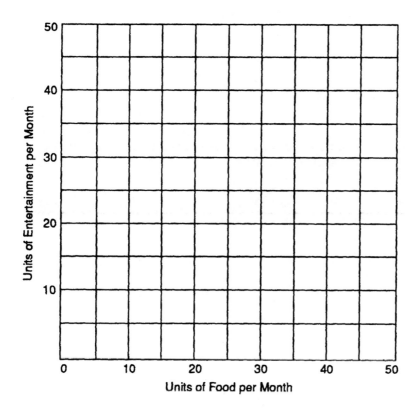

Suppose the consumer is asked to provide the same type of information for some higher level of satisfaction.  In this case the consumer supplies the information given below.

| Units of entertainment per month | Units of food per month |
| --- | --- |
| 40 | 11 |
| 30 | 15 |
| 25 | 18 |
| 15 | 25 |
| 10 | 35 |
| 7 | 45 |

b.  Use this new information and the grid above to plot this additional indifference curve.  Label this curve II.

2.  Suppose that the consumer in problem 1 has a monthly income of $400 and that the price of entertainment is $10 per unit and the price of food is $20 per unit.
   a.  Plot the consumer's budget line on the above grid and label it BL1.

b.  Given the consumer's indifference map and the above prices and income, what combination of entertainment and food will put the consumer at an optimum point?

c.  Suppose that the price of food drops to $10 per unit but the price of entertainment and the consumer's income remain unchanged.  Draw the new budget line in the above grid and label it BL2.

d.  After the change in part (c), which combination of entertainment and food will put the consumer at an optimum point?

3.  Draw a price-consumption curve for each of the following combinations of goods.

a.  Hot dogs and hot dog buns with the price of buns changing.

b.  Coke and Pepsi with the price of Pepsi changing.

c.  Potatoes and guitar strings with the price of guitar strings changing.

### ANSWERS TO APPENDIX B

**COMPLETION QUESTIONS**

1.  indifference; negatively
2.  falls; map
3.  less; more
4.  budget constraint; prices; income; relative prices; income
5.  tangent; indifference; highest
6.  shifts inward (parallel); decrease
7.  remains constant; changes; remains constant
8.  remains constant; remains constant

**TRUE-FALSE QUESTIONS**

1.  F  Total utility stays the same, not marginal utility.
2.  T
3.  F  A linear indifference curve implies a constant marginal rate of substitution.
4.  F  The slope of the budget line reflects relative prices.
5.  F  They are attainable, but not optimal.
6.  F  It is more preferable if it lies above 2.
7.  T
8.  F  Indifference curves are independent of income.
9.  F  The slope stays the same, but the budget line shifts.
10.  T
11.  T
12.  T
13.  T

**MULTIPLE CHOICE QUESTIONS**

1. a;  Every point along the indifference curve is equally desirable to the consumer.
2. d;  Then A, B and C can not be on the same indifference curve because an indifference curve shows "equally preferred" combinations of two goods.
3. c;  We would usually be willing to give up more of one good to get some of the other good.
4. c;  We are substituting between goods so that total satisfaction remains constant.
5. d;  The indifference curve shows the marginal rate of substitution falling.
6. d;  Consumer optimum is reached when the consumer ends up on the highest indifference curve possible given a limited budget.
7. a;  The slope of the budget constraint line shows the price of one good in relation to the price of the other good.
8. b;  If income rises the budget line shifts outward.
9. a;  When a price-consumption curve is derived, money income and price of one good remain constant. The price change in the other good causes a change in both goods in relation to each other.
10. d;  An income-consumption curve is a set of optimum consumption points that would occur if income were increased, nominal and relative prices remaining constant.
11. d  When the price of A rises we can derive the demand curve.

**WORKING WITH GRAPHS**

1.   a. see graph below;   b. see graph below

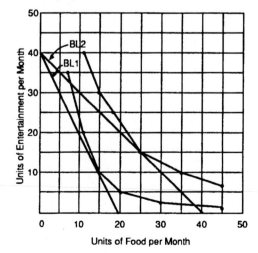

2.    a. see graph above;    b. 10 units of entertainment per month and 15 units of food per month;    c. see graph above;    d. 15 units of entertainment per month and 25 units of food per month.

3.

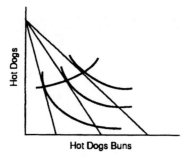

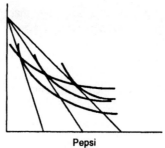

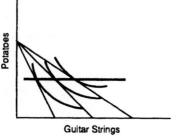

# CHAPTER 8

# EXTENSIONS OF DEMAND, SUPPLY, AND ELASTICITY

## PUTTING THIS CHAPTER INTO PERSPECTIVE

In Chapter 4 you learned how the forces of supply and demand, with buyers and sellers transacting voluntarily, determine market-clearing or equilibrium price. Sellers compete with sellers for sales, and buyers compete with buyers for goods and services. If price is above equilibrium, a surplus exists and seller competition forces price down toward equilibrium; if price is below equilibrium, a shortage exists and buyer competition forces price up toward equilibrium.  Prices adjust until surpluses and shortages are eliminated.

Because resources are scarce, outputs are scarce and somehow scarce outputs must be allocated (or rationed) to people.  Under voluntary exchange, when supply and demand forces are unrestricted, goods and services are allocated to the highest bidders. In effect, goods and services go to those customers who are willing to give up more of *other* goods and services.

In this chapter you learn that (a) markets and intermediaries can reduce the cost of exchanges; (b) the price system of rationing leads to an efficient allocation of resources; (c) if price is not allowed to allocate goods to the highest bidder then some other rationing system must—and will—emerge to determine how a specific good will be allocated; (d) many economic problems faced by farmers can be explained in terms of demand, supply and elasticity.

In Chapter 8, you will apply the theory of demand, supply, and elasticity to evaluate government policies such as rent controls, minimum wage laws, agricultural price supports and import quota policies.

## LEARNING OBJECTIVES

After you have studied this chapter, you should be able to:

1.  define price system, voluntary exchange, intermediary, transactions costs, price controls, price ceiling, price floor, non-price rationing devices, black market, rent control, minimum wage, price support, marketing board and import quota.

2.  appreciate how markets and intermediaries lower the cost of obtaining mutually beneficial exchanges between buyers and sellers.

3.  recognize various methods of rationing goods and services.

4.  understand how the price system of rationing leads to the most efficient allocation of resources.

5.  enumerate several consequences of price ceiling policies, using rent controls as an example.

6.  evaluate a price floor policy, using minimum wage laws as an example.

7.  explain the difference between the short run problem and the long run problem in the farming sector.

8.  illustrate, with the aid of a graph, how the offer to purchase policy supports farm incomes.

9.  understand how elasticity of demand can be used to explain how marketing boards can support the incomes of farmers.

10. apply the concept of elasticity to evaluate a policy of import quotas.


## CHAPTER OUTLINE

1.  In a **price system**, **voluntary exchange** typically determines price; buyers and sellers transact with a minimum amount of governmental interference.
    a.  Under a system of voluntary exchange, the **terms of exchange** (the terms, usually price, under which trade takes place) are set by the forces of supply and demand.
    b.  Markets reduce **transaction costs** (all the costs associated with exchanging, including such costs associated with gathering information and enforcing contracts).
    c.  Under **voluntary exchange,** *both* buyers and sellers are presumed to benefit— otherwise the transactions would not continue.

2. Price reflects relative scarcity and performs a rationing function.
   a. If an input or output becomes scarcer (less scarce), its relative price will rise (fall).
   b. Market or equilibrium prices promote allocative efficiency by ensuring that limited resources and scarce goods and services are allocated to the most valued uses and to the highest bidders.
   c. When prices are prevented from settling at equilibrium levels, resources, goods, and services are allocated according to other **non-price rationing** devices such as cheating, long lines, first-come first-served, political power, and physical force.

3. **Rent controls** include governmentally imposed **price ceilings** on rental apartments, which lead to the following results:
   a. the rental prices are fixed at a level below the equilibrium prices.
   b. a shortage of suitable rental housing space occurs.
   c. **black markets** emerge in the rental housing sector, where prices exceed equilibrium levels.
   d. an inequitable situation arises where landlords prefer to rent to upper income tenants at the expense of lower income households.

4. A legislated **minimum wage** is an example of a **price floor** policy which has the following consequences:
   a. the government fixed wage is set at a level above the equilibrium wage.
   b. a surplus of job seekers occurs, resulting in unemployment.

5. **Price support policies** have been applied to agricultural industries in response to the following problems:
   a. In the short run, a farmer's annual income can fluctuate significantly due to uncontrollable factors such as weather and uncoordinated production of the farmer's vast number of competitors.
   b. In the long run, due to high productivity and low income elasticity of demand, the increase in the supply of farm goods has exceeded the increase in demand for these same farm goods. Consequently, farm incomes have lagged behind the incomes earned in non-farm occupations.

6. One common form of price supports is the **offer to purchase** policy. Like a typical price floor policy, this results in:
   a. a surplus of agricultural output which is purchased by the government.
   b. allocative inefficiency due to overproduction of farm output.
   c. the greatest amount of aid being given to the largest, richest farmers.

7. To avoid surpluses of farm output, governments have often allowed farmers to form **marketing boards** which:
   a. drive up farm prices by restricting farm output
   b. increases total farm revenue in cases where demand is inelastic.
   c. continues to provide the greatest amount of aid to the largest, richest farmers.

8.  Governments also impose quantity restrictions on market transactions.
    a.  Some goods, such as certain drugs and human organs are outright illegal to trade.
    b.  Licensing arrangements, in effect, restrict the quantity of some goods and services.
    c.  An **import quota** is a quantity restriction that prohibits the importation of more than a specified quantity of a particular good in a one-year period.


## KEY TERMS AND CONCEPTS

| | | |
|---|---|---|
| Price system | Price ceiling | Terms of exchange |
| Voluntary exchange | Rent control | Price support policies |
| Transaction costs | Black market | Marketing boards |
| Non-price rationing devices | Price floor | Offer to purchase policy |
| Price controls | Minimum wage | Import quota |


## COMPLETION QUESTIONS
Fill in the blank or circle the correct term.

1.  Resources are scarce; therefore we cannot have all we want at a (zero, positive) price and there will be various ways in which people will (cooperate, compete) to obtain limited resources.

2.  Price performs a(n) _____ function; inputs or outputs go to the _____ bidders, if people are free to exchange voluntarily in markets; if such economic freedoms do not exist, then other (price, non-price) rationing devices will allocate resources, goods and services.

3.  (Price, Non-price) forms of rationing result in an efficient allocation of resources.

4.  Price controls that put a price ceiling on goods and services set the price (below, above) the equilibrium price and result in (surpluses, shortages).

5.  If governments place price (floors, ceilings) on goods, then black markets might emerge.

6.  Rent control is a form of price (floor, ceiling);  rent control (increases, reduces) the future supply of apartment construction, (increases, reduces) tenant mobility, (improves, causes a deterioration in) the quality of the existing stock of apartments, and hurts _____.

7.  A minimum wage policy is an example of a (price ceiling, price floor) policy that results in a situation of (full employment, unemployment).

8. In general, a price floor policy sets the price (below, above) the equilibrium price and results in a (surplus, shortage) situation.

9. The (short-run, long-run) farm problem is unstable incomes; the (short-run, long-run) farm problem is low incomes relative to non-farm incomes.

10. Relative to other sectors agriculture is characterized as a (low productivity, high productivity) sector faced with an (income elastic, income inelastic) demand.

11. The offer to purchase policy results in resources being (underallocated, overallocated) to farm production resulting in (allocative inefficiency, productive inefficiency).

12. A marketing board policy ( enhances, restricts) farm output and will increase farm revenue if demand is (price elastic,price inelastic).

13. By prohibiting the sale and use of tobacco products, the government would cause the supply of cigarettes to shift to the (left, right), makes cigarettes (more, less) scarce, and  causes their relative price to (rise, fall).

14. Import quotas, licensing arrangements, and outright bans on specific goods are forms of government (price, quantity) restrictions.

15. If demand is price inelastic, an import quota imposed by the Canadian government will cause total Canadian dollar spending on foreign goods to (increase, decrease).


**TRUE-FALSE QUESTIONS**
Circle the **T** if the statement if true, the **F** if it is false.  Explain to yourself why a statement is false.

T  F   1.   By raising the costs of production, intermediaries typically raise the price of the final product.

T  F   2.   Non-price rationing devices result in an efficient allocation of resources.

T  F   3.   An effective price ceiling policy will result in a regulated price below the equilibrium price.

T  F   4.   An effective price ceiling policy will result in a surplus of production.

T  F   5.   Rent controls help the poor who are looking for apartments, because rents are lower.

T  F   6.   A minimum wage policy is an example of a price floor.

T  F    7.    Black markets typically result from price floor policies.

T  F    8.    Over the long-run, the high income elasticity of demand for food has increased the income of farmers relative to other occupations.

T  F    9.    An offer to purchase policy provides the greatest amount of aid to the poorer farmers.

T  F   10.   When demand is price inelastic, a quantity restriction policy will result in an increase in total dollar consumer expenditures on the product.

## MULTIPLE CHOICE QUESTIONS
Circle the letter that corresponds to the best answer.

1.    Because resources are scarce,
      a.  buyers compete with buyers for outputs.
      b.  there must be some method for rationing goods.
      c.  people cannot have all they want at a zero price.
      d.  All of the above

2.    If markets are free and prices are flexible,
      a.  equilibrium price cannot be established.
      b.  scarce goods are allocated to the highest bidders.
      c.  chronic shortages will arise.
      d.  chronic surpluses will arise.

3.    Which of the following can influence how a society rations a specific good?
      a.  Price system that rations to the highest bidder
      b.  Political power
      c.  Religion
      d.  All of the above

4.    Prolonged shortages arise if
      a.  demand increases relative to supply.
      b.  price floors are set by governments.
      c.  prices are not allowed to rise to equilibrium.
      d.  buyers are allowed to compete for goods.

5.    Black markets may arise if
      a.  price ceilings exist.
      b.  price floors exist.
      c.  governments do not intervene in the market.
      d.  equilibrium price is too low.

6.   Rent controls
     a.   are a form of price floor.
     b.   encourage new apartment construction.
     c.   can result in slum rental housing space.
     d.   reduce litigation in society.

7.   If an effective minimum wage is imposed, then
     a.   more workers will be unable to find jobs.
     b.   the quantity of labour demanded will fall.
     c.   some workers will move to sectors not covered by minimum wages.
     d.   All of the above.

8.   An offer to purchase policy is
     a.   one in which price is set above equilibrium.
     b.   is an example of a price support policy.
     c.   supported by government purchases of surplus output.
     d.   All of the above.

9.   When marketing boards regulate supply, who is the least likely to lose?
     a.   consumers
     b.   prospective farmers
     c.   foreign farmers
     d.   existing farmers

10.  If the Canadian government imposes import quotas on foreign wines, then
     a.   Canadians will spend more money on foreign wines if it is price elastic.
     b.   Canadians will spend more money on foreign wines if it is price inelastic.
     c.   Canadians will buy more litres of foreign wine.
     d.   All of the above.


**MATCHING**
Choose the numbered item in Column (2) that best matches the term or concept in Column (1).

                    (1)                                              (2)

a.   intermediaries                      1.   quantity restriction
b.   price rationing                     2.   farm price support
c.   price ceiling                       3.   minimum wage law
d.   price floor                         4.   rent control
e.   offer to purchase                   5.   efficient allocation of resources
f.   import quota                        6.   reduce transaction costs
                                         7.   marketing board
                                         8.   subsidy

## WORKING WITH GRAPHS

1.   Consider the graph of the milk market below, then answer the following questions.

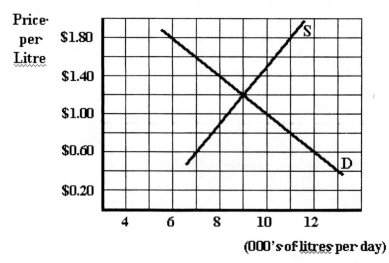

a.    The market-clearing price is _____?

b.    If the government imposes a price ceiling at $0.60, what will be the quantity supplied?  The quantity demanded?  What exists at that price?

c.    Given the quantity that will be forthcoming at the permitted price of $0.60, what will the actual or black market price be?

d.    Other than via a black market transaction, how can the actual price paid by buyers exceed the permitted price, $.60.

e.    Suppose that a newly elected government imposed a price floor of $1.80 per litre on the milk market described above. At this floor price there will be a (shortage, surplus) equal to _____ litres.

2.  Consider the following supply and demand curves for labour, and then answer the questions.

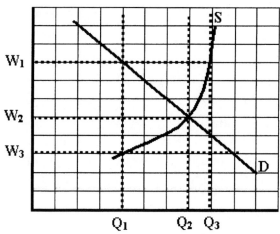

a.  What is the equilibrium wage rate?  The equilibrium quantity of labour?

b.  If the government sets a minimum wage rate at $W_1$, what is the quantity of labour demanded by employers?  The quantity of labour supplied by workers? What exists at the minimum wage rate?

c.  Is there a shortage or surplus of *jobs*?  How might such jobs be allocated (that is, how will employers go about deciding who gets the jobs)?

3.  The table below describes the market demand and supply in a local egg market. Graph the market demand and supply curves using the grid provided below.

| Quantity Demanded Boxes Per Week (000's) | Price per Box | Quantity Supplied: Boxes Per Week (000's) |
|---|---|---|
| 490 | $22 | 530 |
| 500 | $21 | 520 |
| 510 | $20 | 510 |
| 520 | $19 | 500 |
| 530 | $18 | 490 |

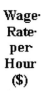

Quantity of Boxes (000's)

a.  What is the market clearing price? Calculate the total revenue (price x quantity) that will be paid to the egg producers assuming the market clearing price.

b.  If the government supports the price at $21 per box, using an offer to purchase policy, there will be a (surplus/shortage) of _____ boxes. Assuming that the the government purchases this (surplus/shortage) at the support price, calculate the total cost to the taxpayers.  Calculate the total revenue that will be received by the egg producers under the offer to purchase policy.

c.  If the government were to replace the offer to purchase policy with a marketing board policy which restricts the weekly egg production to 500,000 boxes, what maximum price per box could the egg producers charge (*TIP*: based on the demand schedule). Assuming this maximum price, calculate the total revenue paid to egg producers under the marketing board policy. Is this total revenue higher than that received under the market clearing price in part a. above? Why?

**PROBLEMS**

1.  In 1979, the rock group "The Who" gave a concert and 11 people died when the gates were opened and the crowd rushed in to get choice seats.  What other method of allocating the scarce resource "choice seats" would have prevented this tragic event?

2.  Currently, homeowners in various Canadian provinces (and U.S states) are experiencing skyrocketing electricity bills and power blackouts. This situation is partly attributable to an overall power shortage as the existing supply of electricity is not keeping up with the increased demand for electricity. In order to get electricity prices lower in the long-run, would you suggest that the provincial governments impose price ceilings on the prices charged by electricity suppliers or should the provincial governments provide subsidies to electricity suppliers? Explain.

## BUSINESS SECTION

### Small Business/Management: Industry Outlook

Demand and supply trends can be applied to develop an industry outlook which is invaluable to the small business owner or to the upper level corporate manager  when making strategic decisions relating to potential expansion plans as well as significant changes in marketing strategies. To illustrate this application, consider the following hypothetical graph which focuses on the *market for dentist services*.

## Market for Dentist Services

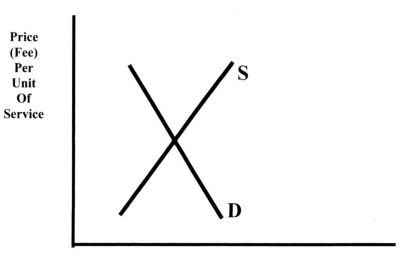

Quantity of Dentist-Provided Services

### Business Application Problem

    a.   For each of the following events determine whether the event will increase **or** decrease the demand **or** the supply of dentist services. Also, for each event, predict whether the event will tend to cause an increase or decrease in the fee (price) that dentists can charge per unit of service.

      i.   Event: The widespread use of fluorides has reduced tooth decay.

      ii.   Event: There has been a significant trend towards preventative practices such as flossing and regular teeth cleaning.

      iii.  Event: More  para-professionals such as dental nurses are performing standard dental procedures such as fillings.

   iv. Event: Compared to previous years, fillings, crowns and bridges are being made with more durable, longer lasting materials.

   v. Event: Schools of Dentistry across the nation are producing dentist graduates at a much faster rate than the growth in the population.

b.  From an existing dentists point of view, do the trends in demand and supply (described in part a. above) suggest a positive or negative industry outlook?

c.  One advantage of trying to predict the industry outlook, is that the business owner and/or the corporate manager may be able to change the outlook by devising strategies aimed at making deliberate changes in the industry demand and/or supply. As an example, for each of the following business strategies, determine whether the event will increase or decrease the demand or the supply of dentist services. Also, for each event, predict whether the event will tend to cause an increase or decrease in the fee (price) that dentists can charge per unit of service.

   i.  Strategy: The National Association of Dentists requires a higher grade point average for a student to qualify for dental school.

   ii  Strategy: The National Association of Dentists increases the standards that foreign dentists must meet in order to practice dentistry nationally.

   iii. Strategy: The National Association of Dentists is successful in lobbying the government to provide subsidized dental care to seniors and those on welfare.

   iv. Strategy: Through anaesthetics, "laughing gas", and hypnosis, dentists are increasingly making ones visit to the "chair" more relaxed and virtually pain free.

   v.  Strategy: It has become common practice for dental secretaries to contact patients to remind them to attend their regular six month checkup.

**ANSWERS TO CHAPTER 8**

## COMPLETION QUESTIONS

1.  zero; compete
2.  rationing; highest; non-price
3.  Price
4.  below, shortages
5.  ceilings
6.  ceiling; reduces; reduces; causes a deterioration in; landlords and low income apartment hunters
7.  price floor, unemployment
8.  above, surplus
9.  short-run, long run
10.  high productivity, income inelastic
11.  overallocated, allocative inefficiency
12.  restricts, inelastic
13.  left; more; rise
14.  quantity
15.  increase

## TRUE-FALSE QUESTIONS

1.  F  Intermediaries typically lower the price of the final product by reducing the transaction costs involved in matching buyers and sellers.
2.  F  Non-price rationing such as "first come first serve" "or providing the scarce good to ones friends results in an inefficient allocation of resources. There is no guarantee that the scarce goods and services end up going to the highest bidders.
3.  T
4.  F  An effective price ceiling policy maintains the price below the equilibrium and results in a shortage of output.
5.  F  To the extent that rent controls result in exorbitant prices being charged in black markets, this policy likely benefits upper income tenants.
6.  T
7.  F  Black markets typically result from price ceiling policies.
8.  F  Over the long-run, the low income elasticity of demand for food helps to contribute to low levels of farm income relative to other occupations.
9.  F  Since the offer to purchase policy supports the price per unit of output, the larger, richer farmers get the greatest amount of aid.
10.  T

## MULTIPLE CHOICE QUESTIONS

1.d;  Due to scarcity, there must be some way of rationing economic goods among competing buyers.
     *TIP* At a zero price people cannot have all they want of an economic good.
2.b;  Equilibrium will eventually be reached, which means that the scarce goods are allocated to the highest bidders.
3.d;  If governments impose price controls, non-price rationing criteria such as political power and religion can replace the price system of rationing.
4.c;  If prices remain below equilibrium, the quantity demanded will exceed quantity supplied, leading to prolonged shortages.
5.a;  Price ceilings cause shortages, which can lead to excessive .prices being charged in black markets.
6.c;  Since rent controls keep the rents below equilibrium, this reduces the     profits accruing to landlords who then have less incentive to properly maintain the apartments.

7.d; Effective minimum wages raise the wage rate above the equilibrium level. This means that the quantity of labour demanded by employers will be less than the quantity supplied of labour by employees. A surplus of labour occurs.

8.d. An offer to purchase policy is designed to support farmer's incomes by keeping the price above equilibrium. This will cause a surplus of output which is purchased by the government.

9.d. Existing farmers can gain in one of two ways. If they stay in business they benefit through higher farm prices. If they decide to sell their farms they can capitalize on selling the quota or license to produce, which makes it more expensive for prospective buyers.

10.b. Import quotas restrict quantity and effectively raise the price of foreign wines. If demand is price inelastic. an increase in price will increase total Canadian dollar expenditures on foreign wines.

## MATCHING

a and 6;   b and 5;   c and 4;   d and 3,   e and 2,   f and 1.

## WORKING WITH GRAPHS

1.  a.  $1.20
    b.  7000 litres;  12,000 litres;  shortage of 5,000 litres
    c.  At a quantity of 7000 litres, the black market price equals $1.60.
    d.  quality deterioration, long lines that increase opportunity costs.
    e.  surplus of 11,000 – 6,000 = 5,000 litres.
2.  a.  $W_2; Q_2$
    b.  $Q_1; Q_3$; surplus of labour, or unemployment
    c.  shortage; family influence, political power, bribes, racial or gender preference
3.  a.  $20; $10,200,000
    b.  surplus; 20,000 boxes, surplus, cost of $420,000; revenue of $10,920,000
    c.  $21; $10,500,000; the total revenue under the marketing board is higher by $300,000, as demand is price inelastic.

## PROBLEMS

1.  Instead of "first-come, first-served seating", ticket sellers could have raised the price of choice seats and used assigned seating.  Shortly thereafter, the city passed a resolution that outlawed first-come, first-served seating.

2.  In the long-run a price ceiling policy would only create additional power shortages. The advantage of providing subsidies is that the supply of electricity would increase which would help to eliminate the shortage situation and thus bring down prices, in the long-run.

## BUSINESS SECTION

    a.  i.   Decrease in demand, fee will decrease
        ii.  Decrease in demand, fee will decrease
        iii. Decrease in demand, fee will decrease
        iv.  Decrease in demand, fee will decrease
        v.   Increase in supply, fee will decrease
    b. Negative outlook as all the events are putting downward pressure on the fees that dentists can charge. In turn this will translate into decreased profit.
    c.  i.   Decrease in supply, fee will increase
        ii.  Decrease in supply, fee will increase
        iii. Increase in demand, fee will increase
        iv.  Increase in demand, fee will increase
        v.   Increase in demand, fee will increase

## ANSWERS TO EXAMPLE QUESTIONS FOR CRITICAL ANALYSIS

I  **EXAMPLE 8-1: Technology and the Death of Intermediaries** (p. 178)
As intermediaries, travel agents can reduce the transaction costs of finding the lowest cost carrier(s) for customers to reach and return from a given destination. On-line services do indeed allow airline customers the advantage of making their own reservations for relatively uncomplicated flights to their destinations. The cost of time spent searching for the best deal for more complicated routes could be quite high for someone who only occasionally flies and is thus unlikely to be familiar with the timetables, or for someone who has a high opportunity cost of time. Travel agents would be valuable to such persons.

II  **EXAMPLE 8-2: Should Shortages in the Ticket Market Be Solved by Scalpers?** (p. 180)
If there are many unsold seats on the day of the game, this would imply a situation where the original ticket purchase price of $150 ends up being above the equilibrium ticket price for Game 4. Scalpers are now facing a surplus of tickets at the price of $150. Due to this surplus, scalpers would have to reduce the price they charge to a level below $150 which would result in a loss for the scalpers.

III  **INTERNATIONAL POLICY EXAMPLE 8-1: Rent Controls in Bombay** (p. 184)
The rent controls, like any typical price ceiling policy, have resulted in a significant shortage - of both commercial and residential rental space. This situation will discourage the entry of new foreign firms into the Bombay area. Since the rent controls have resulted in very high "black market" rents, this makes it very costly for firms and the employees of these firms to operate in Bombay.

IV  **EXAMPLE 8-3: Wheat Farmers and the Canadian Wheat Board** (p. 190)
One advantage the Canadian Wheat Board has is that it controls the supply of Canadian wheat to the world market. If equilibrium prices are low, the Wheat Board can restrict the supply of all Canadian farmers so as gain significant price increases. If half the farmers sold independently, then this would undermine the Wheat Boards ability to convince the other half of the farmers to continue to hold back some of what they produce. Instead of a crop restriction policy, which would drive up both the price and the total revenue (with demand inelastic), each farmer would drive down both the price and the total revenue through price competition.

V  **POLICY EXAMPLE 8-1: Should the Legal Quantity of Cigarettes Supplied Be Set at Zero?** (p. 191)
Psychoactive drugs such as marijuana and cocaine were all legal around the turn of the century. The illegal supply was zero. When these drugs were outlawed, i.e. the legal supply was set at zero, illegal demand developed and the illegal supply increased. The price of these psychoactive drugs increased.

# CHAPTER 9

# THE FINANCIAL ENVIRONMENT OF BUSINESS

## PUTTING THIS CHAPTER INTO PERSPECTIVE

Chapter 9 is the third chapter in Part Two, and it introduces you to the various forms of business organization and provides some background information that will be helpful in Part Three.

Problems arise because a separation of ownership and control exists in large corporations, enabling managers to place their own interests above those of the shareholders. Economists refer to this as the principal-agent problem; also the problems of asymmetric information, adverse selection, and moral hazard are related to financial transactions.

## LEARNING OBJECTIVES

After you have studied this chapter you should be able to

1.   define financial capital, sole proprietorship, partnership, corporation, unlimited liability, limited liability, dividends, share of stock, bond, primary market, secondary market, reinvestment, asymmetric information, adverse selection, moral hazard, principal-agent problem, separation of ownership and control, collateral, incentive-compatible contract, random walk theory, and inside information.

2.   state the distinctions among sole proprietorships, partnerships, and corporations.

3.   state the advantages and disadvantages of  sole proprietorships, partnerships, and corporations.

4.   recognize how owners can reduce the principal-agent problem that arises from the separation of ownership and control.

5.   recognize how asymmetric information can contribute to a moral hazard problem and an adverse selection problem.

6.   enumerate the three principal methods of corporate financing.

7.   distinguish between primary and secondary markets.

8.   predict the consequences of the efficient market theory.


**CHAPTER OUTLINE**

There are three basic forms into which Canadian businesses have chosen to organize: sole proprietorship, partnership, and corporation.

1.   A **sole proprietorship** is owned by a single individual who makes the business decisions, receives all the profits, and is legally responsible for all the debts of the firm.
     a.   Advantages: a **sole proprietorship** is easy to form and dissolve; all decision-making powers reside with the sole proprietor; a sole proprietorship is taxed only once.
     b.   Disadvantages:  the **sole  proprietorship** faces **unlimited liability** for debts of the firm and has limited ability to raise funds; the business normally ceases to exist with the death of the sole proprietor.

2.   A **partnership** is owned by two or more who share profits or losses.
     a.   Advantages:  **partnerships** are easy to form, experience relatively low costs of monitoring job performance, permit more specialization than sole proprietorships, and are only taxed once.
     b.   Disadvantages:  **partnerships** face **unlimited liability** and more difficulty in decision-making (relative to **sole proprietorship**); dissolution of the **partnership** is usually necessary when a partner dies or leaves the **partnership**.

3.   A **corporation** is a legal entity that may conduct business in its own name, just as an individual does.  The owners of the **corporation** are its shareholders.
     a.   Advantages:  shareholders enjoy **limited liability**; a **corporation** continues to exist even if some owners cease to remain owners; a **corporation** has the ability to raise large sums of money for investments.
     b.   Disadvantages:  owners are subject to double taxation because **corporations** pay taxes on profits and shareholders pay taxes on **dividends** received; ownership and control are separated in a **corporation**.
          i.   Professional managers, who may have little or no ownership in the firm, may pursue their own, not shareholder-owner, interests.
          ii.  Shareholders may experience high costs to monitor the behavior of professional managers.

4. Stocks, bonds, and reinvestment of retained earnings are the most important sources of corporate financing.
   a. From the investor's point of view, stocks offer the highest risk (and, therefore, the highest potential rate of return), and the greatest control over the firm's decisions.
   b. Bonds are relatively safer (and yield a correspondingly lower rate of return) and provide little control over decision-making.

5. Both businesses and investors engage in financial transactions in **primary and secondary markets.**
   a. In **primary markets**, purchases and sales of newly issued securities are made.
   b. In **secondary markets**, purchases and sales of previously issued securities are made.

6. Some people believe that the stock market is an efficient market, in the sense that it follows a **random walk**.
   a. The **random walk theory** predicts that the best forecast of tomorrow's stock price is today's price, because today's price incorporates all the information important to stock price determination.
   b. Only **inside information** will permit people to beat the stock market.

7. Technological advances in computers, telecommunications, and travel, along with an increased decentralization and opening of economies, have helped to make the world a global economy; as is always the case in economics, a trade-off exists.

8. Leading the way toward a globalized economy is worldwide financial integration.
   a. Legal and technological changes have blurred the distinctions among financial institutions and between financial and non-financial institutions.
   b. Multinational corporations with a wide array of financial services operate worldwide.
   c. Markets for Canadian government securities, interbank lending and borrowing, foreign exchange trading, and common stock are now operating continuously, in vast quantities, around the clock and around the world; along with technological and legal changes, the Canadian trade deficit has helped to spur such markets.

9. When financial transactions take place, **asymmetric information** may exist.
   a. If asymmetric information exists *before* a transaction takes place, **adverse selection** exists; borrowers who are the worse credit risks know better than lenders that they are poor risks, and such borrowers can outbid other borrowers for funds.
   b. If **asymmetric information** exists *after* a transaction, **moral hazard** may exist; after borrowing funds, the borrowers may be able to use the money to make investments riskier than was otherwise expected by the lender.
   c. A **moral hazard** problem arises *within* a firm; because modern business is characterized by a separation of ownership (stockholders) and control (management) a **principal-agent problem** exists; management has an incentive to pursue its own, and not stockholder, interest.

d. In order to reduce the problems that arise from **asymmetric information**, various countermoves have evolved.
  i. Lenders can reduce the problem of **adverse selection** in general ways.
    (a) Lenders can purchase information from independent businesses who rate the credit worthiness of borrowers.
    (b) Lenders can require borrowers to put up collateral.
  ii. Lenders can reduce the problem of **moral hazard** by requiring an **incentive-compatible contract**, which assures that borrowers also place a good deal of their own assets at risk; such a scheme makes the interests of borrowers and lenders more closely aligned.

## KEY TERMS AND CONCEPTS

| | | |
|---|---|---|
| Financial capital | Share of stock | |
| Separation of ownership and control | | |
| Sole Proprietorship | Bond | Asymmetric information |
| Unlimited liability | Reinvestment | Adverse selection |
| Partnership | Primary market | Moral hazard |
| Corporation | Secondary market | Principal-agent problem |
| Limited liability | Random walk theory | Collateral |
| Dividends | Inside information | Incentive-compatible contract |

## COMPLETION QUESTIONS
Fill in the blank or circle the correct term.

1. The three major forms of Canadian business organizations are _____, _____, and _____.

2. While the highest percentage of Canadian firms are (sole proprietorships, partnerships, corporations), the highest percentage of total business revenue is attributed to (sole proprietorships, partnerships, corporations).

3. A _____ is a legal entity that may conduct business in its own name, just as an individual does; its owners are called (shareholders, bondholders), and such owners enjoy (unlimited, limited, partially limited) liability.

4. The income that corporations earn is taxed (once, twice).

5. When transactions take place, (asymmetric, symmetric) information may exist; if such a situation exists before the transaction occurs, the (adverse selection, moral hazard) problem exists; if it exists after the transaction exists then the (adverse selection, moral hazard) problem exists.

6.  Because modern corporations are characterized by a separation of ownership and (control, risk), a (adverse selection, moral hazard) problem exists.

7.  Lenders can reduce the problem of adverse selection by purchasing information regarding a borrower's (bank history, credit rating); lenders can also require borrowers to put up (building ownership, collateral).

8.  Lenders can reduce the moral hazard problem by requiring a(n) _____ contract, which requires borrowers to assume part of the (ownership rights, risk).

9.  A separation of ownership and control could lead to the _____ problem.

10. The three main sources of corporate finance are _____, _____, and _____; of these a _____ denotes ownership in the corporation and a _____ is a legal claim against the firm, entitling the owner to receive a fixed annual coupon, plus a lump sum (at maturity, each year).

11. Because professional managers usually own a very small percentage of the firms they manage, a separation of ownership and _____ exists; this separation can lead to a situation in which managers can maximize (their own; shareholders') interests.

12. Previously issued stocks and bonds are sold in _____ markets; new issues are sold in _____ markets.

13. According to the efficient markets theory, the stock market is a ____walk; the best prediction of tomorrow's price is (today's price, yesterday's price) .


**TRUE-FALSE QUESTIONS**
Circle the T if the statement is true, the F if it is false.  Explain to yourself why a statement is false.

T  F    1.  Corporations are the most common form of business organization in Canada.

T  F    2.  Sole proprietorships account for the highest percentage of total business revenues in Canada.

T  F    3.  Sole proprietorships and partnerships face unlimited liability for the debts of their firms.

T  F    4.  The main advantage of corporations is that they offer limited liability to shareholders.

T  F   5.   Corporate shareholders are taxed twice on the corporation's earnings.

T  F   6.   A separation of ownership and control often exists in large corporations.

T  F   7.   In large corporations, managers can possibly pursue their own, not shareholders', interests.

T  F   8.   The adverse selection problem results due to asymmetric information after a transaction.

T  F   9.   Borrowers who do not intend to repay loans might be able to outbid honest borrowers for the funds.

T  F  10.   Stocks offer a higher risk and return, relative to bonds, but bonds offer investors greater control over the firm's decisions.

T  F  11.   Reinvestment of retained earnings is the most important source of corporate finance.

T  F  12.   In a secondary market, previously issued securities are bought and sold.

T  F  13.   The principal-agent problem implies that management will pursue the public's interest, not stockholder interests.

T  F  14.   When lenders insist that borrowers put up collateral they are trying to avoid the principal-agent problem.

T  F  15.   According to the efficient market theory, the best prediction of tomorrow's stock price is today's price.

T  F  16.   According to the efficient market theory, the only way to earn abnormal profits (in the long run) is to have inside information.

## MULTIPLE CHOICE QUESTIONS
Circle the letter that corresponds to the best answer.

1.   Which of the following is **NOT** true, concerning a sole proprietorship?
    a.   Most Canadian firms are sole proprietorships.
    b.   They are easy to form and to dissolve.
    c.   They offer limited liability.
    d.   The owner is taxed only once on business income.

2.    Which of the following is a disadvantage of a sole proprietorship?
    a.   Unlimited liability for the firm's debts.
    b.   Limited ability to raise funds.
    c.   The firm ends with the death of the sole proprietor.
    d.   All of the above

3.    Which of the following is **NOT** true, concerning partnerships?
    a.   There are fewer partnerships than sole  proprietorships in Canada.
    b.   They permit more effective specialization than sole proprietorships.
    c.   Business income is taxed only once.
    d.   Partners have limited liability for the firm's debts.

4.    Which of the following is an advantage of partnerships?
    a.   Partners have unlimited liability.
    b.   They enjoy reduced cost in monitoring job performance.
    c.   They must be dissolved if one partner dies.
    d.   All of the above

5.    A corporation
    a.   is a legal entity that conducts business in its own name.
    b.   permits unlimited liability to shareholders.
    c.   must be dissolved if a majority stockholder dies.
    d.   has severely limited abilities to attract financial resources.

6.    According to the efficient market theory, in an efficient market
    a.   only lucky people can earn abnormal profits in the long run.
    b.   tomorrow's price is easily determined.
    c.   only inside information permits abnormal profits.
    d.   a pattern of price changes will emerge.

7.    Regarding asymmetric information:
    a.   if it exists before a transaction, adverse selection may occur.
    b.   it exists only after the transaction.
    c.   it presents a problem that cannot be reduced.
    d.   if it exists after a transaction, adverse selection may occur.

8.    Which of the following helps to reduce the problem of asymmetric information?
    a.   Require borrowers to put up collateral.
    b.   Purchase information regarding the credit rating of borrowers.
    c.   Require an incentive-compatible contract.
    d.   All of the above

9.  Which of the following is **NOT** an example of a problem resulting from asymmetric information?
    a.  moral hazard problem
    b.  efficient markets
    c.  adverse selection problem
    d.  principal-agent problem

10.  Which of the following has **NOT** evolved to solve a problem resulting from asymmetric information?
    a.  collateral
    b.  incentive-compatible contracts
    c.  globalized stock markets
    d.  credit rating agencies

11.  Shareholders
    a.  are the owners of corporations.
    b.  are less at risk than are bondholders.
    c.  are subject to unlimited risk.
    d.  have less control over firm decisions than do bondholders.

12.  In a large corporation
    a.  ownership is usually concentrated in a few hands.
    b.  separation of ownership and control is unlikely.
    c.  managers may try to maximize their own (not shareholders') wealth.
    d.  shareholders are guaranteed a fixed dividend.

**MATCHING**
Choose the item in column (2) that best matches an item in column (1).

(1)

a.  secondary market
b.  share of stock

c.  bond
d.  separation of ownership and control
e.  total profits
f.  corporation
g.  asymmetric information

(2)

1.  corporate debt
2.  purchase and sale of previously issued securities
3.  limited liability
4.  costs random walk theory
5.  corporate ownership
6.  principal-agent problem
7.  unlimited liability
8.  total revenues minus total
9.  adverse selection

**BUSINESS SECTION**

**Finance: Measuring the Growth Performance of a Stock**

Different types of investors have different motives when purchasing a stock. A retired person is often interested in deriving income from the stock by receiving consistently high dividends each year. A young investor typically purchases a stock for its growth potential in terms of providing the investor a large capital gain in the future.

One common measure of a stock's growth potential is the compound annual rate of return (*i*) derived as follows:

$$i = \left(\frac{S}{P}\right)^{\frac{1}{n}} - 1 \times 100$$

*i* = compound annual rate of return
*S* = Selling price of the stock in the future
*P* = purchase price of the stock
*n* = number of annual periods the investor held the stock

Consider the following example. On January 1, 1993 Jerry Attrick purchased 1000 shares of Pfizer Corporation (the manufacturer of Viagra) at a price of $36.25 per share. After holding the shares for 5 ½ years, Jerry sold these 1000 shares on June 30, 1998 at a price of $108.69 per share. Calculate the compound annual rate of return. (*Source:* "Annual Reports," http//www.pfizer.com/main.html

The solution? Compound rate of 22% per year as calculated below:

$$i = \left(\frac{108.69}{36.25}\right)^{\frac{1}{5.5}} - 1 = (2.9873)^{.1818} - 1 = 1.22 - 1 = .22 \times 100 = 22\%$$

**Business Application Problem**

On July 1, 1993 Steve Jaubs purchased 100 shares of Microsoft Corporation at a price of $9.25 per share. Five years later, on July 1, 1998 Steve sold these share at a price of $107.25 per share. Calculate the annual compound rate of return. (*Source:* "Stockholder Information," http://www.microsoft.com)

**ANSWERS TO CHAPTER 9**

**COMPLETION QUESTIONS**

1.   sole proprietorships; partnerships; corporations
2.   sole proprietorships; corporations
3.   corporation; shareholders; limited
4.   twice
5.   asymmetric; adverse selection; moral hazard
6.   control; moral
7.   credit rating; collateral
8.   incentive-compatible; risk
9.   principal-agent
10.  stocks; bonds; reinvestment; stock; bond; maturity
11.  control; their own
12.  secondary; primary
13.  random; today's price

**TRUE-FALSE QUESTIONS**

1.   F   Sole proprietorships account for about 70 percent of total business organizations.
2.   F   Corporations account for the highest percentage of total business revenues.
3.   T
4.   T
5.   T
6.   T
7.   T
8.   F   Asymmetric information is obtained before a transaction.
9.   T
10.  F   Stocks also give investors greater control than bonds.
11.  T
12.  T
13.  F   The principal-agent problem implies that managers pursue their own interests.
14.  F   Lenders are trying to prevent the adverse selection problem.
15.  T
16.  T

**MULTIPLE CHOICE**

1.   c;   The owner is legally responsible for all debts of the firm.
2.   d;   A disadvantage is that it is owned by a single individual who makes decisions and takes the risks.
3.   d;   Partnerships face unlimited liability.
4.   b;   Partnerships are also easy to form and only taxed once.
5.   a;   A corporation permits limited liability. The corporation continues even if some owners cease to remain owners and can raise huge sums of money.
6.   c;   Most public information that you can obtain will prove to have little value.
7.   a;   This is when one side in a transaction has more information than the other side.
8.   d;   Anything that will even the playing field.
9.   b;   Asymmetric information will make markets more inefficient.
10.  c;   All the other options help to solve the problem of asymmetric information.
11.  a;   Shareholders have more control and more limited risk than bondholders.
12.  c.   If the managers have limited ownership in the firm, they may try to maximize their own wealth.

**MATCHING**

a and 2;   b and 4;   c and 1;   d and 5;   e and 8;   f and 3;   g and 9

**BUSINESS SECTION**

1.  Annual compound rate of return is 63.25% per year as calculated below.

$$i = \left(\frac{107.25}{9.25}\right)^{\frac{1}{5}} - 1 = 1.6325 - 1 = .6325 \times 100 = 63.25\%$$

**ANSWERS TO EXAMPLE QUESTIONS FOR CRITICAL ANALYSIS**

**I    EXAMPLE 9-1: How to Read the Financial Press: Stock Prices** (p. 204)
No, up to a point. Some shares of a stock must change hands if there is to be a measured net change in its price. Beyond that, what is more significant is how many shares are being offered for sale compared to the number of offers to buy. Simply looking at the number of shares sold is in itself meaningless because, by definition, the same number were bought.

**II   INTERNATIONAL EXAMPLE 9-1: Moral Hazard and the International Monetary Fund** (p. 207)
It is unlikely that a tightening of funding to the IMF would make countries less vulnerable to financial crisis. While they may welcome IMF relief in a crisis, it is unlikely that they encourage the onset of crisis merely to access the funding. To the extent that financial crises in developing countries are the result of international economic events, a tightening of funding to the IMF would make no difference to the developing countries' vulnerability.

**III  EXAMPLE 9-2: Encouraging Executives to Own a Share of the Company** (p. 208)
Yes. You could find those companies that require their CEO and other managers to own shares. You could then use that information as a guide to investing.

# CHAPTER 10

# THE FIRM: COST AND OUTPUT DETERMINATION

## PUTTING THIS CHAPTER INTO PERSPECTIVE

Chapter 10 is the first chapter in Part Three.  It is an important chapter because the material it contains is essential to the remaining four chapters in Part Three.

Chapter 7 analyzed consumer behavior in detail, and it provided the ingredients for a proper understanding of demand.  Chapter 10 lays the foundation for supply because it analyzes business costs of production.  Many economists refer to microeconomics—the second major topic of this text—as "price theory."  The modern theory of price is that market price is determined by supply and demand; because supply is intimately related to a firm's cost of production, this chapter is obviously important.

In this chapter we analyze again the relationship between "average" and "marginal" concepts; more specifically, Chapter 10 analyzes the relationship between marginal cost and average cost.  As expected, marginal cost pulls and tugs average cost:  if marginal cost is above average cost, then average cost will rise; if marginal cost is below average cost, then average cost will fall; if marginal cost equals average cost, then average cost remains constant.  If you truly understand this, then you can easily see why the marginal cost curve intersects the average variable cost curve and the average total cost curve at their minimum points.

In this chapter we also introduce the law of diminishing returns.  It is important to understand that this law is a purely technological statement; it indicates what happens to output when inputs are changed in a specific way.  By itself the law has nothing to do with costs or profits—each of which, after all, is denominated in money.  The law, however, does have *implications* for firm production costs (and therefore for profits), and you should concentrate on how the law accounts for the upward sloping portion of the marginal cost, the average variable cost, and the average total cost curves.  Pay particular attention to the marginal cost curve; it is the most important because, as we stress again and again, economic decisions are made on the margin.  The profit maximizing firm will compare the marginal cost of producing another unit of output with the marginal benefit of doing so.

Chapter 10 also makes the important distinction between accounting profits and economic profits; it also distinguishes between long-run and short-run cost curves. Note well that it is the law of diminishing returns that determines the shape of the short-run average cost curve, and that it is the existence (or lack thereof) of economies or diseconomies of scale that determines the shape of the long-run average cost curves.

## LEARNING OBJECTIVES

After you have studied this chapter, you should be able to

1.  define firm, explicit costs, implicit costs, accounting profit, normal rate of return, opportunity cost of capital, economic profits, short run, long run, production, production function, law of diminishing (marginal) returns, average physical product, marginal physical product, total costs, fixed costs, variable costs, average fixed costs, average variable cost, average total costs, marginal costs, planning horizon, long-run average cost curve, planning curve, economies of scale, constant returns to scale, diseconomies of scale, minimum efficient scale.

2.  distinguish between accounting profits and economic profits.

3.  distinguish between explicit costs and implicit costs.

4.  distinguish between the firm's short run and its long run.

5.  apply the law of diminishing (marginal) returns to account for the shape of the firm's short-run marginal cost curve, average total cost curve, and average variable cost curve.

6.  classify firm costs as fixed or variable costs.

7.  calculate average total cost, average fixed cost, and marginal cost, given sufficient information.

8.  apply the concepts of economies of scale, diseconomies of scale, and constant returns to scale to predict the shape of a firm's long-run average cost curve.

9.  list reasons for economies of scale and for diseconomies of scale.

## CHAPTER OUTLINE

1.  A **firm** is an organization that brings together different factors of production, such as labour, land, capital, and entrepreneurial skill, to produce a product or service, which it is hoped, can be sold for a profit.

    a. **Accounting profits** equal total revenues minus **explicit costs**.

    b. The opportunity cost of capital, or the **normal rate of return** to invested capital, is the rate of return that must be paid to an investor to induce him or her to invest in a business.

    c. There is also an opportunity cost to labour; single-owner proprietors, after all, could earn wages elsewhere.

       i. There is an opportunity cost to all inputs.

      ii. **Economic profits** equal total revenues minus the opportunity cost of all inputs; stated differently, total profits equal total revenues minus the sum of **explicit and implicit costs**.

2. It is widely assumed by economists that the goal of the firm is to maximize total profits.

3. The short run is defined as that time period in which a firm cannot alter its current size of plant; the long run is that time period in which all factors of production can be varied.

4. **Total costs** are identical to total **fixed costs** plus total **variable costs**.

    a. Total **fixed costs** do not vary with output.

    b. Total **variable costs** are the sum of all those costs that vary with output.

    c. There are several **short-run** average cost curves.

       i. **Average total costs** equal **total costs** divided by output.

      ii. **Average variable costs** equal **total variable costs** divided by output.

      iii. **Average fixed costs** equal **total fixed costs** divided by output.

    d. **Marginal cost** equals the change in **total costs** divided by the change in output.

    e. When **marginal cost** is above average cost, average cost rises; when **marginal cost** is below average cost, average cost falls; when **marginal cost** equals average cost, average cost remains constant.

    f. The **marginal cost** curve intersects the average total cost curve and the **average variable cost** curve at their respective minimum points.

5. The **production function** is a relationship between inputs and outputs; it is a technological, not an economic, relationship.

    a. The **law of diminishing (marginal) returns** comes into play when the firm increases output in the short run.

    b. The **marginal physical product** is the change in total product that occurs when a variable input is increased and all other inputs are held constant.

    c. The **law of diminishing (marginal) returns** implies that the **marginal physical product** of labour eventually falls.

6. Diminishing marginal product causes the **marginal cost** curve, the **average total cost** curve, and the **average variable cost** curve to rise.

7. In the **long run**, all inputs are variable, and **long-run** cost curves must take this into account.

a. The **long-run average cost curve** is the locus of points representing the minimum unit cost of producing any given rate of output, given current technology and resource prices.
b. Another name for the long-run average cost curve is the **planning horizon**.

8. The **long-run average cost** curve is also U-shaped.
   a. Initially a firm experiences **economies of scale** due to specialization, a dimensional factor, or improved productive equipment.
   b. Eventually a firm might experience **diseconomies of scale** because a disproportionate increase in management and staff may be needed, and because the costs of information and communication also grow more than proportionally with output.

9. The **minimum efficient scale** is the lowest rate of output per unit time period at which average costs reach a minimum for a particular firm.

## KEY TERMS AND CONCEPTS

| | | |
|---|---|---|
| Firm | Production | Average total costs |
| Explicit costs | Production function | Marginal costs |
| Accounting profit | Law of diminishing returns | Planning horizon |
| Implicit costs | Average physical product | Long-run average cost curve |
| Normal rate of return | Marginal physical product | Planning curve |
| Opportunity cost of capital | Total costs | Economies of scale |
| Economic profits | Fixed costs | Constant returns to scale |
| Short run | Variable costs | Diseconomies of scale |
| Plant size | Average fixed costs | Minimum efficient scale |
| Long run | Average variable costs | |

## COMPLETION QUESTIONS
Fill in the blank or circle the correct term.

1. (Explicit, Implicit) costs are usually considered by accountants, but (explicit, implicit) costs typically are not.

2. Economists consider implicit costs because such costs (do, do not) include the opportunity costs of the resources used.

3. Accounting profits equal _____ minus _____; economic profits equal _____ minus _____; economic profits are less than accounting profits because economic profits subtract _____ costs from total revenues.

4.  Economists usually assume that the firm's goal is (profit maximization, profit sharing).

5.  Our definition of the short run is the time during which (capital, labour) is fixed, but (capital, labour) is variable; in the long run (no, all) factors are variable.

6.  Fixed costs (do, do not) vary with output; variable costs (do, do not) vary with output; _____ and _____ are examples of fixed costs; _____ and _____ are examples of variable costs.

7.  Short-run average cost curves eventually are upward sloping due to _____; at the minimum of the average total cost curve, marginal cost is (less than, greater than, equal to) average total cost; if marginal cost exceeds average total cost, then average total cost will (fall, rise, remain constant).

8.  Because of diminishing (marginal) returns, in the (short, long) run the marginal product of labour will eventually (fall, rise, remain constant).

9.  The long-run cost curve may also be U-shaped, because initially as a firm expands its scale of operations, it realizes _____ of scale; then it may realize _____ returns to scale; eventually it realizes _____ of scale.

10.  Reasons for economies of scale include _____, _____, and _____; a firm might experience diseconomies of scale due to _____ and _____.

**TRUE-FALSE QUESTIONS**
Circle the **T** if the statement is true, the **F** if it is false.  Explain to yourself why a statement is false.

T  F  1.  Accountants typically do not consider implicit costs.

T  F  2.  Explicit costs include the opportunity cost of a resource.

T  F  3.  Accounting profits equal total revenues minus explicit costs.

T  F  4.  Accounting profits always exceed economic profits.

T  F  5.  Economists usually assume that the firm's goal is to maximize profits.

T  F  6.  Short-run cost curves that include variable costs eventually reflect the influence of the law of diminishing marginal returns.

T  F    7.    Fixed costs vary with output.

T  F    8.    Eventually, as output expands, the short-run marginal cost curve must rise.

T  F    9.    When average costs exceed marginal cost, marginal cost must be rising.

T  F   10.    At the minimum average total cost output level, marginal cost equals average total cost.

T  F   11.    In the short run, the supply of labour to the firm is usually fixed.

T  F   12.    Because of the law of diminishing marginal returns, the marginal product of labour will rise.

T  F   13.    Long-run cost curves are U-shaped due to the law of diminishing returns.


## MULTIPLE CHOICE QUESTIONS
Circle the letter that corresponds to the best answer.

1.    Explicit costs
      a.   are considered by accountants.
      b.   are greater than implicit costs.
      c.   are considered irrelevant by economists.
      d.   are considered by accountants, but not by economists.

2.    Implicit costs
      a.   are considered important to accountants, but not to economists.
      b.   are usually less than explicit costs.
      c.   include the opportunity costs of resources.
      d.   are considered irrelevant by businesses.

3.    Accounting profits
      a.   equal total revenues minus explicit costs.
      b.   exceed economic profits.
      c.   do not take implicit costs into account.
      d.   All of the above

4.    The opportunity cost of capital is
      a.   an explicit cost of doing business.
      b.   not an important cost of doing business.
      c.   the normal rate of return on capital invested in a business.
      d.   purely a technological concept.

5.    Which of the following is unlike the others because it is not explicit?
      a.   wages
      b.   opportunity cost of capital
      c.   taxes
      d.   rent

6.    *Analogy*: Rent is to explicit costs as _____ are to implicit costs.
      a.   labour services of a proprietor
      b.   taxes
      c.   wages
      d.   accounting profits

7.    Which of the following goals of the firm is most widely assumed by economists?
      a.   staff maximization
      b.   sales maximization
      c.   growth maximization
      d.   profit maximization

8.    In the short run, for our purposes,
      a.   all factors are variable.
      b.   labour is variable.
      c.   capital is variable
      d.   both capital and labour are variable.

9.    The long run
      a.   permits the variation of all factors of production.
      b.   is different for different firms.
      c.   permits a firm to avoid the consequences of the law of diminishing returns.
      d.   All of the above

10.   Fixed costs
      a.   vary with output.
      b.   do not vary with output.
      c.   reflect the effect of diminishing returns.
      d.   include labour and raw material costs.

11.   Which cost is most unlike the others because it is not fixed?
      a.   rent
      b.   wages
      c.   opportunity cost of capital
      d.   interest payments on borrowed money

12.   If marginal cost is above average total cost, then average total cost
      a.   will rise.
      b.   will fall.
      c.   will remain constant.
      d.   cannot be calculated.

13.  At that output where average total cost is at a minimum,
     a.  marginal cost equals average total cost.
     b.  marginal cost equals average variable cost.
     c.  average total cost is rising.
     d.  total cost is constant.

14.  Which short-run curve is **NOT** U-shaped?
     a.  average total cost
     b.  marginal cost
     c.  average variable cost
     d.  average fixed cost

15.  The production function
     a.  is a technological relationship.
     b.  is not an economic relationship.
     c.  relates output to inputs.
     d.  All of the above

16.  Because of the law of diminishing marginal returns,
     a.  long-run average cost eventually rises.
     b.  marginal cost falls.
     c.  the marginal product of labour eventually falls.
     d.  the average total cost curve falls.

17.  Which is **NOT** due to the law of diminishing marginal returns?
     a.  rising short-run marginal cost
     b.  rising long-run average total cost
     c.  rising short-run average variable cost
     d.  rising short-run average total cost

18.  *Analogy*: Diminishing returns is to rising short-run average total costs as _____ is
     to rising long-run average total costs.
     a.  economies of scale
     b.  diseconomies of scale
     c.  law of diminishing returns
     d.  constant returns to scale

19.  Which of the following helps to account for a U-shaped short-run average total cost
     curve?
     a.  economies of scale
     b.  diseconomies of scale
     c.  law of diminishing (marginal) returns
     d.  constant returns to scale

20. A firm might experience diseconomies of scale due to
    a. disproportionate rises in specialization.
    b. dimensional factors.
    c. information and communication costs that rise disproportionately.
    d. the ability to use larger-volume machinery that is efficient only at large outputs.

21. If the minimum efficient scale is relatively low, then
    a. there will likely be a relatively large number of firms in the industry.
    b. there will likely be a relatively small number of firms in the industry.
    c. economies of scale are very great.
    d. long-run average costs decline over broad ranges of output.

## MATCHING
Choose the item in column (2) that best matches an item in column (1).

| (1) | (2) |
|-----|-----|
| a. long run | 1. falling long-run average cost |
| b. short run | 2. explicit cost |
| c. fixed cost | 3. fixed plant size |
| d. variable cost | 4. diminishing marginal product |
| e. opportunity cost of capital | 5. planning curve |
| f. economies of scale | 6. wages of labourers |
| g. diseconomies of scale | 7. implicit cost |
| h. law of diminishing returns | 8. all factors variable |
| | 9. rising long-run average cost |
| | 10. overhead |

## WORKING WITH GRAPHS

1. Assume that the High Rise Bakery produces a single product: loaves of bread. Further assume that the bread is produced using a fixed plant size, with ten ovens and varying quantities of labour. John Doe notices that as he hires additional workers, the total output of bread goes up for a while. Then he finds that after hiring several additional workers, the workers begin to get in one another's way and extra output begins to decline. John knows the principles of economics and something about diminishing marginal physical product. Given the information below, calculate the marginal physical product of John's bakers. Graph total and marginal products on the next page and tell John how many bakers he can employ before diminishing marginal returns set in. (Plot the marginal product at the midpoint between the numbers of bakers employed.)

| Bakers | Output (loaves per day) | Marginal product |
|--------|-------------------------|------------------|
| 0 | 0 | |
| 1 | 8 | _____ |
| 2 | 19 | _____ |
| 3 | 32 | _____ |
| 4 | 45 | _____ |
| 5 | 60 | _____ |
| 6 | 71 | _____ |
| 7 | 75 | _____ |
| 8 | 77 | _____ |
| 9 | 77 | _____ |
| 10 | 75 | _____ |
| 11 | 65 | _____ |

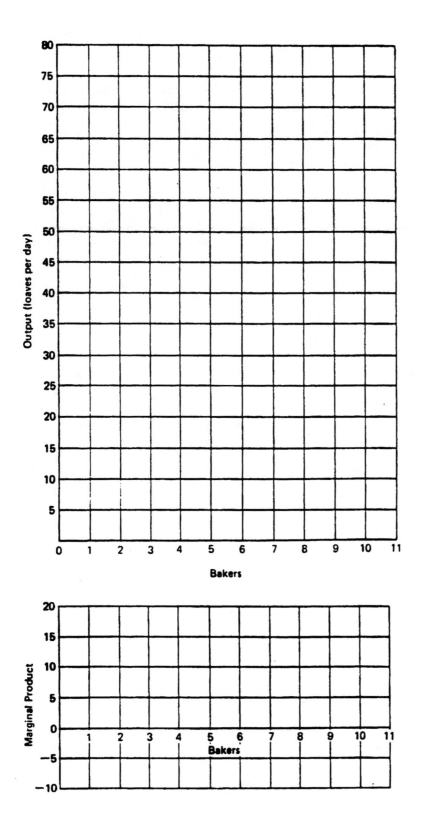

2. Complete the following table of cost figures and then graph the information on the graphs provided below.  Assume total fixed costs are $3.

| Output | Total variable costs | Total costs | Average variable cost | Average total cost | Marginal cost |
|---|---|---|---|---|---|
| 0 | 0.00 | 3.00 | _____ | _____ | _____ |
| 1 | 3.00 | _____ | _____ | _____ | _____ |
| 2 | _____ | _____ | _____ | 4.00 | _____ |
| 3 | _____ | 9.20 | _____ | _____ | _____ |
| 4 | _____ | _____ | _____ | _____ | 2.30 |
| 5 | _____ | _____ | 2.38 | _____ | _____ |
| 6 | _____ | _____ | _____ | _____ | 5.00 |
| 7 | 23.90 | _____ | _____ | _____ | _____ |
| 8 | _____ | 36.90 | _____ | _____ | _____ |

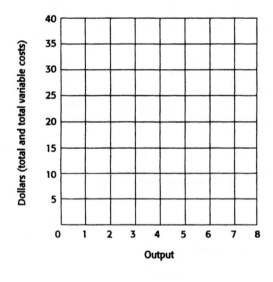

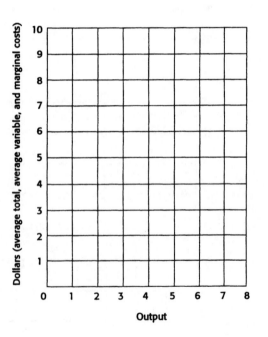

3.Use the graph below to answer the questions that follow.

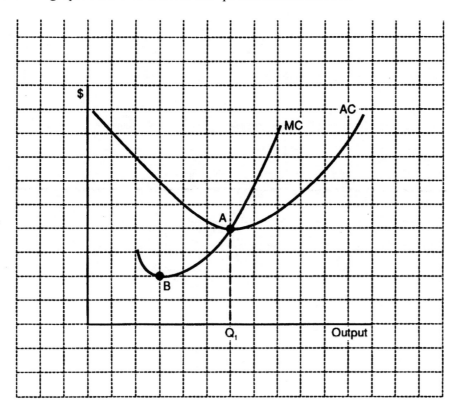

a.  At what point do diminishing marginal returns begin?

b.  At any output less than $Q_1$, why is AC falling?

c.  At any output greater than $Q_1$, why is AC rising?

d.  What is AC doing at the exact output $Q_1$?

4.  Use the graph below to answer the questions that follow.  Assume that A and B are minimum points.

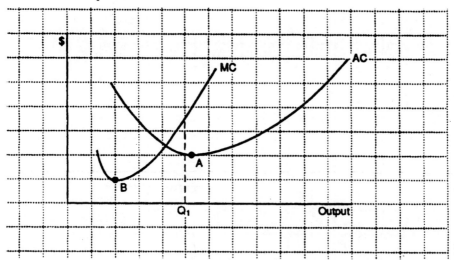

*a.  Something is wrong with the graph above.  What is it?

b.  According to the graph above, what is happening at output $Q_1$, with respect to MC and AC?  Is this possible?

## PROBLEMS

1.  Mr. Delinski owns his own car repair business.  His annual total revenues are $200,000, and his total explicit costs are $160,000.  Upon further investigation it is discovered that Mr. Delinski did not include an estimate of the worth of his own wages (which were $35,000 at a former job) in calculating his annual total profits of $40,000.  Nor, it seems, did he estimate the annual rate of return that he could have earned on the $100,000 of his own savings that he used to enter his business. His savings were previously invested in mutual funds earning 10% interest per year. Calculate his accounting profit? Calculate his economic profit? Does the car repair business provide him with a "normal rate of return"?

2.  Fill in the information in each blank below so that the equation is correct.  (Note:  Q is quantity of output.)

a.  TC = TFC + _____

b.  AFC = _____ - AVC

c.  ATC = (TVC/Q) + _____

d.  TFC = Q x _____

e.  AVC = (TC/Q) - _____ /Q

f.  TVC = (Q x ATC) - Q x _____

## BUSINESS SECTION

### Entrepreneurship/Accounting

### Break Even Quantity and Target Profit Quantity: Fixed vs. Variable Costs

The **break even quantity** (BEQ) refers to the amount of a product that a firm must sell in order to have Total Revenue just cover Total Cost. The BEQ is a good application of fixed and variable costs and can be determined by using the following formula:

$$BEQ = \frac{Total\ Fixed\ Cost}{Price - Average\ Variable\ Cost}$$

The **target profit quantity** (TPQ) refers to the amount of a product that a firm must sell in order to achieve a desired level of profit. The TPQ can be determined by using the following formula:

$$TPQ = \frac{Total\ Fixed\ Cost + Target\ Profit}{Price - Average\ Variable\ Cost}$$

*Note:* In both applications above, average variable cost is assumed to be constant in the relevant quantity range.

### Business Application Problem 1
To help pay for a three  month summer visit at Banff National Park, Shelley Kopps plans to set up a Buffalo Burger stand in a popular tourist site. Shelley estimates her costs as follows:

**Fixed Costs Per Month**

| | |
|---|---|
| Depreciation on barbecue | $100.00 |
| Site rental | $ 50.00 |
| Shelley's monthly wage (paid to herself) | $1000.00 |

**Variable Costs Per Buffalo Burger**

| | |
|---|---|
| Pattie | $1.07 |
| Bun | $.13 |
| Garnish | $.10 |
| Condiment | $.09 |
| Propane | $.02 |

If Shelley plans to charge a price of $4.95 per Buffalo Burger, determine the following:

a. How many Buffalo Burgers must Shelley sell per month in order to break even. How many burgers per day does this imply, assuming 30 days in a typical month.

b. How many Buffalo Burgers per month must Shelley sell in order to achieve a monthly profit of $1500. How many burgers per day does this imply, assuming 30 days in a typical month.

## Business Application Problem 2

In order to finance his way through college, Otto Matic plans to operate 5 cold beverage vending machines at 5 different locations on campus. Otto will rent each machine at $42 per month and can rent each college location at $30 per month. He can hire a co-op student to stock and service all 5 machines at  a total wage of $400 per month. The vending machine will dispense the cold beverages in cans. Through a local supplier, Otto can purchase each can at $.30 per can and he plans to charge a price of $1.00 per can.

a. Considering all 5 machines, how many cans must Otto sell per month to just break even. How many cans per location per day does this imply (30 days in a typical month).

b. Considering all 5 machines, how many cans per month must Otto sell to achieve a profit of $2000 per month. How many cans per location per day does this imply (30 days in a month).

## ANSWERS TO CHAPTER 10

### COMPLETION QUESTIONS

1.    Explicit; implicit
2.    do
3.    total revenues; explicit costs; total revenues; implicit plus explicit costs; implicit
4.    profit maximization
5.    capital; labour; all
6.    do not; do; rent; interest payments on mortgages; wages; raw material costs
7.    diminishing (marginal) returns; equal to; rise
8.    short; fall
9.    economies; constant; diseconomies
10.    specialization; dimensional factors; improved productive equipment; disproportionate requirements for managers and staff; disproportionate costs of information and communication

**TRUE-FALSE QUESTIONS**

1.   T
2.   F    Implicit costs include the opportunity cost of a resource.
3.   T
4.   T
5.   T
6.   T
7.   F    By definition, they are fixed.
8.   T
9.   F    Average costs can be increasing while marginal costs are decreasing.
10.  T
11.  F    Capital is fixed in the short run.
12.  F    Marginal product of labour falls due to the law of diminishing returns.
13.  F    Diminishing marginal returns occur in the short run.

**MULTIPLE CHOICE QUESTIONS**

1.  a;   Explicit costs are money payments that would be found on an income statement.
2.  c;   Implicit costs are what the resources could have been used for.
3.  d;   Accounting profits would be found on a typical income statement. Total revenue – total costs where total costs are explicit costs.
4.  c;   An implicit cost of doing business.
5.  b;   All others would be found on an income statement.
6.  a;   All others would be found on an income statement.
7.  d;   Businesses want to maximize profits.
8.  b;   Labour would vary while capital would be considered fixed.
9.  d;   In the long run they can change the plant size and other factors.
10. b;   Fixed costs are not related to output.
11. b;   The number of workers will tend to vary with production.
12. a;   If the cost of producing one more unit is increasing, this will increase average total cost.
13. a;   Marginal cost intersects average variable cost and average total cost at their lowest point.
14. d;   Average fixed cost decreases as quantity increases.
15. d;   The production function is a technological not and economic issue.
16. c;   Labour is variable, if added to fixed it will eventually fall.
17. b;   In the long run, all inputs are variable.
18. b;   Diseconomies cause long run average total costs to increase because of the lack of communication and red tape.
19. c;   Adding variable input to a fixed input will initially decrease costs but as fixed input reaches its maximum, costs will increase.
20. c;   The firm has too much red tape.
21. a;   More firms will be able to compete as it will be easy to reach their lowest costs.

**MATCHING**

a and 8;   b and 3;   c and 10;   d and 6;   e and 7;   f and 1;   g and 9;   h and 4

**WORKING WITH GRAPHS**

1.    Marginal product:  8; 11; 13; 13; 15; 11; 4; 2; 0; -2; -10
      Diminishing returns set in when John hires the sixth baker.

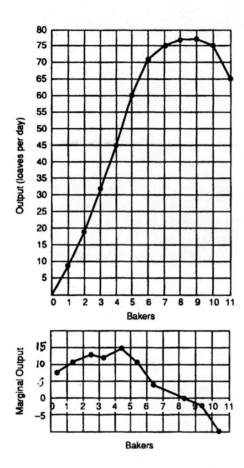

2.

| Output | Total variable costs | Total costs | Average variable cost | Average total cost | Marginal cost |
|--------|----------------------|-------------|-----------------------|--------------------|---------------|
| 0 | 0.00 | 3.00 | -- | -- | -- |
| 1 | 3.00 | 6.00 | 3.00 | 6.00 | 3.00 |
| 2 | 5.00 | 8.00 | 2.50 | 4.00 | 2.00 |
| 3 | 6.20 | 9.20 | 2.07 | 3.07 | 1.20 |
| 4 | 8.50 | 11.50 | 2.13 | 2.88 | 2.30 |
| 5 | 11.90 | 14.90 | 2.38 | 2.98 | 3.40 |
| 6 | 16.90 | 19.90 | 2.82 | 3.32 | 5.00 |
| 7 | 23.90 | 26.90 | 3.41 | 3.84 | 7.00 |
| 8 | 33.90 | 36.90 | 4.24 | 4.61 | 10.00 |

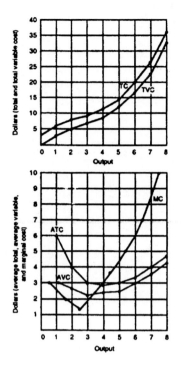

3.   a.   B
     b. MC is below AC, due to specialization
     c. MC is above AC
     d. AC is constant, because MC = AC.
4.   a.   MC cuts the AC curve to the left of AC's minimum point.
  b.   MC > AC, yet AC is falling.  No.

## PROBLEMS

1.   Accounting profit = 40,000. Economic profit = -5,000 including his lost wages. If he is not covering all explicit and implicit costs, he might consider working for someone else and earning interest on his money, unless he really enjoys being his own boss, that is.
2.   a. TVC  b. ATC  c. AFC  d. AFC  e. TFC  f. AFC

## BUSINESS SECTION

1.   a.   Monthly BEQ = 1,150 / (4.95 – 1.41) = 324.85 or 325 burgers per month;
         325/30 =10.8 or 11 burgers per day .
     b.   Monthly TPQ = 2,650/ (4.95 – 1.41) = 748.58 or 749 burgers per month;
         749/30 = 24.96 or 25 burgers per day.
2.   a.   BEQ for all 5 machines = 760/.70 = 1,085.71 or 1086 cans per month;
         (1086/5)/30 = 7  cans per location per day.
     b.   TPQ for all 5 machines = (760 + 2,000)/.70 = 3942.86 or 3943 cans per month; (39436/5)/30
         = 26 cans per location per day.

## ANSWERS TO EXAMPLE QUESTIONS FOR CRITICAL ANALYSIS

**I    INTERNATIONAL EXAMPLE 10-1: Europeans Use More Capital** (p. 219)

A firm decides to use more machines when it is cheaper to do so than to use an additional amount of labour to produce a given increase in output. Alternatively, more machines are used when marginal product per last dollar spent on a machine is greater than the marginal product per last dollar spent on labour.

**II    EXAMPLE 10-1: The Cost of Driving a Car** (p. 227)

Total fixed costs are the insurance, license and registration, and financing charges. Total variable costs are equal to the total cost of $6,071.12 less the total fixed costs. An average total cost is 44.7 cents, 39.8 cents, or 36.1 cents per kilometer. Marginal cost is the additional cost of driving one more kilometer.

**III   EXAMPLE 10-2: Goods Versus Ideas** (p. 233)

The long-run average cost curve for ideas would be close to zero. The cost of the idea would occur in the short run. After the idea has been implemented, the costs reach zero.

# CHAPTER 11

# PERFECT COMPETITION

## PUTTING THIS CHAPTER INTO PERSPECTIVE

Chapter 11 is the first of three chapters (the others are Chapters 12 and 13) that are concerned with how firms determine price and output under different market structures. The market structures studied are perfect competition (the subject of this chapter), monopoly (Chapter 12), monopolistic competition (Chapter 13), and oligopoly (also in Chapter 13). Alternatively stated, in Chapter 11 you will be introduced to the field of economics called industrial organization. Industrial organization studies how the firm's industry environment affects the firm's behaviour and performance.

Your understanding of the economic analysis of firms operating in various market structures will be facilitated if you see the "big picture." In effect, the same pattern of methodology can be found under each market structure analysis.  First note well the specific characteristics of each particular market structure; memorize those characteristics and then try to see how each one helps to make the specific market structure unique.

Secondly, try to determine the firm's short-run (and then long-run) behaviour in terms of equilibrium output, price, and profit levels.  You might find it helpful to know that regardless of the model we analyze, the firm's equilibrium output will occur where marginal benefit (MB) equals marginal cost (MC). Under different circumstances, the MB to an economic agent (firm, consumer, employer, labourer, etc.) will be called different things; so too will the specific economic agent's MC be called different things in different models and situations.   Nevertheless, our assumption of the goal of maximization usually allows us to predict the optimal decision point.  For example, in this chapter the competitive firm's MB is its selling price, or its marginal revenue; the marginal cost of a particular output is found on its marginal cost curve.  The competitive firm maximizes at the point where MB = MC; that is, it produces up to the point where Price = MC or where Price equals Marginal Revenue. Thus, the profit maximizing output for the competitive firm is at that level for which MR = MC. (Note: you should always be able to show why the economic agent is not maximizing if MB > MC or if MB < MC.)

The final component of our "pattern" is to assess the specific market in terms of key socio-economic goals (i.e. the firm's performance). That is, is the firm allocatively efficient? Is output at a level at which productive efficiency is achieved?  Do economic or "excess" profits persist in the long run? Is the typical firm innovative?

If you try to see the pattern of analysis you may save yourself a lot of study time, and you can more easily *compare* the various market structures (a task which your instructor may well ask you to perform).


## LEARNING OBJECTIVES

After you have studied this chapter, you should be able to

1.   define industrial organization, price taker, total revenues, marginal revenue, short-run shutdown price, short-run break-even price, short-run firm supply curve, long-run industry supply curve, constant-cost industry, increasing-cost industry, decreasing-cost industry, long-run equilibrium, marginal-cost pricing.

2.   list  and explain four characteristics of the perfect competition market structure.

3.   recognize the shape of a competitive firm's demand curve and provide reasons for its shape.

4.   determine a perfect competitor's optimal output rate, using total revenues and total costs related information.

5.   determine a perfect competitor's optimal output rate, using per unit revenue and per unit cost related information.

6.   calculate the value of a perfect competitor's short-run profits, given sufficient information.

7.   recognize and determine the perfectly competitive firm's short-run shutdown price and its short-run break-even price.

8.   recognize a perfectly competitive firm's short-run supply curve and recognize how an *industry* short-run supply curve is derived.

9.   distinguish among constant-cost, increasing-cost, and decreasing-cost industries.

10.   recognize the long-run equilibrium position for a firm in a perfectly competitive industry.

11.   indicate why a perfectly competitive market structure is allocatively efficient.

12.   indicate why a perfectly competitive market structure is productively efficient.

13.   explain why a perfectly competitive market structure may contribute to an equitable distribution of income.

14.   recognize that market failures such as externalities and public goods affect the socio-economic performance of the perfect competition model.


## CHAPTER OUTLINE

1.   There are four major characteristics of the **perfect competition market structure**: a large number of buyers and sellers, homogeneous product, unimpeded industry exit and entry, and equally good information for both buyers and sellers.

2.   Because in the perfect competition model many firms produce a homogeneous product, a single firm's demand curve is perfectly elastic at the "going" market price. That is, each firm is a **price taker**.

3.   In order to predict how much the perfect competitor will produce, we assume that it wants to maximize total profits. Using the **total revenues** and total costs approach:
     a.   Total revenues equal quantity sold times price per unit.
     b.   In the short run, total costs are the sum of total fixed costs and total variable costs.
     c.   Total revenues minus total costs equal total profits.
     d.   The **profit maximizing output** level is that output level where the largest difference between total revenues and total costs occurs.

4.   In order to predict how much the **perfect competitor** will produce, we assume that it wants to maximize total profits. Using the unit cost approach:
     a.   **Marginal revenue** is the change in total revenues when producing (selling) one more unit of output. That is, marginal revenue is the extra revenue in selling one more unit of output.
     b.   Marginal cost is the change in total costs when producing (selling) one more unit of output. That is, marginal cost is the extra cost in selling one more unit of output.
     c.   Total profits are maximized at that rate of output where marginal revenue equals marginal cost.
     d.   The profit per unit is determined by comparing the price with the average total cost.

5.   The firm's **short-run shutdown price** occurs at its minimum average variable cost value; at a higher price the firm should produce and contribute to payment of fixed costs; it should not produce at a lower price.

6. The firm's **short-run break-even price** is found at the minimum point on its average total cost curve; at a higher price the firm will earn abnormal profits; at a lower price it suffers economic losses; at the minimum point, economic profits equal zero. When the firm breaks even, the firm just earns a normal profit.

7. Because a normal rate of return to investment is included in the average total cost curve, the "profits" we calculate are economic profits.

8. The firm's short-run supply curve is its marginal cost curve above the short-run shutdown point.

9. The short-run **industry supply curve** is derived by summing horizontally all of the firm supply curves; the industry supply curve shifts when non-price determinants of supply change.

10. In a competitive market, the "going" price is set where the market demand curve intersects the industry supply curve.

11. In the long run, because abnormal industry profits induce entry and because negative industry profits induce exit, firms in a competitive industry will earn zero economic profits.
    a. Long-run supply curves relate price and quantity supplied after firms have time to enter or exit from an industry.
    b. A constant-cost industry is one whose long-run supply curve is horizontal, because input prices are unaffected by output.
    c. An **increasing-cost industry** is one whose long-run supply curve is positively sloped, because the price of specialized (or essential) inputs rises as industry output increases.
    d. A **decreasing-cost industry** is one whose long-run supply curve is negatively sloped, because specialized input prices fall as industry output expands.

12. In a perfectly competitive industry, a firm operates where price equals marginal revenue equals marginal cost equals long-run minimum average total cost—in the long run.
    a. Perfectly competitive industries are allocatively efficient from society's point of view because for such industries price equals marginal cost in long-run equilibrium.
    b. They are also productively efficient because in long-run equilibrium the output rate is produced at minimum average cost.
    c. In the long-run perfect competition promotes an equitable distribution of income to the extent that upper income shareholders earn just a normal profit or rate of return.

13. If **market failure** due to externalities or public goods applies to the industry, a perfectly competitive market structure will lead to a sub-optimal allocation of resources.

## KEY TERMS AND CONCEPTS

Perfect competition
Price taker
Total revenues
Industrial organization
Perfectly competitive firm
Marginal revenue
Signals
Short-run shutdown price
Short-run breakeven price

Market structure
Industry supply curve
Long-run industry supply curve
Constant-cost industry
Increasing-cost industry
Decreasing-cost industry
Marginal cost pricing
Market failure
Profit-maximizing rate of production

## COMPLETION QUESTIONS
Fill in the blank or circle the correct term.

1.  The four major characteristics of a perfect competition market structure are
    _____, _____, _____, and _____.

2.  The demand curve facing a perfect competitor is _____ elastic.
    This means that the individual firm is a (price maker, price taker)

3.  We assume that the goal of the firm is to _____; if so, the
    perfect competitor should produce up to the point where marginal revenue (MR)
    equals _____; total profits are defined as _____ minus
    _____.

4.  Marginal revenue equals _____ divided by _____.

5.  Because we include the opportunity cost of capital as a cost of production, the
    profits we define are (accounting, economic) profits.

6.  If the firm's selling price cannot cover its short-run variable costs, then it should
    _____; if selling price equals minimum average total
    cost, the firm is just _____, and its economic profits are
    (negative, positive, zero).

7.  If the firm is earning zero economic profits, it (would, would not) continue to
    operate.

8.  The competitive firm's short-run supply curve is the portion of its _____
    curve lying above minimum AVC; the industry short-run supply curve is derived
    by _____ all the firm supply curves.

9.    In the long run, a firm in a perfectly competitive industry will earn exactly zero economic profits. This is true because if economic profits are positive, some firms will _____ the industry and price will fall; if economic profits are negative, some firms will _____ the industry and price will rise.

10.   If an industry expands and input prices do not change, such an industry is a(n) _____-cost industry and the long-run supply curve is horizontal; if input prices rise, the industry is a(n) _____-cost industry and the long-run industry supply curve is _____ sloping; if input prices fall, the industry is a(n) _____-cost industry and the industry's long-run supply curve is _____ sloping.

11.   In the long run a perfectly competitive firm will earn (negative, positive, zero) economic profits. Its price will be (greater than, less than, equal to) marginal cost, and output (will, will not) be produced at minimum average total cost. From society's point of view, all of this is (efficient, inefficient).

12.   Suppose Product X entails external costs. If this product is produced under a perfect competition market structure it will tend to be (efficiently produced, over produced) from a social viewpoint.

13.   Since perfect competition firms tend to make zero economic profits in the long-run, this acts as a(n) (incentive, disincentive) to undertake expensive research and development.

**TRUE-FALSE QUESTIONS**
Circle the **T** if the statement is true, the **F** if it is false. Explain to yourself why a statement is false.

T   F   1.    A firm in a perfectly competitive industry is a price taker.

T   F   2.    Because firms in a perfectly competitive industry are all price takers, price cannot change in that industry.

T   F   3.    The demand curve facing a perfect competitor is perfectly elastic.

T   F   4.    The perfectly competitive firm attempts to maximize marginal profits.

T   F   5.    The maximum profit output level occurs at the point where the firm's marginal cost equals its marginal revenue.

T   F   6.    Average revenue minus average cost equals total profits.

T  F    7.    If price is below minimum average variable costs in the short run, the firm will shut down, assuming output is where MR = MC.

T  F    8.    If price is below minimum average total cost, economic profits will be negative, assuming that output is where MR = MC.

T  F    9.    The firm's short-run supply curve is its average variable cost curve.

T  F   10.   The industry supply curve is derived by summing horizontally all the firm supply curves.

T  F   11.   Because of the law of diminishing returns, the firm's short-run supply curve will be upward sloping.

T  F   12.   Because of free exit and entry, long-run accounting profits for a perfect competitor must be zero.

T  F   13.   A constant-cost industry has an upward sloping long-run industry supply curve.

T  F   14.   If demand falls in a decreasing-cost industry, in the long-run both output and price will fall.

T  F   15.   In the long-run equilibrium situation, the perfectly competitive firm will earn zero economic profits and produce at minimum average cost.

T  F   16.   Because of excessive competition, the perfectly competitive industry is believed to be inefficient from society's point of view.

T  F   17.   Perfect competition promotes allocative efficiency when sources of market failure (externalities, public goods etc.) are present.


## MULTIPLE CHOICE QUESTIONS
Circle the letter that corresponds to the best answer.

1.    Which of the following is **NOT** a characteristic of the perfect competition market structure?
    a.   equally good information for both buyers and sellers
    b.   homogeneous product
    c.   large number of buyers and sellers
    d.   restricted entry and exit

2.    In the perfect competition model
      a.  each seller is a price taker.
      b.  all firms together can affect price.
      c.  all firms produce a homogeneous product.
      d.  All of the above

3.    The demand curve facing the perfect competitor is
      a.  perfectly elastic.
      b.  vertical at the going price.
      c.  perfectly inelastic.
      d.  negatively sloped.

4.    The perfect competitor
      a.  can sell all it wants to sell at the going price.
      b.  can sell nothing at a price higher than the going price.
      c.  faces a perfectly elastic demand curve.
      d.  All of the above

5.    We assume the firm wants to maximize _____ profits.
      a.  marginal
      b.  average
      c.  total
      d.  fixed

6.    The firm maximizes total profits at that output at which
      a.  $MC = MR$.
      b.  $MR < MC$.
      c.  $P = AC$.
      d.  $MR > MC$.

7.    In which of these cases are economic profits negative?
      a.  Total revenues exceed total costs.
      b.  Average revenues exceed average costs.
      c.  Price is below minimum average total cost.
      d.  Average revenue is equal to price.

8.    The competitive firm's short-run total profits equal
      a.  average revenue minus average cost times quantity sold.
      b.  average revenue minus average cost.
      c.  price minus marginal cost.
      d.  price minus average variable cost.

9. A firm should shut down when
   a. price is below average cost.
   b. price is above average variable cost.
   c. price is below. average variable cost.
   d. None of the above.

10. At the short-run break-even price,
   a. accounting profits equal economic profits.
   b. economic profits are negative.
   c. economic profits are zero.
   d. accounting profits are zero.

11. The firm's short-run supply curve is its
   a. marginal cost curve above the shutdown point.
   b. average cost curve, above its minimum point.
   c. average variable cost curve, above the shutdown point.
   d. marginal revenue curve.

12. The industry supply curve is derived by summing horizontally all the firms'
   a. marginal cost curves above their shutdown points.
   b. average revenue curves.
   c. total revenue curves.
   d. marginal revenue curves.

13. Which of the following will **NOT** shift the industry supply curve?
   a. change in price
   b. change in the cost of raw materials
   c. change in number of firms in the industry
   d. change in wage rates

14. If economic profits are negative in an industry, then
   a. firms will enter that industry.
   b. some firms will exit from that industry.
   c. price is above minimum average total costs.
   d. accounting profits must also be negative.

15. If demand falls in an increasing-cost industry, then in the long run
   a. price will fall.
   b. price will return to its previous level.
   c. output will rise.
   d. output will return to its previous level.

16.   In a decreasing cost industry, the long-run industry supply curve is
a.   downward sloping.
b.   upward sloping.
c.   horizontal.
d.   perpendicular.

17.   In long-run equilibrium, a competitive firm
a.   earns zero economic profits.
b.   produces at minimum average cost.
c.   produces where price equals marginal cost.
d.   All of the above

18.   The marginal cost of producing good A
a.   includes fixed costs.
b.   represents the opportunity cost to society of producing one more unit of good A.
c.   is found by reading the average variable cost curve.
d.   includes only labour costs.

**MATCHING**
Choose the numbered item in Column (2) that best matches the term or concept in Column (1).

(1)

a.   price taker
b.   profit maximizing output
c.   profit per unit
d.   short-run shutdown price
e.   short-run break even price
f.   short run supply curve
g.   decreasing cost industry
h.   productive efficiency
i.   allocative efficiency

(2)

1.  rising long-run industry supply curve
2.  minimum average cost
3.  price equals marginal cost
4.  perfectly elastic demand
5.  marginal cost curve above min AVC
6.  price equals minimum AVC
7.  price equals average cost
8.  marginal revenue equals marginal cost
9.  price minus average cost
10. price minus average fixed cost
11. falling long-run industry supply curve
12. perfectly elastic demand

**WORKING WITH GRAPHS**

1.  Use the graphs below to answer the questions that follow. Assume that the graphs describe a firm operating under perfect competition.

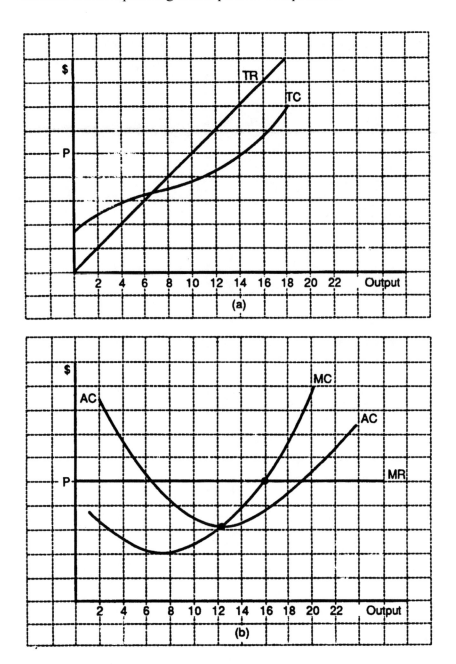

a.  The total revenue curve is linear; therefore its slope is a _____; its slope equals what economic concept?

b.  The slope of a tangent to a point on the TC curve is defined as what?

c.  The firm tries to (minimize, maximize) the positive difference between TR and TC.  At what output level does that occur?

d.  In panel (b), what is the firm's profit-maximizing output?  Why?

e.  How are your answers to parts c and d related?

2.  Use the following graph to answer the questions that follow. Assume that the firm is a profit maximizer operating in a purely competitive market.

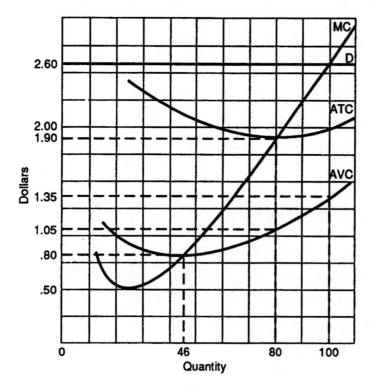

a.  How many units of output will the firm produce and sell? Why?

b.  What is price at this level of output? Why?

c.  What is the average cost at this level of output?

d.  What is the profit per unit at this level of output? Explain.

e.  What is the amount of total profits at this level of output? Explain.

f.  What is break-even point price? Explain.

g.  What is the shut-down point price? Explain.

h.  Assuming that the ATC curve is the long-run average cost curve, predict the price in the long-run. Explain.

3.  The following graph describes a perfectly competitive firm selling natural gas on a daily basis. Assume that the daily total fixed cost is $680.00.

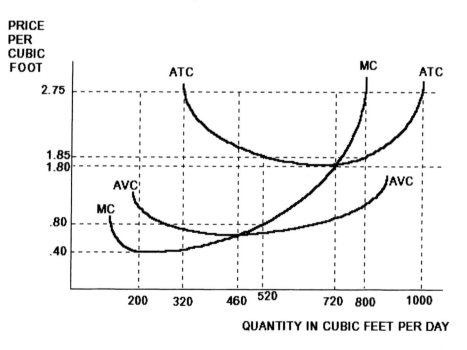

a. If the market sets a price of $2.75 per cubic foot:
   i.  Find the daily quantity level that maximizes total profits.

   ii.  What is the dollar amount of the daily maximum profit?

b. If the market sets a price of $0.40 per cubic foot:
   i.   Find the daily quantity level that maximizes total profits.

   ii.  What is the dollar amount of the daily maximum profit (or minimum dollar loss)?

c. If the market sets a price of $0.80 per cubic foot, and there are 100 identical firms in the industry (including this firm), what would be the daily market supply? Show your work.

d. Assuming that the ATC curve in the graph is also the long-run average cost curve, predict the long-run price. Explain.

## PROBLEMS

1.  Suppose you are hired as an economic consultant for Profmax Consulting Company. Your job is to advise the company's clients on the appropriate action to take in the short run in order to maximize the profits (or minimize the losses) of each firm. The firms you are to analyze produce different products, and each operates independently in a different perfectly competitive market. You may assume that each is currently operating at an output level where marginal cost is increasing. Fill in the missing information, and make your suggestions about the appropriate action for each firm by placing one of the following symbols in the last row of the table of information that follows.

    C   =  currently operating at the correct level of output
    I   =  increase the level of output
    D   =  decrease the level of output
    SD  =  shut down the plant

| Firm | A | B | C | D | E | F | G |
|------|------|------|------|------|------|------|------|
| Price | $0.50 | _____ | $3.50 | _____ | $3.00 | $5.00 | _____ |
| Output | _____ | 300 | 750 | 700 | _____ | _____ | 1000 |
| TR | $500 | $300 | _____ | $2800 | $1800 | $4000 | $5000 |
| TC | _____ | $525 | $2625 | $2975 | _____ | _____ | _____ |
| TFC | _____ | _____ | _____ | _____ | $180 | $1200 | _____ |
| TVC | $300 | _____ | _____ | $2450 | _____ | _____ | $3000 |
| ATC | $0.40 | _____ | Minimum | _____ | _____ | $5.50 | $5.50 |
| AVC | _____ | $1.20 | $3.00 | _____ | $2.00 | Minimum | _____ |
| MC | $0.40 | $1.00 | _____ | $4.00 | $3.50 | _____ | $5.75 |
| Suggestion | _____ | _____ | _____ | _____ | _____ | _____ | _____ |

2.  The following table describes the per unit costs at different daily production levels for Apex Ltd. which produces a standard recycling box for homeowners.

| Q<br># boxes<br>per day | Average<br>Variable<br>Cost ($) | Marginal<br>Cost<br>$ | Average<br>Total<br>Cost ($) |
|------|------|------|------|
| 0 | ----- | ----- | ----- |
| 1 | 4 | 4 | 24 |
| 2 | 6 | 8 | 16 |
| 3 | 8 | 12 | 14.67 |
| 4 | 10 | 16 | 15 |
| 5 | 12 | 20 | 16 |

a.  Based on the per unit costs above, complete the table below. Assume that there are 100 identical firms (including Apex) that supply the recycling box in the industry. The table below refers to short-run supply.

| Price<br>per box | Individual<br>Firm Supply | Market<br>Supply | Market<br>Demand |
|------|------|------|------|
| 21 | _____ | _____ | 200 |
| 13 | _____ | _____ | 300 |
| 5 | _____ | _____ | 400 |
| 3 | _____ | _____ | 1000 |

b.    What will be the short-run equilibrium price and equilibrium quantity in this recycling box industry?

## BUSINESS SECTION

### Accounting: Short Run Analysis: Tools of a Cost Accountant

### Business Application Problem

Moniques  is a purely competitive firm that manufactures pulp in Quebec. The  price of pulp is determined  on a worldwide market in response to demand and supply forces.

At the end of every month, Ted Baxter, the cost accountant at Moniques, compares the projected pulp price with the company's short run unit costs in order to determine the optimum production level for the next month. Once the optimum production schedule is determined, other important decisions  can be made such as the number of shifts to operate, man-hours of labour to employ and the amount of raw materials to purchase. As well, the monthly profit or loss can be projected, which is important from a cash flow point of view.

Given the current plant facility and related commitments, the total monthly fixed cost is $250,000. The other relevant costs depend on the monthly production level and are described in the table below. Note that in the table below, the full capacity of the plant is 6,000 tons per month.

| Monthly Production Rate in Tonnes (Q) | Total Variable Cost (TVC) | Average Variable Cost (AVC) | Marginal Cost Per Tonne (MC) | Average Total Cost (ATC) |
|---|---|---|---|---|
| 0 | $0 | ------------------ | ------------------ | ------------------ |
| 1000 | $124,000 | | | |
| 2000 | $240,000 | | | |
| 3000 | $375,000 | | | |
| 4000 | $540,000 | | | |
| 5000 | $750,000 | | | |
| 6000 | $1,020,000 | | | |

a.  Complete the table above.

b.  Due to a major union strike at competitive plants in the U.S., Ted projects that, in September the price of pulp will increase to $230 per ton. Base on this projection and the cost information above,  determine the profit maximizing (or loss minimizing) September production rate, in tons. At this production rate, calculate the total monthly profit, in dollars.

c. In October the U.S. labour dispute was settled. As well, new competitive pulp plants started operation. As a result, the projected October price for pulp is only $140 per ton. Based on this projected price and the cost information above, determine the profit maximizing (or loss minimizing) October production rate, in tons. At this production rate, calculate the total monthly profit, in dollars.

d. In November the Asian economies, major buyers of Moniques pulp, went into a recession. As a result, the November price dropped to $118 per ton. Base on the $118 price and the cost information above, determine the profit maximizing (or loss minimizing) November production rate, in tons. At this production rate, calculate the total monthly profit, in dollars.

e. In general, in the short run, is the best production rate always going to be where Moniques achieves the lowest cost per ton of pulp? Explain.

f. In general, in the short run, should Ted always shut down the plant when he projects a loss? Explain.

**ANSWERS TO CHAPTER 11**

**COMPLETION QUESTIONS**

1. large number of buyers and sellers; homogeneous product; equally good information for both buyers and sellers; and easy entry or exit
2. perfectly; price taker
3. maximize total profits; marginal cost (MC); total revenues; total costs
4. change in total revenue; change in output
5. economic
6. shut down; breaking even; zero
7. would
8. MC; summing horizontally
9. enter; exit
10. constant; increasing; upward; decreasing; downward
11. zero; equal to; will; efficient
12. overproduced
13. disincentive

**TRUE-FALSE**

1. T
2. F   Price is a constant to an *individual* firm, but not to the group of firms.
3. T
4. F   Firms attempt to maximize *total* profits.
5. T
6. F   Total revenues minus total costs equal total profits.
7. T
8. T
9. F   The firm's marginal cost curve above minimum AVC is its short-run supply curve.
10. T
11. T
12. F   Long-run *economic* profits must be zero.
13. F   The long-run industry supply curve is horizontal.
14. F   Price will rise.
15. T
16. F   It is efficient because P = MC and production is at minimum average cost, in the long run.
17. F   Perfect competition will tend to over-produce or under-produce the product in cases of market failure.

**MULTIPLE CHOICE QUESTIONS**

1.d; There is easy (not restricted) entry and exit in perfect competition.
2.d; In perfect competition, since there are a large number of firms selling a homogeneous
     product, each individual firm is a price taker. However, all firms, taken together,
     can affect the price.
     *TIP:* In perfect competition the market (not the individual firm) sets the price.
3.a; In perfect competition, there are a large numbers of competitors producing an
     identical product. Therefore, if a firm increases its price just a minute amount above
     the "going price," the firm's quantity demanded will fall to zero. This is a perfectly
     elastic demand situation.
     *TIP*: Recall that a perfectly elastic demand curve is a horizontal demand curve.
4.   d; Since any one perfect competitor's total output is such a small fraction of the industry output, the
     firm can sell all it wants to sell at the going price.
5.c; A firm is in business to maximize total not average profits.
6.a; If a firm operates at a quantity where MR<MC, the firm is not maximizing total
     profits as if it reduced its output, the extra cost would fall more than the extra
     revenue, which adds to profit. If a firm operates at a quantity where MR>MC, the
     firm is also not maximizing total profits as if it increased its output, the extra revenue  would
     increase more than the extra costs which adds to profit. If a firm operates where P = AC, the
     economic profit would be zero.
7.c; If the price per unit that the firm receives is below the cost per unit (average cost) of
     selling the product, a negative economic profit will result.
     *TIP:* In economics, average cost includes the opportunity cost of capital or a normal
     profit amount.
8.a; Average revenue is the same as price. Therefore, (AR – AC) x Q is the same as
     (P – AC) x Q or (Profit per unit) x Q which equals total profit.
9.c; If price is below average variable cost, the firm should shutdown with a loss equal to
     its total fixed costs. If the firm decides to operate it will simply add to its total losses as each extra
     unit of output will lead to an additional loss, since variable costs per unit of output exceed the price
     per unit of output sold.

10.c; At the short run break even price, total revenues equal total cost or price equals
    to average cost. Since costs include the opportunity cost of capital or a normal profit
    amount, the economic profit is zero (not the accounting profit)

11.a; The firm's short-run supply curve is its marginal cost curve above minimum average
    variable cost. In other words, at each possible price, the firm produces where the
    price equals marginal cost or "out to its marginal cost curve."
    *TIP:* Recall that the firm will shutdown if its price goes below its average variable
    cost.

12.a; The firm's supply curve is the portion of its marginal cost curve above min AVC.
    Since the industry consists of all the individual firms, the industry supply curve is
    derived by summing horizontally all the firms' marginal cost curves (above
    min AVC).

13.a; A change in price will cause movement along the industry supply curve, not a shift.

14.b; If economic profits are negative in an industry, then some firms are not even making a normal profit in
    this industry. This means that these firms could make a better profit return in some other industry.

15.a; In an increasing cost industry, the long run industry supply curve is upward sloping.
    *TIP:* Sketch an upward sloping supply curve. If you shift the demand curve leftward
    (decrease in demand) you will see that the equilibrium price will fall.

16.a; An increase in industry output leads to a reduction in long-run marginal costs and
    therefore the supply curve is downward sloping.

17.d; In long-run equilibrium, the price is equal to marginal cost is equal to average cost.
    When price equals average cost, economic profits are zero.

18.b; The marginal cost of producing good A represents the opportunity cost to society of
    producing one more unit of good A. This meaning of marginal cost helps to
    understand why allocative efficiency occurs when price equals marginal cost.

## MATCHING

a and 12;  b and 8;  c and 9;  d and 6;  e and 7;  f and 5;  g and 11;  h and 2;  i and 3;

## WORKING WITH GRAPHS

1.  a.  constant; marginal revenue or price
    b.  marginal cost
    c.  maximize; 16 units of output
    d.  16 units of output; because MC = MR at that output level
    e.  If the firm produces where MR = MC which is at 16 units of output, this will
        maximize total profits.
2.  a.  100 units; this is where MR = MC or where profits are at a maximum (recall D = P = MR)
    b.  Price is the same as the height of the D curve, which is $2.60
    c.  Average cost is $2.00 which is the height of the ATC curve at Q = 100.
    d.  Profit per unit = price – average cost = $2.60 - $2.00 = $0.60 per unit.
    e.  Total profit = (P – ATC) x Q = (profit per unit) x quantity = $0.60 x 100 = $60.00
    f.  The break even point price is $1.90 where the price line would just be tangent to the average cost
        curve.
    g.  The shut down point price is $0.80 where the price line would just be tangent to  the average
        variable cost curve.
    h.  In the long-run, in perfect competition, the price just equals minimum average cost which would be
        at a price of $1.90.
3.  a.  i. 800   ii.   (2.75-1.85)x800 = $720
    b.  i. shutdown  ii.   total fixed costs = $680
    c.  520x100 = 5200
    d.  long run price = min ATC = $1.80

## PROBLEMS

1.

| Firm | A | B | C | D | E | F | G |
|------|------|------|------|------|------|------|------|
| Price | $0.50 | $1.00 | $3.50 | $4.00 | $3.00 | $5.00 | $5.00 |
| Output | 1000 | 300 | 750 | 700 | 600 | 800 | 1000 |
| TR | $500 | $300 | $2625 | $2800 | $1800 | $4000 | $5000 |
| TC | $400 | $525 | $2625 | $2975 | $1380 | $4400 | $5500 |
| TFC | $100 | $165 | $375 | $525 | $180 | $1200 | $2500 |
| TVC | $300 | $360 | $2250 | $2450 | $1200 | $3200 | $3000 |
| ATC | $0.40 | $1.75 | Minimum | $4.25 | $2.30 | $5.50 | $5.50 |
| AVC | $0.30 | $1.20 | $3.00 | $3.50 | $2.00 | Minimum | $3.00 |
| MC | $0.40 | $1.00 | $3.50 | $4.00 | $3.50 | $4.00 | $5.75 |
| | | | | | | | |
| Suggestion | I | SD | C | C | D | I | D |

2. a.  Individual Supply:    5, 3, 1, 0
       Market Supply:       500, 300, 100, 0
   b.  Equilibrium price = $13; equilibrium quantity is 300 boxes.

## BUSINESS SECTION

1. a.  Starting at Q=1000:   AVC:    124, 120, 125, 135, 150, 170
                            MC:     124, 116, 135, 165, 210, 270
                            ATC:    374, 245, 208.33, 197.50, 200, 211.67
   b.  Profit maximizing quantity = 5000 tons per month; total profit = $150,000
       per month.
   c.  Loss minimizing quantity = 3000 tons per month; total loss = $204,990 per month.
   d.  Loss minimizing quantity 0 tons per month (shutdown); total loss = $250,000 per
       month
   e.  No. as the example above shows, in the short run, as prices change, profit
       maximization criteria will dictate varying optimal production levels. As an example in part b.
       above, the profit maximizing level is at q= 5000 tonnes. The minimum cost per unit occurs at q =
       4000 tonnes.
   f.  No. As part c. above illustrates, if Moniques operates at 3000 tons per month the
       loss per month is $204,990 compared to a loss of $250,000 per month if the firm
       shutdown. In this case a savings of $45,010 a month occurs by operating.

## ANSWERS TO EXAMPLE QUESTIONS FOR CRITICAL ANALYSIS

I.  **INTERNATIONAL EXAMPLE 11-1: The Global Market** (p. 243)
    No, it does not. A coal buyer will not want the commodity called "coal", but will want
    a given grade of coal. Within that grade, all producers' coal will be homogeneous.

II. **EXAMPLE 11-1: Whittling Away at Apple's Profit Margins** (p. 258)
    By not licensing its operating system and by keeping its computer prices high, Apple
    lost market share when the cost of PCs based on MS-DOS kept falling. The quantity
    of IBM-compatibles demanded increased because they became relatively cheaper to
    produce. With Windows and Windows 95 (later Windows 98) for the PC market,
    Apple no longer had a competitive advantage in the graphics interface, and there was a great deal of
    software for other applications for the PC that was not available for the
    Macintosh computers.

# CHAPTER 12

# MONOPOLY

## PUTTING THIS CHAPTER INTO PERSPECTIVE

Chapter 12 is the second chapter devoted to the study of industrial organization; the first was Chapter 11, which analyzed the perfect competition model. Chapter 12 introduces the monopoly market structure, and you should be able to compare the perfect competition model to the monopoly model. Here we follow the "pattern" of analysis suggested in Chapter 11 of this student learning guide.

First, we consider the characteristics of the monopoly market structure. In the monopoly model, one firm produces a homogeneous product and entry into the industry is impeded for one reason or another. Contrast this market structure with perfect competition, in which *many* firms produce a homogeneous product and entry into the industry is easy.

Because there is only one firm in the monopoly market structure, the firm's demand curve is the market demand curve; like all market demand curves, the monopolist's demand curve is negatively sloped. This, of course, is to be contrasted with the perfectly elastic demand curve facing the perfect competitor. Stated differently, there are many close substitutes for the output of the perfect competitor (who is a price taker), but there are no close substitutes for the output of the monopolist (who is a price searcher).

The second part of the pattern of analysis leads us to determine the equilibrium output-price combination. Because we assume that the monopolist desires to maximize profit, we (as usual) predict that the firm will produce output up to the point where the marginal benefit (MB) equals the marginal cost (MC) of doing so. In this chapter, we assume that the cost of the monopolist is not unlike that of the perfect competitor; therefore, its rising marginal cost is found by reading the marginal cost curve.

The marginal benefit to the monopolist of producing one more unit of output is a bit more troublesome. As was true for the perfect competitor, for the monopolist the marginal benefit equals the marginal revenue. Unlike the situation under perfect competition, however, under monopoly marginal revenue falls, because the monopolist's demand curve is downward sloping. For the monopolist, the profit maximizing output level is where *marginal revenue equals marginal cost*.

Once the profit maximizing output is determined, the monopolist's price is already determined; the quantity produced can be sold only at one price, read from the monopolist's demand curve. The profit per unit is equal to the price per unit minus the average cost per unit, at the profit maximizing output level. Total profits are computed by multiplying the profit per unit by the profit maximizing output level. Note that all of this assumes that the monopolist sells all of its output at the same price.  If we relax that assumption, as we do near the end of Chapter 12, then we can analyze price discrimination.

Because entry into the monopoly industry is impeded, it is possible (but not necessary) for the monopolist to earn economic profits even in the long run—unlike the perfect competitor, who operates in an industry in which entry is easy.

At the end of the chapter, we consider whether the monopoly market structure is socially desirable. In equilibrium, price exceeds marginal cost for the last unit produced. This suggests a situation of allocative inefficiency where the monopolist underallocates resources to the product. The monopolist may be productively inefficient to the extent that the firm does not produce at minimum average cost. The existence of barriers to entry may provide the monopoly firm and its shareholders with positive economic profits in the long-run. This may result in an inequitable distribution of income with upper income shareholders benefiting at the expense of lower income consumers who are forced to pay the high monopoly prices.

In certain situations, a monopoly market structure may benefit society. If large economies of scale exist, a monopoly firm may be more productively efficient that a competitive firm. Monopoly practices such as patent protection may provide incentives for innovation and technological progress.

## LEARNING OBJECTIVES

After you have studied this chapter, you should be able to

1.  define monopolist, barriers to entry, natural monopoly, license, franchise, patent, tariff, predatory behaviour, price searcher, price discrimination, price differentiation, allocative inefficiency, productive inefficiency, long run economic profit.

2.  list the characteristics of a monopoly and distinguish them from the characteristics of the perfectly competitive firm.

3.  list possible barriers to entry into an industry.

4.  distinguish between the monopolist's demand curve and the perfect competitor's demand curve.

5.  describe the relation between price and marginal revenue in a monopoly situation.

6.  recognize some misconceptions concerning monopoly.

7.  determine the profit maximizing output for the monopolist, given sufficient information; and determine the price that a monopolist would charge, given the profit-maximizing output.

8.  calculate a monopolist's total profits, given sufficient information.

9.  distinguish between price discrimination and price differentiation, and list the conditions necessary for price discrimination.

10.  list and explain the social costs and possible social benefits that may result from a monopoly situation.


**CHAPTER OUTLINE**

1.  A **monopolist** is a single supplier that constitutes an entire industry; the monopolist produces a good for which there are no close substitutes.

2.  Barriers to entry are impediments that prevent new firms from entering an industry; there are numerous potential barriers to entry.
    a.  Some monopolists gain power through the exclusive ownership of a raw material that is essential to produce a good.
    b.  If an enormous capital investment is required to enter an industry, such a sum could be a barrier to entry.
    c.  Licenses and franchises also constitute potential barriers to entry.
    d.  Patents issued to inventors constitute, for a time, effective barriers to entry.
    e.  If economies of scale are great relative to market demand, new entrants into an industry will be discouraged; persistent economies of scale could lead to a **natural monopoly**.
    f.  The existing monopoly firm may engage in predatory behaviour tactics such as pricing the product below average cost to deter the entry of new firms.
    g.  If **tariffs** on imports are sufficiently high, then producers can gain some measure of monopoly power.

3.  The monopolist faces the industry demand curve because the monopolist is the entire industry; examples of monopolies include local electric power companies and the post office.

4.  It is instructive to compare the monopolist with the perfect competitor.
    a.  The perfect competitor's demand curve is perfectly elastic at the "going" price; price is the same as average revenue, and average revenue equals marginal revenue in this model.
    b.  The monopolist's demand curve is negatively sloped; price (or average revenue) falls, and therefore marginal revenue is less than price because the monopolist must lower its price on all the units it sells, and not just on the marginal unit. Since the monopolist must now determine the best price, we call the monopolist a **price searcher**.

5.  Since the monopolist's demand curve is negatively sloped, price elasticity of demand will vary along the curve. In the lower price ranges, demand is inelastic, and an increase in price will increase total revenue. At some point, demand will become unit elastic, in which case an increase in price will leave total revenue unchanged. If the monopolist continues to increase the price, demand becomes inelastic and total revenue will fall. As one can see, it is a misconception to think that the monopolist will always maximize profits by charging the highest price possible.

6.  By assuming that the monopolist wants to maximize total profits and that the short-run cost curves are similar in shape to those of the perfect competitor, we can determine the monopolist's optimal output-price combination.
    a.  The monopolist's total revenue curve is nonlinear (unlike the perfect competitor's); optimal output exists where the positive difference between total costs and total revenues is maximized.
    b.  Stated differently, optimal output exists where MR = MC.
    c.  If MR > MC, the firm can increase total profits by increasing output; if MC > MR, then the firm can increase total profits by reducing output.
    d.  Once the profit-maximizing output is determined, the monopolist's price is already determined; it is read on the demand curve at that quantity.

7.  Graphically, total profits are calculated by subtracting the average cost (at the profit maximizing level) from the price (at the profit maximizing level) and multiplying that value by the quantity produced.

8.  If the monopolist's average cost curve lies entirely above its demand curve, it will experience economic losses.

9.  If the monopolist can prevent the resale of its homogeneous output and if it can separate its customers into different markets with different price elasticities, then it can **price discriminate**—and earn higher profits. The strategy is to charge higher prices in the inelastic markets and lower prices in the elastic markets.

10. The social costs of a monopoly situation often include both allocative and productive inefficiency. If excess profits persist in the long run, an inequitable distribution of income can result.

11. A monopolist may benefit society in terms of achieving economies of scale and product and cost related innovations.


## KEY TERMS AND CONCEPTS

Monopolist                          Price discrimination
Natural monopoly                    Price differentiation
Price searcher                      Tariffs


## COMPLETION QUESTIONS
Fill in the blank or circle the correct term.

1.  A monopolist is a _____ supplier that constitutes the entire industry; its demand curve is _____ sloped.

2.  Before a monopolist can earn long-run monopoly profits, there must be _____ to entry.

3.  Examples of barriers to entry include _____, _____, _____, _____, and _____.

4.  Because the perfect competitor's demand curve is perfectly elastic, its selling price is constant; therefore its average revenue (falls, rises, remains constant) and its marginal revenue (falls, rises, remains constant).

5.  Because the monopolist's demand curve is negatively sloped, its selling price falls with output; therefore its average revenue (falls, rises, remains constant) and its marginal revenue (falls, rises, remains constant).

6.  If a monopolist must charge the same price to everyone, when it produces more, its marginal revenue will be (less than, greater than, equal to) its price.

7.  When marginal revenue equals zero, total revenue is (minimized, maximized); at that point on the demand curve, the price elasticity of demand equals the number _____; at a higher price total revenues would fall, and therefore demand is (elastic, inelastic); at a lower price total revenues would fall, and therefore demand is _____.

8.  One misconception about monopoly is that the monopolist can sell any quantity that it chooses to, at any _____; instead the monopolist can sell any specific quantity at only one price.   Another misconception is that a monopolist must earn economic profits; it will not, however, if the _____ curve is above the monopolist's demand curve.

9.  The monopolist maximizes total profits at that output for which _____ equals _____; given its profit-maximizing output, the monopolist (need not, must) charge a price  consistent with that quantity.

10.  If a monopolist need not charge the same price to everyone, then it can _____, and its profits will rise; a monopolist can charge different prices to different groups if it can prevent the _____ of its product.

11.  A monopolist charges a price that is too _____, and it produces an output that is too _____; therefore monopoly is (less, more) allocatively efficient than perfect competition.

12.  If a monopolist does not produce at minimum average cost, it is (allocatively, productively) inefficient.


**TRUE-FALSE QUESTIONS**
Circle the T if the statement is true, the F if it is false.  Explain to yourself why a statement is false.

T  F    1.   A monopolist is a price taker.

T  F    2.   The more broadly we define an industry, the less likely it is to be a monopoly.

T  F    3.   The monopolist's marginal revenue curve lies below its demand, or average revenue, curve.

T  F    4.   Because there are no close substitutes for a monopolist's output, its demand curve is inelastic throughout

T  F    5.   At that output for which total revenue is maximized, price elasticity of demand equals 1.

T  F    6.   The profit maximizing monopolist will never produce on the inelastic portion of its demand curve.

T  F    7.   Total profits are maximized where total revenue equals total costs.

T  F    8.   If MR > MC, the firm can increase profits if it produces less.

T  F    9.    Total profits equal price minus average total cost.

T  F   10.   A monopolist can select only one profit-maximizing price, given the output it chooses to produce, assuming no price discrimination.

T  F   11.   A monopolist must charge the same price to all buyers.

T  F   12.   If possible, a monopolist will charge a higher price to a price inelastic group than to a price elastic group.

T  F   13.   A monopolist tends to produce too little and to sell at a price that is too high.

T  F   14.   Because of easy entry , a monopolist cannot earn long-run profits.


**MULTIPLE CHOICE QUESTIONS**
Circle the letter that corresponds to the best answer.

1.    Which of the following is *not*  a characteristic of the monopoly market structure?
      a.   one seller
      b.   homogeneous product
      c.   restricted entry
      d.   price taker

2.    Which of the following is a potential barrier to entry?
      a.   government license requirement
      b.   sole ownership of a key resource
      c.   great economies of scale, relative to demand
      d.   All of the above

3.    Which is **NOT** true about monopolies?
      a.   linear total revenue curve
      b.   may earn long-run economic profits
      c.   negatively sloped demand curve
      d.   marginal revenue below price

4.    The firm maximizes total profits at that output level where
      a.   total revenue equals total cost.
      b.   marginal revenue equals marginal cost.
      c.   the elasticity of demand equals 1.
      d.   All of the above

5.    Once a monopolist produces a profit-maximizing output,
    a.  the price is determined for it, given its demand curve.
    b.  it can select any price it wants.
    c.  its competitors select price.
    d.  price cannot be determined.

6.    If MR < MC, then the firm
    a.  is maximizing total profits.
    b.  can increase total profits by producing more.
    c.  can increase total profits by producing less.
    d.  is maximizing total revenues.

7.    Assume that at a given output a monopolist's marginal revenue is $10 per unit and
    its marginal cost is $5.  If the monopolist increases output, then
    a.  price, marginal cost, and total profit will fall.
    b.  price will fall, marginal cost will rise, and total profit will rise.
    c.  price will rise, marginal cost will fall, and total profit will rise.
    d.  price, marginal cost, and total profit will rise.

8.    Monopoly total profits
    a.  equals (average revenue - average cost) times quantity sold.
    b.  equals price times quantity sold.
    c.  exists only in the short run.
    d.  exists because no entry barriers exist.

9.    A monopolist will price discriminate if
    a.  price differentiation exists.
    b.  it can separate markets by different price elasticities of demand and prevent
        resales.
    c.  it chooses to maximize average revenues.
    d.  all buyers have the same price elasticity of demand.

10.   Which of the following is price differentiation?
    a.  Students pay a higher rental price for apartments than do non-students because
        they cause more damage.
    b.  Women pay higher prices for haircuts because it takes longer to cut their hair.
    c.  People in ghetto areas pay higher prices for individual items because costs are
        greater in such areas.
    d.  All of the above.

11.   Which one of the following statements does NOT typically apply to a monopoly.
    a.  The firm can make economic profits in the long-run.
    b.  The firm tends to restrict output and drive up the price.
    c.  The firm tends to be productively inefficient.
    d.  The firm tends to produce too much of the product, from society's view.

**MATCHING**
Choose the numbered item in Column (2) that best matches the term or concept in Column (1).

(1)    (2)

a.  monopolist
b.  natural monopoly
c.  predatory behaviour
d.  price searcher
e.  price discrimination
f.  price differentiation

1.  price taker
2.  firm with a downward sloping demand curve
3.  barrier to entry based on import taxes
4.  single firm in the industry
5.  price differences based on cost differences
6.  price differences based on willingness to pay
7.  barrier to entry due to economies of scale
8.  deterring entry by severe price cutting

**WORKING WITH GRAPHS**

1.  Suppose you are given the demand schedule for a monopolist and the total cost figures below.  Plot the monopolist's demand curve, marginal revenue curve, and marginal cost curve on the graph provided.  Determine the profit maximizing level of output for the monopolist. What is the amount of maximum profit? Plot the marginal revenue and marginal cost against the midpoint of the quantity range. That is, plot the MR of the $1^{st}$ unit of output against the quantity level of 0.5 and the MR of the $2^{nd}$ unit of output against the quantity level of 1.5 etc. Do the same for the marginal cost.

| Output per unit of time | Price | Total Cost |
|---|---|---|
| 0 | $ 32 | $ 12 |
| 1 | 28 | 20 |
| 2 | 24 | 25 |
| 3 | 20 | 31 |
| 4 | 16 | 41 |
| 5 | 12 | 56 |
| 6 | 8 | 79 |
| 7 | 4 | 117 |

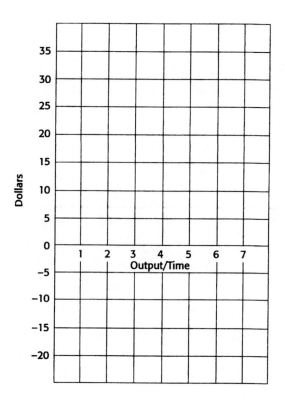

2.  Suppose you are given the graphical summary of a monopolist below.  Answer the following questions using this information.

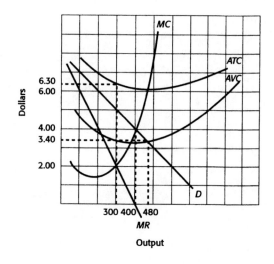

a.  The optimal short-run output level for the monopolist is _____.

b.  At the optimal level of output, marginal cost is _____.

c.  At the optimal level of output, total cost is _____.

d.  At the optimal level of output, price is _____ and total revenue is _____.

e.  The monopolist is earning a (profit, loss) of _____ in the given situation.

f.  Suppose that the above graph represented a competitive industry and the demand curve given was the market demand curve for the entire industry. The competitive level of output would be _____, sold at a price of _____.

g.  Based on your answers above, the monopolist tends to (overproduce, underproduce) in order to drive (down, up) the price.

## PROBLEMS

1.  Indicate whether the following may characterize the perfect competitor (PC), the monopolist (M), or both (B).

_____  a.  perfectly elastic demand curve

_____  b.  increasing marginal cost curve

_____  c.  downward sloping demand curve

_____  d.  linear total revenue curve

_____  e.  total profit maximizer

_____  f.  possibility of earning long-run economic profits

_____  g.  price exceeds marginal revenue at each output level

_____  h.  homogeneous output

_____  i.  price discriminator

_____  j.  barriers to entry

_____  k.  free exit and entry

_____ l.  price searcher

_____ m. price taker

_____ n.  produces where marginal revenue equals marginal cost

_____ o.  price equals marginal cost for the last unit produced.

_____ p.  long-run equilibrium at minimum AC

_____ q.  price equals marginal revenue at each quantity level.

_____ r.  price equals average revenue at each quantity level.


## BUSINESS SECTION
## Accounting: Production, Pricing, and Profit Under Different Monopoly Situations

### Business Application Problem

By obtaining a patent on a new acupuncture treatment that provides long lasting relief for back pain, Dr. Kildare has achieved a monopoly situation. The following table describes the demand and cost behaviour associated with providing this treatment. The quantity in the first column of the table refers to the number of treatments provided per day. The $300 marginal cost showing in the table refers to the extra cost of providing the first treatment of the day. Since the doctor finds each treatment physically demanding, there is a point where diminishing returns sets in and thus marginal cost eventually increases.

| Quantity: # treatments per day | Price per treatment ($'s) | Total Revenue ($'s) | Marginal Revenue ($'s) | Average Total Cost ($'s) | Marginal Cost ($'s) |
|---|---|---|---|---|---|
| 0 | | | | | |
| 1 | $720 | | | $420 | $300 |
| 2 | $660 | | | $350 | $280 |
| 3 | $580 | | | $300 | $200 |
| 4 | $500 | | | $350 | $500 |
| 5 | $420 | | | $420 | $700 |
| 6 | $340 | | | $510 | $960 |
| 7 | $260 | | | $620 | $1,280 |
| 8 | $180 | | | $750 | $1,660 |

a. Complete the total revenue and marginal revenue columns in the table above.

b. Assuming that the monopoly firm (Dr. Kildare) is not regulated and does not price discriminate:
   i. Find the profit maximizing quantity level. Explain.



   ii. Calculate the total dollar profit earned at the profit maximizing level.



c. Assuming that the monopoly firm is regulated so as to receive a "fair profit":
   i. Find the "fair profit" price (imposed by the government)? Explain.



   ii. What would be the amount of economic profit earned under the "fair profit" form of regulation? Briefly explain.



d. Assuming that the monopoly firm practices perfect price discrimination:

   i. Determine the profit maximizing quantity level.



   ii. Calculate the total daily dollar profit at the profit maximizing level.



## ANSWERS TO CHAPTER 12

### COMPLETION QUESTIONS

1. single; negatively
2. barriers
3. ownership of resources without close substitutes; large capital requirements to enter industry; legally required licenses or franchises; patents, economies of scale; safety and quality regulation; high tariffs
4. remains constant; remains constant
5. falls; falls
6. less than
7. maximized; 1; elastic; inelastic
8. price; average total cost
9. MR; MC; must
10. price discriminate; resale
11. high; low; less
12. productively inefficient

**TRUE-FALSE QUESTIONS**

1.  F  A monopolist is a price searcher.
2.  T
3.  T
4.  F  A monopolist's demand curve has various ranges of elasticity as it is negatively sloped.
5.  T
6.  T
7.  F  Profit maximization occurs where MR = MC; if TR = TC, then economic profits are zero.
8.  F  If MR > MC, profits will rise if the firm produces more. An additional unit will add more to revenue than to cost.
9.  F  Profit per unit equals price minus average total cost.
10.  T
11.  F  A monopolist can price discriminate under certain conditions.
12.  T
13.  T
14.  F  Because of barriers to entry a monopolist can earn long-run economic profits.

**MULTIPLE CHOICE QUESTIONS**

1.d; The monopolist's demand curve is the industry demand curve which is negatively sloped. Therefore the monopolist will affect the price when it varies the level of output. This means that the monopolist is a price searcher, not a price taker.

2.d; If a firm has secured an exclusive government license to produce a product, or is the sole ownership of a resource crucial to producing a product, or experiences economies of scale from expanding its size, this can prevent other firms from competing with the existing firm.

3.a; The linear total revenue curve applies to a perfectly competitive firm which faces a fixed price as the firm's quantity sold increases. The monopolist's total revenue curve is curved because it faces a negatively sloped demand curve, where the price falls as the quantity sold increases.

4.b; The firm maximizes total profits at the output level where the positive difference between total revenue and total cost is the greatest. This profit maximizing level is also where marginal revenue equals marginal cost.

5.a; Since the typical monopolist faces a negatively sloped demand curve, once the quantity level is determined, a unique price is determined by the demand curve.

6.c; If MR is less than MC, then if the firm reduces its output by one unit, the cost will be reduced by more than the loss in revenue, which will add to the firm's profit..

7.b; If the monopolist increases output by one unit, the extra revenue will be $10 while the extra cost will only be $5, so total profit will increase by $5. As the quantity increases, the price will decrease, as the demand curve is negatively sloped. As the quantity increases, the marginal cost will increase, as the marginal cost curve is positively sloped.

8.a; (Average revenue - average cost) times quantity sold is the same as (profit per unit) times quantity sold which equals total profits.

9.b; If a monopolist can separate markets based on elasticity, it can increase total revenue by increasing the price in the inelastic markets and decreasing the price in the elastic markets. For this to be successful, the monopolist must be able to prevent customers from reselling from the low price to the high priced markets.

10.d; All of the above are examples of price differentiation, as in each case, the differences in prices are based on cost differences.

11.d. Since the monopolist produces to the point where the price exceed marginal cost, the firm underproduces (not overproduces) the product.

**MATCHING**

a and 4;  b and 7;  c and 8;  d and 2;  e and 6;  f and 5

**WORKING WITH GRAPHS**

1.

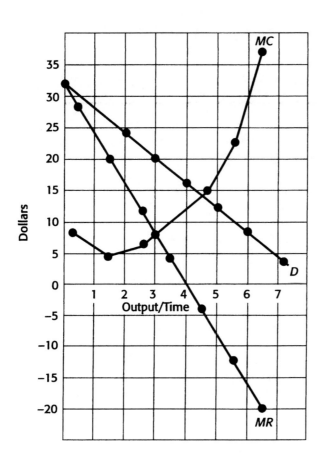

The profit-maximizing level of output is 3 units sold at a price of $20 each. This can be seen graphically. Total profits equal TR – TC = $60 – $31 =$29 at that output.

2.    a. 300;  b. $2;  c. $1890;  d. $5, $1500;  e. loss, $390;   f. 400, $4;  g. under, up.

**PROBLEMS**

1.    a. PC      b. B      c. M        d. PC      e. B       f. M       g. M       h. B       i. M
      j. M       k. PC     l. M       m. PC      n. B       o. PC      p. PC      q. PC      r. B

**BUSINESS SECTION**

| 1. | a.TR: | 0 | 720 | 1320 | 1740 | | 2000 | 2100 | 2040 | 1820 | 1440 |
|----|-------|---|-----|------|------|--|------|------|------|------|------|
| | MR: | | 720 | 600 | 420 | | 260 | 100 | (60) | (220) | (380) |

     b.        i. Q = 3; ii. Total maximum profit = $840

     c.        i.Q = 5; ii.   Economic profit = 0, so the doctor just earns a normal profit.

     d.        i.Q = 4; ii.   Total maximum profit = $1060

**ANSWERS TO EXAMPLE QUESTIONS FOR CRITICAL ANALYSIS**

**I.**    **EXAMPLE 12-1: "Intel Inside"** (p. 270)

It is likely that Intel would spend less. The reason is that the very large investment in R&D creates a barrier to entry in two ways. First, the amount of money that a potential competitor must spend to compete with Intel would be great enough that few could afford it, and the payback period would be very long. Second the high rate of spending on R&D results in new patents which form a legal barrier. The resulting high rate of development of new chips makes use of Intel's expired patents worthless for potential customers.

**II**    **POLICY EXAMPLE 12-1: Should Canada Post Remain a Monopoly—Or Does It Matter?** (p. 272)

One way would be to get a legal ban put on the use of e-mail and the sending of messages by fax machines. This is not likely. Canada Post could compete by offering these services to those who do not own a fax machine or a personal computer. As well, since the emerging e-commerce industries involve the delivering of goods to one's home by courier, Canada Post could increase its presence in the Canadian courier industry.

**III**    **INTERNATIONAL POLICY EXAMPLE 12-1: Patents as Intellectual Property** (p. 273)

A trademark is associated with a given company's product. A competitor can make a similar product and sell it under a different name. The competitor is simply not allowed to use the same name or, in some cases, a name which would mislead buyers into thinking that they had bought the first company's trademarked product. The actual type of good is not protected by the trademark.

**IV**    **INTERNATIONAL EXAMPLE 12-1: Fuji Film Price Discrimination** (p. 284)

Price discrimination would have benefited Canadian consumers who would have been paying a lower price for film. Fuji would have been making higher profits so its shareholders and workers would also have benefited.

# CHAPTER 13

# MONOPOLISTIC COMPETITION AND OLIGOPOLY

## PUTTING THIS CHAPTER INTO PERSPECTIVE

Chapter 13 is the third chapter that deals with market structures; Chapter 11 analyzed the perfect competition model and Chapter 12 analyzed the monopoly model.  Chapter 13 examines two more market structures—monopolistic competition and oligopoly. Because this is a long chapter we suggest that you break it into several parts; let the first part cover the monopolistic competition model and the second part cover the oligopoly model (and the issues and applications).

In the monopolistic competition model the assumptions are (1) a significant number of sellers in a highly competitive (but not perfectly competitive) market, (2) product differentiation, and (3) easy entry into the industry.

Because of assumptions 1 through 3, the monopolistic competitor has some control over its selling price.  This means that its demand curve is negatively sloped, which in turn means that its marginal revenue curve must be below its demand curve and that in equilibrium, price must exceed marginal cost.  In short, assumptions 1 through 3 imply that monopolistic competition is allocatively inefficient because such assumptions necessitate that in equilibrium the price exceeds marginal cost, for the last unit produced.

Because of easy entry we know that in the long run the typical monopolistic competitor will earn zero economic profits.  This means that the demand (average revenue) curve must be tangent to the monopolistic competitor's average cost curve. Furthermore, because the demand curve is negatively sloped, the demand curve must be tangent to the AC curve somewhere to the left of the AC's minimum point resulting in excess capacity. This gives us another reason to believe that the monopolistic competition model leads to productive inefficiency, as the equilibrium output will not be produced at minimum average cost.

In an oligopoly market structure there a few large firms dominating the total sales in the industry. Put differently, there is a high concentration ratio in oligopoly. The high level of concentration can be caused by barriers to entry such as large economies of scale, ownership of key raw materials, patents and predatory behaviour.

Because there is interdependence among oligopolistic competitors, it is difficult to predict the price/output outcome resulting from their behavior. As a consequence economists have developed an approach, called game theory, that gives some insights into the oligopoly model.  Your text introduces you to this interesting topic.

If we assume that an oligopolist's rivals will find it in their own interest to match a price decrease but to ignore a price increase, then a kinked demand curve for each oligopolist is the result.  The demand curve is negatively sloped, the marginal revenue curve is below it—and discontinuous. This situation implies price rigidity, where the marginal costs can change significantly without the oligopoly firm changing its price.

In other oligopoly situations the firms may adopt cooperative pricing strategies by forming cartels or practicing price leadership.

In order to avoid price competition many oligopoly industries engage in non-price forms of competition such as product differentiation and advertising. In some cases the existing oligopoly firms may engage in behaviour which deters the entry of new competitors.

To the extent that an oligopoly industry acts somewhat like a monopoly situation, allocative inefficiency, productive inefficiency and excess profits may result. In other cases, the oligopoly firms may promote both productive efficiency and innovation.


## LEARNING OBJECTIVES

After you have studied this chapter you should be able to

1.  define monopolistic competition, product differentiation, oligopoly, strategic dependence, concentration ratio, horizontal and vertical mergers, best response function, game theory, cooperative and non-cooperative games, zero sum, positive sum, and negative sum games, strategy, dominant strategy, prisoner's dilemma, payoff matrix, opportunistic behavior, tit-for-tat strategic behavior, price war, price leadership, limit-pricing model, and entry-deterrence strategy.

2.  list the characteristics of the monopolistic competition market structure.

3.  distinguish between the monopolistic competitor's demand curve and the perfect competitor's demand curve

4.  compare the long run equilibrium for monopolistic competition with perfect competition.

5.  list the characteristics of the oligopoly  market structure

6.  list three reasons for the existence of oligopolies.

7.  calculate concentration ratios and recognize their limitations.

8.  given a payoff table, identify a dominant strategy, opportunistic behaviour, and a tit for tat strategy.

9.  distinguish among zero sum, positive sum, and negative sum games.

10. explain the assumptions leading to a kinked demand curve and enumerate criticisms of the kinked demand curve model.

11. recognize three ways that existing oligopolists deter entry into the industry.

12. list three reasons why oligopoly firms engage in product differentiation

13. identify the social benefits and costs of advertising.

14. evaluate oligopoly from a social viewpoint.


**CHAPTER OUTLINE**

1.  The theory of *monopolistic competition* was developed simultaneously by Edward Chamberlin and Joan Robinson in 1933; we analyze Chamberlin's model.
    a.  There are three characteristics of **monopolistic competition**:  a significant number of sellers in a highly competitive market, **product differentiation**,  and easy entry.
    b.  Although there are many sellers, there are not as many as there are in the perfect competition model; each monopolistic competitor has a little control over its price, but collusion is difficult and each firm acts independently of the others.
    c.  Perhaps the most important feature of this model is product differentiation.
        i.   Differentiation refers to differences in physical or image characteristics.
        ii.  Each separate differentiated product has close substitutes.
    d.  Because the monopolistic competitor has at least some monopoly power, it may be profitable for it to advertise.
    e.  In the long run, entry into such a market structure is easy.

2.  It is possible to predict the optimal price-output combination of the monopolistic competitor.
    a.  The monopolistic competitor's demand curve is downward sloping; therefore its marginal revenue curve lies below its demand curve.
    b.  Short-run equilibrium exists where MR = MC; economic profits or losses are possible in the short run.
    c.  In the long run, because of free entry, the monopolistic competitor must earn exactly zero economic profits.

3.  For the monopolistic competitor, allocative inefficiency exists because price exceeds marginal cost. In the long run the typical firm's rate of output lies to the left of the minimum point on the ATC curve resulting in excess capacity.

4.  **Oligopoly** is a market situation in which there are a very few sellers, each of which expects a reaction from its rivals to changes in its price and quantity; there are three major characteristics of oligopolies; few large firms, **interdependence**, barriers to entry.

5.  There are at least three reasons for the emergence of oligopolistic industries: economies of scale, barriers to entry, and **horizontal or vertical merger**.
    a.  Four- or eight-firm **concentration ratios** are often calculated to determine the extent to which an industry is "monopolized."
    b.  Over time some industries experience drastic changes (up or down) in their concentration ratios; others show little change.

6.  Before an oligopoly situation can be analyzed with respect to price and output, specific assumptions about rival reactions must be made; a different model arises with each assumption regarding the oligopolist's **best response function**.

7.  Because there is interdependence among oligopolistic competitors economists have developed an approach, called **game theory**, to describe how such firms interact rationally.
    a.  If firms collude and form a **cartel**, the game is referred to as **cooperative game**.
    b.  If cartels are too expensive to form or enforce, then a **noncooperative game** is played among oligopolists.
    c.  Games are classified as being **zero sum**, **positive sum**, or **negative sum**.

8.  Oligopolistic decision makers derive a strategy, or rule used to make a choice; a **dominant strategy** is one that always yields the highest benefit, regardless of what the other oligopolists do.

9.  The most famous example of game theory is called the **prisoner's dilemma** in which it can be shown that (under specified conditions) in situations in which there is more than one party to a crime, the dominant strategy for each prisoner is to confess.

10. A **payoff matrix** indicates the consequences of the strategies chosen by the players in the game.

11. Another oligopoly model results from assuming that rivals will match a price reduction, but ignore a price increase.
    a.  In such a situation, for the oligopolist the price elasticity of demand above the current price will be very high, and the price elasticity of demand below the current price will be very low; the result is a kinked demand curve and a discontinuous marginal revenue curve.
    b.  One implication of the kinked demand curve model is price rigidity; any change in marginal costs in the discontinuous gap of the marginal revenue curve will leave price unaltered.
    c.  One criticism of this analysis is that it offers no explanation of how the current price was established; empirical evidence indicates that oligopolies tend to change price more frequently than do monopolies.

12. On occasion smaller rivals may set price too far below the price leader and a **price war** results.

13. Sometimes even if no formal cartel arises among oligopolists, tacit collusion in the form of **price leadership** can occur; the largest firm announces its price and smaller competitors then follow this lead.

14. Strategic decision making could lead to pricing or investing policies that deter entry by potential competitors; **entry-deterrence strategies** include threats of a price war, investment in excess capacity by existing firms, inducing governments to restrict entry, and raising switching costs to customers.

15. The **limit-pricing model** suggests that existing oligopolists collude to set the highest price they can without encouraging entry into the industry.

16. In order to avoid direct price competition oligopoly firms often engage in non-price forms of competition such as product differentiation and innovation.

17. To the extent that an oligopoly industry acts somewhat like a monopoly situation, allocative inefficiency, productive inefficiency and excess profits may result. In other cases, the oligopoly firms may promote both productive efficiency and innovation.

## KEY TERMS AND CONCEPTS

Monopolistic competition
Product differentiation
Strategic dependence
Oligopoly
Concentration ratio
Horizontal merger
Vertical merger
Game theory
Best response function

Prisoner's dilemma
Opportunistic behavior
Tit-for-tat
Zero sum game
Positive sum game
Negative sum game
Price war
Cooperative game
Entry-deterrence strategy

Non-cooperative game
Payoff matrix
Dominant strategies
Conglomerate merger
Strategy
Cartel
Limit pricing model
Price leadership

## COMPLETION QUESTIONS
Fill in the blank or circle the correct term.

1.  The three characteristics of monopolistic competition are _____,
    _____, and _____.

2.  Under monopolistic competition, collusion is (easy, difficult); each firm (must,
    need not) take into account the reactions of rivals, and each firm has (a little, much,
    no) control over its selling price.

3.  The demand curve for the monopolistic competitor is _____ sloped;
    therefore its marginal revenue curve is (below, above) its demand, or AR curve;
    therefore in equilibrium price must be (less than, greater than, equal to) marginal
    cost; therefore allocative (inefficiency, efficiency) exists in the monopolistic
    competition market structure.

4.  In the long run, ease of entry causes the monopolistic competitor to earn
    _____ economic profits; therefore its negatively sloped demand curve
    must be (above, below, tangent to) its ATC curve.  As a consequence, in long-run
    equilibrium, output must be produced at a cost (below, above, at) minimum
    average total cost.

5.  Three key characteristics of oligopoly are _____, _____;
    and _____; oligopolies may emerge because of _____,
    _____ and _____.

6.  Concentration ratios (fall, rise) as the definition of "industry" is narrowed, and they
    _____ as the definition is broadened.

7.   Economists have developed an approach to analyze the interdependence among oligopolists called _____ theory; if oligopolists collude and form a cartel this is a _____ game; if cartels are too expensive to form or enforce then oligopolists will play a _____ game.

8.   Games are referred to as _____ sum if one player's benefit is exactly equal to the expense of the other, _____ sum if the sum of the players' benefit is positive, and _____ sum if the sum of the players' benefit is negative.

9.   The most famous example of game theory is _____ in which the dominant strategy of prisoners is to (confess, not confess).

10.  Assume that firm B is an oligopolist.  If its rivals match its price reductions but ignore its price increases, firm B will have a _____ demand curve; its marginal revenue curve will be _____; firm B probably (will, will not) change its price very often.  Because its demand curve is negatively sloped, in equilibrium firm B's (P = MC, P > MC, P < MC) and from society's point of view it will produce (too little, too much, just enough) and its price will be (too low, too high, just right).

11.  Even if no formal cartel arises in an oligopolistic industry, tacit collusion in the form of _____ leadership may result; occasionally such a system breaks down and a price _____ results.

12.  Existing oligopolists can use the following strategies to deter entry: _____, _____, and _____; the _____ model suggests that existing firms set the highest price they can without encouraging entry.

13.  Three reasons why oligopoly firms engage in advertising are _____, _____, _____.

14.  Advertising can benefit consumers to the extent that it provides _____ to buyers, that it (promotes, discourages) economies of scale, and to the extent that it (promotes, discourages) new improved products.


**TRUE-FALSE QUESTIONS**
Circle the **T** if the statement is true, the **F** if it is false.  Explain to yourself why a statement is false.

T   F    1.   The monopolistic competitor must take into account the reactions of its competitors.

T  F    2.   The most important feature of the monopolistic competitive market is product differentiation.

T  F    3.   Product differentiation exists in the wheat industry.

T  F    4.   The monopolistic competitor has a negatively sloped demand curve.

T  F    5.   The monopolistic competition model leads to allocative efficiency because in the long run P = MC.

T  F    6.   The main characteristic of the oligopoly market structure is that an oligopolist must consider the reaction of its rivals.

T  F    7.   Perhaps the strongest reason for the existence of oligopolies is economies of scale relative to market demand.

T  F    8.   Concentration ratios provide an accurate measure of the degree of monopoly power in an industry.

T  F    9.   A dominant strategy is one that is always preferred by a player, regardless of what other players do.

T  F    10.  Price wars result because all players are in a positive sum game.

T  F    11.  If an oligopolist's rivals match all of its price changes, its demand curve will be kinked.

T  F    12.  Cartels are usually expensive to set up and enforce.

T  F    13.  Collusion may be found in both formal and tacit arrangements.

T  F    14.  The limit-pricing model suggests that oligopolists set price at the highest price they can.

T  F    15.  Advertising can act as a barrier to entry.

## MULTIPLE CHOICE QUESTIONS
Circle the letter that corresponds to the best answer.

1.   Which is *not* a characteristic of monopolistic competition?
   a.  significant number of sellers
   b.  differentiated products
   c.  advertising
   d.  must take into account rival's reaction to price changes

2.  Under monopolistic competition, collusion is
    a.  easy.
    b.  difficult.
    c.  impossible.
    d.  nonexistent.

3.  Which firm has the **LEAST** control over price?
    a.  perfect competitor
    b.  monopolistic competitor
    c.  oligopolist
    d.  monopolist

4.  Product differentiation is the *central* feature of the _____ model.
    a.  monopoly
    b.  oligopoly
    c.  monopolistic competition
    d.  perfect competition

5.  Only when a firm's demand curve is negatively sloped will
    a.  its MR curve lie below its demand curve.
    b.  in equilibrium, MR = MC.
    c.  economic profits equal zero in the long run.
    d.  All of the above

6.  For the monopolistic competitor, in the long run
    a.  the demand curve must be tangent to the ATC curve.
    b.  output is too high, from society's point of view.
    c.  output is produced to the right of the minimum ATC point.
    d.  economic profits can be positive.

7.  Which firms must have zero economic profits in the long run?
    a.  monopolist, perfect competitor
    b.  oligopolist, monopolistic competitor
    c.  perfect competitor, monopolistic competitor
    d.  perfect competitor, oligopolist

8.  The *best* explanation for the existence of oligopolies is
    a.  no economies of scale exist.
    b.  large economies of scale relative to market demand.
    c.  advertising.
    d.  one firm has exclusive ownership of an important raw material.

9.    In an oligopolistic industry, entry will result if
      a.  normal profits exist.
      b.  the industry LAC curve is below the market demand curve.
      c.  the industry LAC curve is above the market demand curve.
      d.  advertising is permitted.

10.   Which market structure is most **UNLIKE** the others, regarding its demand curve?
      a.  perfect competition
      b.  oligopoly
      c.  monopolistic competition
      d.  monopoly

11.   Which firm's demand curve is most inelastic?
      a.  oligopolist
      b.  perfect competition
      c.  monopolist
      d.  monopolistic competition

12.   *Analogy*:  Product differentiation is to monopolistic competition as _____ is to oligopoly.
      a.  competition
      b.  interdependence
      c.  advertising
      d.  economies of scale

13.   In which of the following will the players' sum of benefits be positive?
      a.  negative sum game
      b.  zero sum game
      c.  positive sum game
      d.  prisoner's dilemma

14.   If oligopoly B's rivals ignore its price increases but match its price decreases, then B's demand curve will be
      a.  discontinuous.
      b.  kinked at the going price.
      c.  below its marginal revenue curve.
      d.  proportionate to the industry demand curve.

15.   The kinked demand curve theory
      a.  is supported by empirical evidence.
      b.  requires that an oligopolist's rivals exactly match its price changes.
      c.  predicts price rigidity.
      d.  requires collusion.

16.  Which of the following is a strategy to deter entry by potential competitors?
a.  raising switching costs to customers
b.  investment in excess capacity by existing firms
c.  limit-pricing strategy
d.  All of the above

17.  Advertising
a.  attempts to increase demand for one's product.
b.  helps to differentiate one's product.
c.  can lead to more information for buyers.
d.  All of the above

18.  In long-run equilibrium for the oligopolist,
a.  MR = MC.
b.  P = MR.
c.  economic profits can be positive.
d.  All of the above

**MATCHING**
Choose the numbered item in Column (2) that best matches the term or concept in Column (1).

(1)

a.  product differentiation
b.  positive sum game
c.  price rigidity
d.  low concentration ratio
e.  price taker
f.  interdependence
g.  zero sum game

(2)

1.  horizontal demand curve
2.  all players benefit
3.  one competitor
4.  ones gain is another's loss
5.  kinked demand curve
6.  many competitors in an industry
7.  all players lose
8.  negative sloped demand curve
9.  game theory

**WORKING WITH GRAPHS**

1.    Use the graph of a monopolistic competitor below to answer each of the following
      questions.

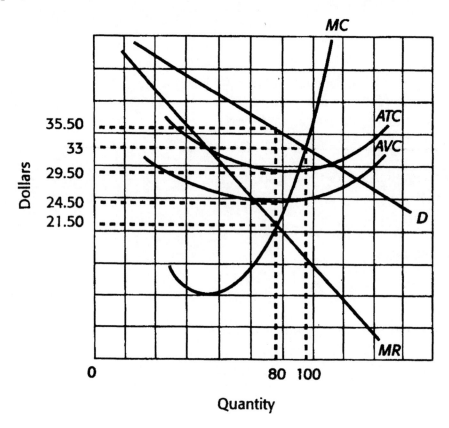

a.   At what level of output will this firm operate? _____

b.   What is marginal revenue at this level of output? _____

c.   What price will this firm charge for its product? _____

d.   What  is total revenue at this level of output? _____

e.   What is the firm's average total cost in equilibrium? _____

f.   What  is the firm's total cost at this level of output? _____

g.   Is the firm making profits or incurring losses? _____

h.   What are the profits or losses at this level of output? _____

2.    Use the graph of the oligopolist below to answer each of the questions that follow.

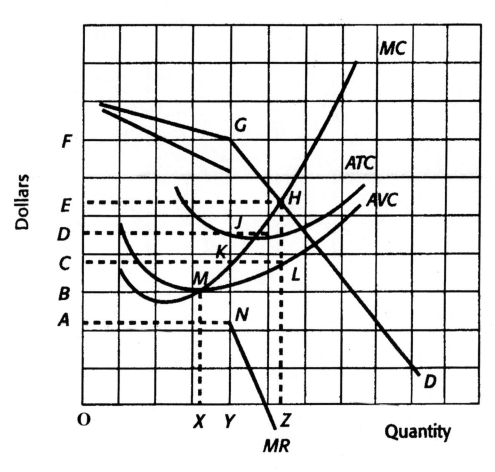

a.   At what level of output will this firm operate? _____

b.   What is the marginal cost at this level of output? _____

c.   What price will the firm charge for its product? _____

d.   The area of what rectangle equals total revenue? _____

e.   What is the firm's average cost? _____

f.    The area of what rectangle is equal to the firm's total cost? _____

g.   The area of what rectangle is equal to the firm's profit? _____

h.   Suppose the firm is operating at an output level of Y units.  How low would
      marginal costs at Y units of output have to drop before the firm would lower its
      price? _____

3    Use the graphs below to answer the questions that follow.

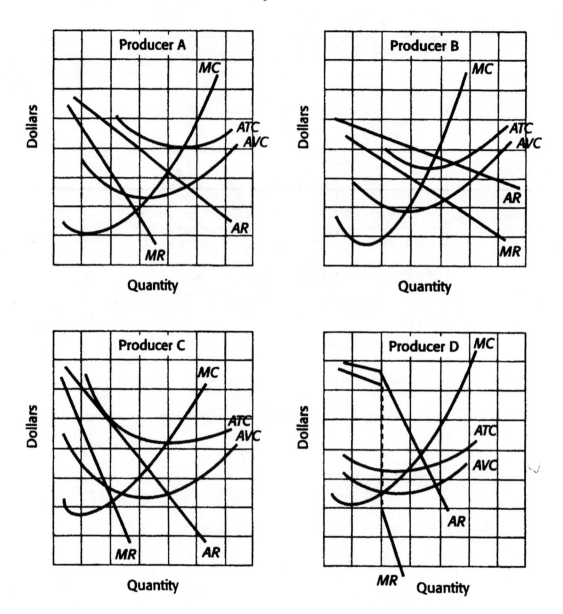

a.  Which of the producers is a monopolistic competitor making positive economic profits? _____
b.  Which of the producers appears to be in an industry that may have reached a long-run equilibrium? _____
c.  Which of the producers is most likely to leave the industry in which it is currently operating? _____
d.  If costs increase by a small amount, which producer is most likely to maintain its present price-quantity combination? _____
e.  Which of the producers is in an industry that is most likely to attract additional firms? _____

f.  Which of the producers is most probably in the industry with the fewest competitors? _____
g.  If all the firms in Producer C's industry are currently in a similar situation, what will most probably happen if there is a decrease in demand for the products of that industry? _____
h.  Which producer(s) is/are incurring short-run losses? _____
i.  Which producer is in the industry that is most probably characterized by some type of barrier to entry? _____

**PROBLEMS**

1.  Consider the table below, then answer the questions that follow.  All information is for domestic firms.

| Domestic Firms in Industry A | Annual Sales |
|---|---|
| 1 | $2,000,000 |
| 2 | 1,500,000 |
| 3 | 1,400,000 |
| 4 | 1,100,000 |
| 5 | 1,000,000 |
| 6 | 700,000 |
| 7 | 200,000 |
| 8 | 100,000 |
| 9-20 (remaining firms) | 1,000,000 |

a.  What is the 4-firm concentration ratio?

b.  What is the 8-firm concentration ratio?

c.  What would happen to the four firm concentration ratio in industry A if Firm 4 and Firm 5 merged?

d.  What would happen to the concentration ratios if the sales of imported goods in Industries A and B that are sold in domestic markets were included?

2.    Let PC = perfect competition, M = monopoly, MC = monopolistic competition, and O = oligopoly.  Indicate by writing down the appropriate initials which of the following may be consistent with one, several, or all of those markets.

_____    a.  profit maximizer
_____    b.  advertising
_____    c.  long-run economic profits
_____    d.  allocative inefficiency
_____    e.  P > MC in equilibrium
_____    f.  product differentiation
_____    g.  large economies of scale relative to market demand
_____    h.  long-run equilibrium at minimum ATC
_____    i.  short-run economic profits
_____    j.  easy entry
_____    k.  few firms
_____    l.  interdependence of firms
_____    m.  ability to set price

**BUSINESS SECTION**
**Marketing: The Marketing Mix:  The " 4P's"**

In order to enhance revenue and profit, firms operating under monopolistic competition and oligopoly may engage in product differentiation as well as price competition. In marketing terms, these firms attempt to create an effective *marketing mix* based on the needs and wants of the target market(s).

The *marketing mix* refers to the development of appropriate strategies for each of the "4P's" – *product, place, promotion* and *price. Product* focuses on attributes such as design features, quality, types of services offered, guarantees, warranties, packaging, and style.  *Place* refers to the selection and management of marketing channels and the physical distribution of products. In short, *place* is concerned with getting the product or service to the customer conveniently. *Promotion* refers the methods which the firm uses in order to enhance the target market's awareness and knowledge of the product or service being offered. These methods can include advertising, sales promotion, personal selling, and public relations. *Price* not only refers to the regular price of the product or service, but as well, includes discounts, allowances, credit terms, and methods of payment allowed.

**Business Application Problem**

Steve Boyd has just started a business called InfoMutual which will provide monthly Canadian mutual fund information to sophisticated investors as well as to other firms which sell mutual funds – brokers, banks and other financial advisors.

Which one of the "4P's" best relates to each of the following:

a.  After considering other alternatives such as  mail and fax, Steve decides to  distribute his mutual fund information through an Internet (web) site.

b.  In addition to providing the latest information relating to each Canadian mutual fund's performance, Steve plans to conduct sophisticated statistical analysis measuring the risk related to each type of fund. The  analysis will also relate the each mutual fund's performance with other mutual funds as well as with economy wide factors.

c.  In order to make his service known to prospective customers, Steve decides to register InfoMutual with major Internet  search engines such as Yahoo, Lycos, and Alta Vista.

d.  Steve rejects the idea of charging a monthly fee. Instead customers can access his monthly information by paying a six-month or a one-year subscription fee.

e.  Every quarter, Steve plans to provide detailed research reports to paid subscribers. These reports will profile a specific family of funds.

f.  Steve plans to offer a cheaper educational subscription rate for those  business schools in colleges and universities that purchase a "site license" for his services.

g.  InfoMutual will regularly participate in popular investor, broker chat room discussions on the Internet in order to increase consumer awareness of the new company.

h.  In order to make it convenient to pay for InfoMutual's subscription fee, each new customer will be provided with a free one-month  temporary password. This free month of full service, should provide ample time for the customer to arrange for the secure payment of the subscription fee.

i.  Steve plans to have animated ads  appear on other popular online news and sports Internet sites.

# ANSWERS TO CHAPTER 13

## COMPLETION QUESTIONS

1.  significant number of sellers; differentiated product; easy entry.
2.  difficult; need not; a little
3.  negatively; below; greater than; inefficiency
4.  zero; tangent to; above
5.  small number of firms; interdependence; economies of scale; product differentiation and advertising; merger
6.  rise; fall
7.  game; cooperative; noncooperative
8.  zero; positive; negative
9.  the prisoner's dilemma; confess
10. kinked; below its demand curve and discontinuous; will not; P > MC; too little; too high
11. price; war
12. threats of price wars; investment in excess capacity; get government to restrict entry; limit-pricing.
13. increase entry barriers; increase industry demand; more difficult for competitors to copy effective ad strategy.
14. valuable information, promotes, promotes.

## TRUE-FALSE

1.  F  There are so many rivals, they can be ignored.
2.  T
3.  F  Wheat is largely homogeneous.
4.  T
5.  F  Allocative inefficiency exists because the monopolistic competitor's demand curve is negatively sloped; therefore, P > MC in equilibrium.
6.  T
7.  T
8.  F  They are very inaccurate, if only because inter-industry competition exists; foreign competition exists too.
9.  T
10. F  They result when price leadership strategies break down and result in a negative sum game.
11. F  Its demand curve will be proportionate to the industry demand curve.
12. T
13. T
14. F  They set price at the highest level that *will still discourage entry*.
15. T

## MULTIPLE CHOICE QUESTIONS

1.d; Since there are a significant number of sellers in monopolistic competition, it would be too difficult to take into account rival's reaction to price changes.
2.b; Collusion is difficult because of the large number of sellers.
3.a; The perfect competitor sells a product which is identical to its many competitors. This makes it a price taker.
4.c; Product differentiation is the *central* feature of monopolistic competition. This feature means that the monopolistic competitor has some control over price.
5.a; When a firm's demand curve is negatively sloped, the firm must lower the price on all units to sell an extra unit. This makes the marginal revenue of the extra unit fall below the price.

6.a; Due to easy entry in monopolistic competition, the demand curve is tangent to the ATC curve in the long-run. This implies a situation of excess capacity and normal profits in the long run.

7.c; Ease of entry allows firms to enter if there are profits and leave if there are losses.

8.b; When there are large economies of scale relative to market demand, only a few large competitors (oligopoly) can compete in the market..

9.b; Price will be greater that ATC therefore positive economic profits will attract new entrants.

10.a; The demand curve is perfectly elastic as the firm has no control over price in perfect competition.

11.c; A monopoly faces the least number of close substitutes and therefore faces the most inelastic demand curve.

12.b; Because there a just a few large firms competing in an oligopoly industry, there is strong interdependence. If one firm lowers its price, its competitor will be very much affected. Interdependence is unique to oligopoly.

13.c; A positive sum game is one where all the players, as a whole, end up being better off.

14.b; If oligopoly B's rivals ignore its price increases but match its price decreases, then this results in the demand curve being kinked at the going price. In this case, if the price is raised, the demand curve will become very elastic. If the price is lowered the demand curve switches to being relatively inelastic.

15.c; Rivals will match a price decrease but ignore a price increase, making it unattractive to change the price from the status quo (price rigidity).

16.d; All will prevent entry of new firms.

17.d; Advertising can help to differentiate a product (more inelastic), as well as increase (shift) the demand in favour of the firm's product.

18.c; Economic profits can be positive in oligopoly due to barriers to entry.

## MATCHING

a and 8;   b and 2;   c and 5;   d and 6;   e and 1;   f and 9;   g and 4

## WORKING WITH GRAPHS

1.   a. 80;   b. 21.50;   c. 35.50;   d. 2840;   e. 29.50;   f. 2360;   g. profits;   h. 480
2.   a. 0Y;   b. 0C;   c. 0F;   d. 0FGY;   e. 0D;   f. 0DJY;   g. DFGJ;   h. below 0A
3.   a. B;   b. C;   c. A;   d. D;   e. B;   f. D;   g. some firms will exit the industry;
     h. A;   i. D;

## PROBLEMS

1.   a. 67% (6/9)   b. 89% (8/9)   c. It would increase.   d. They would fall.
2.   a. PC, M, MC, O;   b. M, MC, O;   c. M, O;   d. M, MC, O;   e. M, MC, O;
     f. MC, O;   g. M, O;   h. PC;   i. PC, M, MC, O;   j. PC, MC;   k. O;   l. O;
     m. M, MC, O

## BUSINESS SECTION

a.  place        b.  product      c.  promotion        d.  price        e.  product
f.  price        g.  promotion    h.  price            i.  promotion

## ANSWERS TO EXAMPLE QUESTIONS FOR CRITICAL ANALYSIS

I.    **EXAMPLE 13-1: Product Differentiation in the Canadian Apparel Industry** (p. 297)
The Canadian apparel industry would be classed under monopolistic competition, based on reading this example. A key feature of monopolistic competition is product differentiation. As the example explains, Eddie Bauer offers many different colours and fitness styles for its jean product. Eddie Bauer also offers product differentiation in the form of its virtual dressing room and its reminder service for upcoming birthdays, anniversaries etc. Similarly, Winterco practices product differentiation in the form of its distinctive outerwear styles, its brand names and its on-line contests.

II.   **EXAMPLE 13-2: The Prisoners' Dilemma** (p. 304)
Yes. Assume that two firms, A and B, agree to share the market and charge a high monopoly profit maximizing price. Assume that there are now four possibilities.
1. Both stick to the price agreement and each make $100 in profits.
2. Both ignore the agreement, charge lower prices, and each makes $40 in profits.
3. *A* sticks to the agreement while *B* ignores and lowers the price. *A* makes a profit of $30 and *B* makes a profit of $120.
4. *B* sticks to the agreement while *A* ignores and lowers the price. *B* makes a profit of $30 and *A* makes a profit of $120.
The dominant strategy is for neither to stick to the agreement, if cannot be enforced.

III.  **INTERNATIONAL EXAMPLE 13-1: Collapsing Oil Prices** (p. 307)
Saudi Arabia, as the largest oil producer, can have the largest impact on oil production and prices. Since all OPEC members know this, they will be less likely to cheat when it is clear that Saudi Arabia will practice a tit-for-tat strategy and flood the market for oil if it finds one or more members of the cartel cheating.

IV.   **INTERNATIONAL EXAMPLE 13-2: OPEC As Strong As Ever** (p. 307)
Yes, in 1999 and 2000, OPEC adopted a cooperative pricing strategy. The text points out that after practicing the tit-for-tat strategy, oligopolists can appreciate how a cooperative pricing strategy can improve profits over a prolonged period of time.

V.    **EXAMPLE 13-3: Do Pet Products Have Nine Lives?** (p. 310)
The demand for 9-Lives cat food is price elastic. The percentage change in quantity demanded is $-8/(23+15)/2 = 42$ percent. Therefore, the coefficient of price elasticity of demand is $42/22 = 1.9$.

VI.   **EXAMPLE 13-4: Air Wars** (p. 311)
Air Canada and Canadian Airlines could not match Greyhound's fares and still retain their "frills" service – frequent flyer plans, business class service and so on. So they fought back by offering the frills that Greyhound did not, trying to appeal to those customers who wanted more than just transportation.

VII.  **POLICY EXAMPLE 13-1: Conspiracy to Fix Snow Removal Prices in Quebec** (p. 312)
By agreeing, in advance, which company will submit the winning bid, the industry is acting like a monopoly.

**VIII. INTERNATIONAL EXAMPLE 13-3: Diamond Cartel Forever?** (p. 313)
The "rarity" of diamonds makes this stone very appealing to many consumers, especially the richer ones. This suggests that the demand for diamonds is relatively inelastic. A cartel seeks to restrict output and therefore keeps diamonds rare and "precious." Economically speaking, since the demand for diamonds is inelastic, a lower quantity and a higher price will increase the cartels total revenue and profit.

**IX. EXAMPLE 13-5: High Switching Costs in the Credit World** (p. 314)
The Bank of Montreal offers Air Miles for every dollar charged to its MasterCard. The Royal Bank's Visa Classic II allows the card holder to accumulate points towards the purchase of merchandise at various approved stores. These benefits to cardholders can serve as an effective switching cost.

**X. EXAMPLE 13-6: Can Advertising Lead to Efficiency?** (p. 316)
This is a chicken and egg type of question. It is likely that the firm that initially advertises and attracts new customers is able to grow larger. As it gets larger, it can stock a wider selection of products. A larger advertising budget allows the firm to attract still more customers and so on.

# CHAPTER 14

# REGULATION AND COMPETITON POLICY

## PUTTING THIS CHAPTER INTO PERSPECTIVE

Chapter 14 is the last chapter in Part Three, which deals with market structure, and it revisits the monopoly model. You should not have much trouble with this chapter because it presents relatively little new theory; much of what you have learned in previous chapters of Part Three is discussed again in Chapter 14.

Natural monopoly describes a situation in which significant economies of scale (relative to industry demand) lead to persisting declines in average cost and marginal cost. Therefore the first firm to expand in size will reap tremendous cost advantages and will price its output so as to drive out all competitors. Presumably, after it has attained monopoly status, it will maximize profits by charging a higher price and producing a lower output than social efficiency requires. (Interestingly enough, because of the advantages of economies of scale, it is possible that it would produce more, at a lower price, than would the perfect competition market structure.)

There are two basic approaches for coming to grips with a natural monopoly: competition policy and regulation. Competition, in essence, attempts to prevent the monopoly from arising in the first place; it makes "monopolizing" actions illegal. The regulation approach is to permit the monopoly to emerge (indeed, to *help* it to do so) and then to force it to behave in socially desirable ways.

One form of regulation forces the monopolist to price at the firm's marginal cost of output. Unfortunately (as your text points out), in such a situation marginal cost is below average cost; hence the monopolist would suffer economic losses. In order to deal with that problem, natural monopolists are regulated via rate regulation, which takes two forms. First, there is "cost of service" regulation, which requires the natural monopolist to charge according to the *average* cost of production (rather than the marginal cost, and therefore is socially inefficient). Second is the "rate of return" regulation which permits the natural monopolist to earn only a "normal" or competitive rate of return on the investment in the business.

This chapter also analyzes the behavior of regulators. The model maintains that regulators are just like the rest of us: they usually, but not always, do things that are in their own self-interest—and not society's. Two hypotheses are presented: the capture hypothesis and the share the gains/share the pains theory.

After examining the costs of regulation, this chapter proceeds to examine the alternate policies of de-regulation and Canadian competition policy.

## LEARNING OBJECTIVES

After you have studied this chapter, you should be able to

1. define natural monopoly, marginal cost pricing, average cost pricing, cost-of-service regulation, rate-of-return regulation, creative response, capture hypothesis, share the gains/share the pains theory, deregulation, and theory of contestable markets.

2. indicate the problem with requiring a natural monopolist to engage in marginal cost pricing and list two ways to counter this problem.

3. distinguish between cost-of-service regulation and rate-of-return regulation, and answer questions that indicate an understanding of the difficulties involved with such regulation.

4. apply the regulator behavior model to predict the behavior of regulators.

5. understand the general idea behind competition policy.

## CHAPTER OUTLINE

1. A natural monopoly arises when there are large economies of scale relative to industry demand and one firm can produce at a lower cost than can be achieved by multiple firms.

2. When long-run average costs are falling, the long-run marginal cost curve is below the long-run average cost curve; the first firm to take advantage of decreasing costs can drive out all competitors by underpricing them.
   a. If regulators force the natural monopolist to engage in **marginal cost pricing**, the firm will suffer economic losses and will shut down.
   b. In such a situation, regulators might subsidize the natural monopolist to engage in marginal cost pricing.

3.  There are three types of government regulation:  regulation of natural monopolies, regulation of inherently competitive industries, and social regulation.
    a.  Economic regulation typically concerns controlling prices that regulated enterprises are allowed to charge.
        i.  **Cost-of-service regulation** allows regulated companies to charge in accordance with actual average costs.
        ii.  **Rate-of-return regulation** allows regulated firms to earn a normal rate of return on their investment in the business.
    b.  Regulators can control prices, but because quality is difficult to measure and control, regulated firms can change their price per constant-quality unit when forced to underprice services.
    c.  Regulated firms engage in **creative response**, which is a response to a regulation that conforms to the letter of the law while undermining its spirit.

4.  The regulator behavior model suggests that regulation benefits firms already in a regulated industry—not potential entrants or consumers.
    a.  The **capture hypothesis** predicts that regulators will eventually be controlled by the special interests of the industry that is being regulated.
    b.  The **share the gains/share the pains** theory maintains that regulators must take into account the demands of three groups:  legislators, firms in the industry, and consumers of the regulated industry.

5.  **Deregulation** can create costs and benefits.
    a.  In the short run firms and workers can be hurt by deregulation, but the long-run effects are largely beneficial.
    b.  The **contestable market theory** suggests that regulation should be concerned with ease of entry into an industry—and not with the current structure of an industry.

6.  Competition policy attempts to prevent the emergence of monopoly and monopolistic behavior.
    a.  In 1889 the Act for the Protection and Suppression of Combinations was passed; which made it illegal to unduly restrict competition in the marketplace.
    b.  In 1910 the Anticombines Act set out procedures for reporting and investigating alleged crime.
    c.  In 1960, anti-competitive behaviour was made a civil offense instead of a criminal offense.
    d.  The Competition Act of 1986 was aimed at maintaining and encouraging an efficient and competitive Canadian economy.

7.  Competition law has evolved to apply to three main offenses: price fixing that unduly restricted competition; mergers or monopolies acting contrary to the public interest; and unfair trade practices.

## KEY TERMS AND CONCEPTS

Creative response
Marginal cost pricing
Average cost pricing
Rate-of-return regulation
Share the gains/share the pains theory

Cost-of-service regulation
Capture hypothesis
Deregulation
Theory of contestable markets

## COMPLETION QUESTIONS
Fill in the blank or circle the correct term.

1. A natural monopoly arises when there are large _____ of scale relative to _____; in such a case the firm's average total costs persistently _____ and its marginal cost curve lies (below, above) its average cost curve; the first firm to expand will be able to offer a price that is _____ than those of its rivals and drive them out of business.

2. If a natural monopolist were forced to engage in marginal cost pricing for social efficiency, that firm would experience _____ economic profits; in order to counter that, regulators might _____ the natural monopolist.

3. There are three types of government regulation of _____, _____, and _____.

4. Cost of service regulation requires firms to charge customers based on actual (marginal, average) costs; rate-of-return regulation permits regulated firms to earn _____ profits. Because price is easier to measure and regulate than quality, regulated firms can (lower, raise) the price per constant-quality unit even if price is constant.

5. Regulated firms often try to avoid the effects of regulation, so they react to regulation by making a _____ response; that is they follow the letter, but not the spirit, of a regulation.

6. The regulator behavior model suggests that much regulation is for the benefit of (consumers, firms already in the industry); two such theories are _____ and _____.

7. One predictable short-run result of deregulation is _____; long-run results include _____ and _____.

8.  The contestable markets theory suggests that regulation should be more concerned with the _____ into an industry and not the current _____ of the industry.

9.  The Act for the Protection and Suppression of Combinations in Restraint Trade made it a criminal offense to act to unduly restrict _____ in the marketplace.

10. The Anti-Combines Act set out procedures for _____ complaints of restrictive trade practice.

11. The _____ Act is aimed at maintaining and encouraging competition in Canada.

12. Anti-trust law covers three main offences: _____ ; _____ ; and _____ .

## TRUE-FALSE QUESTIONS

Circle the **T** if the statement is true, the **F** if it is false.  Explain to yourself why a statement is false.

T  F   1.  Natural monopolies arise mainly due to large economies of scale.

T  F   2.  If a natural monopolist is required to engage in marginal cost pricing, it will earn abnormal profits.

T  F   3.  Regulated firms often follow the letter of a rule, but violate its spirit.

T  F   4.  Regulators can easily regulate the price per constant-quality unit of regulated firms.

T  F   5.  According to the regulator behavior theory, regulators are mostly concerned with the well-being of consumers.

T  F   6.  Everyone benefits from deregulation.

T  F   7.  Traditionally in Canada, inherently competitive industries have not been regulated.

T  F   8.  One predictable result of deregulation is bankruptcy for the less efficient firms.

T  F   9.  Under the Combines Investigation Act in 1976, offenses were made civil rather than criminal.

T F 10. The Competition Act classifies anti-competitive behaviour as "abuse of dominant position".

## MULTIPLE CHOICE QUESTIONS
Circle the letter that corresponds to the best answer.

1. A natural monopoly results because
   a. of large economies of scale.
   b. of persisting declining average and marginal costs.
   c. the largest firm can underprice its competitors.
   d. All of the above

2. If the natural monopolist were forced to price at marginal cost, it would earn
   a. abnormal profits.
   b. economic profits.
   c. economic losses.
   d. zero economic profit.

3. Which of the following is **NOT** a recognized type of government regulation?
   a. regulation of natural monopolies
   b. regulation for the benefit of the Senate
   c. regulation of inherently competitive industries
   d. regulation for public welfare across all industries

4. Which of the following is probably the most difficult to regulate?
   a. price
   b. output
   c. quality
   d. profit

5. Which of the following is **NOT** consistent with the regulator behavior model?
   a. Regulators are concerned with benefiting themselves.
   b. Regulators are concerned with benefiting vocal customers.
   c. Regulators are concerned with benefiting firms already in the industry.
   d. Regulators are concerned with benefiting potential entrants into an industry.

6. If an industry is deregulated,
   a. short-run costs to some existing producers can be significant.
   b. all producers would be hurt.
   c. all consumers would be helped.
   d. All of the above

7.    Which of the following is a predictable consequence of deregulation?
      a.  increased bankruptcies in the short run
      b.  long-run abnormal profits
      c.  Long-run price is even greater than MC.
      d.  short-run misallocation of resources

8.    The contestable market theory maintains that regulators should be primarily concerned with
      a.  the degree to which entry into an industry is possible.
      b.  concentration ratios.
      c.  profits today.
      d.  past profits.

**MATCHING**

Choose the numbered item in Column (2) that best matches the term or concept in Column (1).

                (1)                                              (2)

a.  natural monopoly                          1.  positive economic profits
b.  marginal cost pricing                     2.  behavior of regulated firms
c.  creative response                         3.  behavior of regulators
d.  capture hypothesis                        4.  ease of entry into industry
e.  contestable markets                       5.  persistent fall in long run AC
f.  Competition Act                           6.  prohibits restrictive trade practices
                                              7.  allocative efficiency

**WORKING WITH GRAPHS**

1.    Suppose you are an analyst for a regulatory board that is in charge of the regulation of local monopolies.  Given the information in the graph that follows, answer the list of questions submitted by your supervisor.

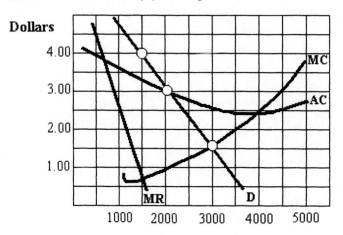

a.  If this monopolist is not regulated, what will be the level of output? _____ price? _____ total revenue? _____ total costs? _____ profit or loss? _____

b.  If this monopolist is regulated by marginal cost pricing, what will be the level of output? _____ price? _____ total revenue? _____ total costs? _____ profits or loss? _____ Will the monopoly need a subsidy? _____ If so, how much? _____

c.  If cost-of-service regulation is imposed on this monopolist, what will be the level of output? _____ price? _____ total revenue? _____ total costs? _____ profit or loss? _____

## BUSINESS SECTION

### Marketing: Restrictive Trade Practices

In creating an effective marketing mix  - price, product, promotion, place- a firm must consider "non-controllable environmental variables" such as the legal climate. In Canada, the federal Competition Act is an important aspect of the legal climate to consider in developing the marketing mix. Some of the *restrictive trade practices* listed below are prohibited under the Competition Act.

- Price discrimination
- Predatory pricing
- Resale price maintenance
- False or misleading representations or claims (in a material respect)
- Exclusive dealing
- Tied selling
- Referral selling
- Bait and switch selling (non-availability of advertised specials)
- Pyramid selling (multi-level marketing practice)

### Business Application Problem

Match each of the following hypothetical trade practices to one of the restrictive trade practices listed above. To answer this question the student is encouraged to visit one of the following web sites:
"The Competition Act" at http://canada.justice.gc.ca/STABLE/EN/Laws/Chap/C/C-34.html or: "The Competition Bureau" at  http://strategis.ic.gc.ca/SSG/ct01135e.html

a.  A door to door vacuum salesperson  provides a customer with a written promise to sell a new vacuum at 20% off the regular price The customer will only receive the discount to the extent that the salesperson is successful in selling another vacuum to the customer's friend. The customer has provided the salesperson with the friend's name and address.

b.  A retailer of software can only obtain the most popular operating software from a software manufacturer if the retailer also agrees to buy other software products offered by the same software manufacturer.

c.  Every week for a period of two years, Quality Carpets placed newspaper ads that claimed that they were closing out immediately.

d.  The deep discounts (sometimes below cost) offered by a major airline causes the only other competitor to go out of business.

e.  A large gas refining company will only sell gas to Zaks Gas Station if Zak promises to never buy gas from any other gas refining company.

f.  A small clothing retailer claims that it pays a higher cost per jean in a shipment of 1000 designer jeans  than a large department store retailer pays (in the same market area) for the same shipment for the same brand of jean sold by the same manufacturer.

g.  Advanced Electronics places a full-page ad featuring a 5-day half price sale for all of its brand name CD's. On the first day of the sale, one hour after opening the doors, all of the brand name CD's were sold out. The purpose of the sale was to get customers interested in buying the new CD players that had just arrived in the store.

h.  An appliance manufacturer refuses to continue to sell a leading brand of microwave ovens to an appliance retailer. The reason given was that the retailer priced the microwaves at a price below the retail price suggested by the manufacturer.

i.  Leo's Furniture Mart displays a "50% off" sales ticket on a brand of Italian leather sofas. The ticket indicates a discounted price of $2,500. A customer who purchased the sofa found out later that the regular price of the sofa was $3,000.

# ANSWERS TO CHAPTER 14

## COMPLETION QUESTIONS

1. economies; industry demand; fall; below; lower
2. negative; subsidize
3. natural monopoly; inherently competitive industries; social regulation
4. average; normal; raise
5. creative
6. firms already in the industry; capture theory; share the gains/share the pains theory
7. increased bankruptcies; prices closer to marginal cost; smaller abnormal profits
8. degree to which entry is permitted; market structure
9. competition
10. investigating
11. Competition
12. price fixing; mergers or monopolies acting contrary to public interest; unfair trade practices

## TRUE-FALSE QUESTIONS

1. T
2. F    It will realize losses.
3. T
4. F    It is difficult to regulate quality.
5. F    They, like the rest of us, are assumed to be concerned with their own well-being.
6. F    Some firms and workers are hurt in the short run from de-regulation.
7. F    Inherently competitive industries such as trucking and airlines have been regulated.
8. T
9. T
10. T

## MULTIPLE CHOICE QUESTIONS

1.d; In a natural monopoly, the marginal cost is continually below the long run average cost, causing the average cost to continue to decline as the one dominant firm expands. This means that the largest firm can underprice its competitors.
2.c; In a natural monopoly, where the marginal cost is below the average cost, setting the price equal to marginal cost will result in economic losses for the firm.
3.b; The three types of regulation are regulation of natural monopolies, inherently competitive industries, public welfare across all industries.
4.c; Since quality is not easily measured, it is the most difficult to regulate.
5.d; Since potential entrants are typically not yet identified, the regulators are least likely to be responsive to this group.
6.a; Since deregulation typically implies increased competition, certain  firms who were not efficient under regulation, will find it difficult to survive.
7.a; Some firms will not be able to compete without having the government protect them from competition.
8.a; The contestable market theory maintains that, even in cases where there are just a few existing competitors, deregulation can bring about a more competitive result due to the threat of new entrants.

## MATCHING

a and 5;   b and 7;   c and 2;   d and 3,   e and 4,   f and 6

**WORKING WITH GRAPHS**

1.    a.    1500 units, $4.00, $6,000, $4,875 = 3.25x 1500, profit of $1,125 = 6000-4875.
      b.    3000 units, $1.50, $4500, $7500, loss of $3000, yes, $3000
      c.    2000 units, $3, $6000, $6000, $0

**BUSINESS SECTION**

1.    a   Referral selling      b.   Tied sales                    c.  False/misleading claims
      d.  Predatory pricing   e.   Exclusive dealing          f.  Price discrimination
      g.  Bait and switch      h.   Resale price maintenance   i.  False/misleading claims

**ANSWERS TO EXAMPLE QUESTIONS FOR CRITICAL ANALYSIS**

I.    **INTERNATIONAL POLICY EXAMPLE 14-1: European Post Offices: Natural Monopolies and How to Evade Them** (p. 328)
      No firm competes with Canada Post in delivering first class mail at the price of a postage stamp. It is likely that this is one area where the postal service is a natural monopoly and probably would not need protection. In other areas of service, it is likely that the postal services are not natural monopolies.

II.   **POLICY EXAMPLE 14-1: Can the CRTC Effectively Regulate Cable TV?** (p. 330)
      The CRTC would have to be able to block transmission of the American channels if it were to enforce Canadian content regulations. Given the increasing effectiveness and decreasing cost of satellite dishes, it is unlikely the CRTC would be successful.

III.  **EXAMPLE 14-1: The Effectiveness of Auto Safety Regulations** (p. 332)
      The purpose of the safety regulations was to make automobile accidents less dangerous and reduce the number of injuries and deaths by eliminating certain hazardous features and by the addition of safety devices to cars. The regulators did not consider that ceteris paribus conditions would not continue as a result of the regulations. The unintended effect of having safer cars has been an increase in reckless driving and more accidents, which has increased, or at least not reduced, the number of injuries. Regulation to achieve a certain goal does not take into account that people's likely response can have effects that were unforeseen and not intended.

IV.   **POLICY EXAMPLE 14-2: The Ontario Energy Competition Act of 1998** (p. 335)
      The fact that the government expects to continue to regulate the distribution and transmission of electricity, suggests that this segment of the electricity sector is subject to significant economies of scale. Since the generation of electricity has been influenced by factors such as small turbine technology, this segment of the electricity sector is no longer characterized as a natural monopoly situation.

V.    **EXAMPLE 14-2: Cutting Through the "Red Tape"** (p. 336)
      Costs attached to reviewing and revising regulations are mainly the opportunity costs of labour. Civil servants must research the effects of the regulation and then devise improvements. This is a time consuming task.

VI.   **POLICY EXAMPLE 14-3: Breaking the Tight Grip of Interac** (p. 338)

      The widening access to Interac will decrease the demand for each competitor's system. Service charges (the price of using the system) should rise.

# CHAPTER 15

# LABOUR DEMAND AND SUPPLY

## PUTTING THIS CHAPTER INTO PERSPECTIVE

Much of what you learned in Part Three can be applied to Part Four.  Most fundamentally, you can apply the maximization or rational behaviour model that you learned earlier.  Recall that a rational person—supplier, buyer, owner, or manager of a firm—will undertake any activity up to the point where the marginal benefit (MB) of doing so equals the marginal cost (MC) of doing so.  For this model to work, eventually marginal cost must rise relative to marginal benefit.  If MB > MC, then maximizing behaviour requires that the person (or firm) do more; if MC > MB, then maximizing behaviour requires that less be done.  If MB = MC (and MC is rising relative to MB), then the person or firm is maximizing. The trick is to identify the MB and the MC of any activity.

The first input market structure analyzed in Chapter 15 is perfect competition in both the product market and the labour market.  The activity in question is hiring labour; as usual we assume that the firm wants to maximize profits.  The firm's marginal benefit from hiring labour is the marginal physical product of labour multiplied by the price of the good sold (MRP); thus MB = MRP.  The MRP falls because the marginal physical product of labour falls (due to the law of diminishing marginal returns) and price, P, is constant because the firm is a price taker.  The marginal cost of hiring labour is the wage rate, which is constant because the firm is a price taker in the labour market, too.  Predictably, the firm hires labour up to the point where MB = MC, as in this model where the MRP of labour equals the wage rate, respectively.

The second major model analyzed in Chapter 15 assumes perfect competition in the labour market, but imperfect competition (monopoly, actually, but the conclusions are the same for monopolistic competition and oligopoly) in the product market.  Because an imperfect competitor must reduce price in order to sell more, in this model marginal benefit is more complicated.  The MB for hiring labour is marginal revenue (MR) multiplied by the marginal physical product, or MRP, of labour.  Recall that if demand is negatively sloped, then price, P, must exceed MR.  Because we assume perfect competition in the labour market, the firm is there a price taker; hence the MC of hiring labour is again the wage rate, W.  Thus the profit maximizing quantity of labour to hire occurs where MB equals MC, or in this model MRP of labour = W. Note that in this model, MR, or MRP, falls for two reasons: the marginal physical product of labour falls due to diminishing returns, and price falls because the firm is a monopolist in the product market and faces a downward-sloping demand curve.

In Chapter 15 the industry demand for labour curve is also derived; so too is an industry supply of labour curve. Wage rates are determined, of course, at the intersection of the industry demand for labour curve and the industry supply of labour curve.


## LEARNING OBJECTIVES

After you have studied this chapter you should be able to

1.  define marginal physical product of labour, marginal revenue product, marginal factor cost, derived demand, and labour market signaling.

2.  determine the profit-maximizing quantity of labour to hire for a firm that is a perfect competitor in both the product and the labour market.

3.  determine the profit-maximizing quantity of labour to hire for a firm that is a perfect competitor in the labour market and a monopolist in the product market.

4.  distinguish between the MRP of labour curve for a perfect competitor and the MRP of labour curve for a monopolist.

5.  list four determinants of the price elasticity of demand for an input.

6.  determine the equilibrium wage rate, given the supply of labour and the demand for labour.

7.  list three factors that cause the total demand curve for labour to shift.

8.  list two factors that cause the total supply of labour curve to shift.

9.  recognize the minimum total cost condition for producing a given rate of output.


## CHAPTER OUTLINE

1.  What is the profit-maximizing quantity of labour to hire for a firm that is a perfect competitor in both the labour market and the product market?
    a.  The **marginal physical product of labour** is the change in total output accounted for by hiring one worker, holding all other factors of production constant.
    b.  Because of the law of diminishing returns, the **marginal physical product of labour** eventually declines.

    c.  Because this firm is in a competitive labour market, it is a price taker; it can hire as much labour as it wants to hire at the going wage rate.

    d.  The marginal benefit from hiring one more unit of labour is that labourer's **marginal physical product** multiplied by the firm's constant product selling price, or the **marginal revenue product (MRP).**

    e.  The profit maximizing rule for hiring is to hire labourers up to the point where the wage rate equals the MRP of labour.

2.  The demand for labour is a **derived demand**; labourers (or other inputs) are desired only because they can be used to produce products that are expected to be sold at a profit.

3.  The market demand for labour curve is negatively sloped.

4.  There are four principal determinants of the price elasticity of demand for an input. The price elasticity of demand for a variable input will be greater

    a.  the greater the price elasticity of demand for the final product.

    b.  the easier it is to substitute for that variable input.

    c.  the larger the proportion of total costs accounted for by a particular variable input.

    d.  the longer the time period being considered.

5.  The industry supply of labour curve is upward sloping from left to right.

    a.  As wage rates rise in an industry, more labourers are willing to accept jobs there.

    b.  Nevertheless, the individual firm faces a horizontal supply curve at the going wage rate.

6.  The equilibrium market wage rate is determined where the industry demand for labour curve intersects the industry supply of labour curve.

7.  When nonwage determinants of the supply of and the demand for labour change, those curves shift.

    a.  The labour demand curve shifts if there is a change in (1) the demand for the final product, (2) labour productivity, or (3) the price of related factors of production.

    b.  The labour supply curve shifts if there is a change in the (1) alternative wage rate offered in other industries, or (2) nonmonetary aspects of the occupation under study.

8.  What is the profit-maximizing quantity of labour to hire for a firm that is a perfect competitor in the labour market but a monopolist in the product market?

    a.  Such a firm's demand for labour (or any other input) is negatively sloped because (1) the **marginal physical product** falls and (2) the price (and, therefore, MR) falls as output increases.

    b.  Such a firm's MB curve, or demand curve, is its MRP curve, which equals labour's **marginal physical product** multiplied by the firm's MR; thus MRP = MR x MPP.

c. Given the going market wage rate, this firm hires up to the point where MRP equals the wage rate.
d. The monopolist hires fewer workers than a perfectly competitive producer would, other things being constant.

9. How much of *each* variable factor should the firm use when combining those factors to produce a given output?
   a. The firm will hire all variable inputs up to the point where each input's MRP equals its price.
   b. In order to minimize the total cost of producing a given output, the firm should equate the ratios of each factor's **marginal physical product** to its respective price; this condition is referred to as the *least-cost combination of resources*.

## KEY TERMS AND CONCEPTS

Marginal physical product (MPP) of labour
Marginal revenue product (MRP)
Marginal factor cost (MFC)

Derived demand
Labour market signalling

## COMPLETION QUESTIONS
Fill in the blank or circle the correct term.

1. To a firm that is a perfect competitor in both the labour and the product market, the marginal benefit from hiring labour equals labour's _____ times _____, or MRP.

2. A competitive firm's MRP curve is negatively sloped because labour's _____ falls, due to the law of (demand, diminishing returns).

3. To such a competitive firm, the marginal cost of hiring labour is the (normal, wage) rate, which (falls, rises, remains constant) as the firm hires more labourers; in the labour market, such a firm is a price (taker, maker).

4. The competitive firm hires labour up to the point where _____ equals the (normal, wage) rate; at that point it is maximizing (accounting, total) profits.

5. The demand for labour is a _____ demand; therefore if the product's selling price increases, the competitive firm's demand for labour curve will shift to the (left, right); the market demand curve for labour will be (negatively, positively) sloped.

6. The supply of labour to a competitive firm is (inelastic, perfectly elastic), therefore its labour supply curve is (vertical, horizontal); the supply of labour curve for the industry, however, is (negatively, positively) sloped.

7.  Assume a firm is a perfect competitor in the labour market but a monopolist in the product market. Its marginal benefit from hiring labour equals _____ times _____, or MRP of labour. This firm's MRP curve is negatively sloped because _____ falls due to the law of (demand, diminishing returns) and because _____ falls due to the fact that this firm must reduce its (price, workers) as it produces more. This firm will hire labour up to the point where _____ equals the (hiring, wage) rate.

**TRUE-FALSE QUESTIONS**
Circle the **T** if the statement is true, the **F** if it is false. Explain to yourself why a statement is false.

T  F    1.  A firm that is a competitor in all markets will discover that its demand for labour curve is horizontal at the going wage rate.

T  F    2.  A competitive firm will hire labour up to the point where MRP equals the going wage rate.

T  F    3.  The marginal physical product of labour declines due to diseconomies of scale.

T  F    4.  Because the demand for labour is a derived demand, it shifts when wage rates change.

T  F    5.  The price elasticity of demand for labour will be higher the lower is the price elasticity of demand for the final good.

T  F    6.  A competitive firm's supply of labour curve is perfectly elastic, but the entire industry supply of labour curve is upward sloping.

T  F    7.  If labour productivity rises, the demand for labour increases.

T  F    8.  A firm that is a competitor in the labour market but a monopolist in the product market hires labour up to the point where the MRP of labour equals the going wage rate.

T  F    9.  If a firm suddenly monopolizes a perfectly competitive industry, more workers will be hired.

T  F   10.  If a competitive firm hires two factors of production it will hire up to the point where the MRP of one factor divided by that factor's price equals the MRP of the other factor divided by that factor's price.

**MULTIPLE CHOICE QUESTIONS**
Circle the letter that corresponds to the best answer.

1.  Which of the following is **NOT** true about a firm that is a perfect competitor in all markets?
    a.  Its supply of labour curve is perfectly elastic.
    b.  Its demand for labour curve is downward sloping.
    c.  Its price falls as it produces more output.
    d.  Its marginal physical product of labour falls as it hires more labour.

2.  For a firm that is a perfect competitor in all markets, the profit-maximizing quantity of labour to hire occurs where
    a.  a falling MRP equals a rising wage rate.
    b.  a rising MRP equals a rising wage rate.
    c.  a falling MRP equals a falling wage rate.
    d.  a falling MRP equals a constant wage rate.

3.  A firm that is a perfect competitor in all markets finds that its MRP for labour falls because as it hires more labour
    a.  the marginal physical product of labour falls.
    b.  the price of output falls as output increases.
    c.  Both of the above
    d.  None of the above

4.  The marginal factor cost of labour
    a.  equals the going wage rate to a competitive firm.
    b.  equals the change in wage rates divided by the change in labour.
    c.  rises for the competitive firm.
    d.  equals the change in total cost divided by the change in wage rates.

5.  The demand for labour
    a.  is a derived demand.
    b.  shifts as selling price of the good produced changes.
    c.  shifts to the right if labour productivity increases.
    d.  All of the above

6.  Which of the following will **NOT** lead to a relatively high price elasticity of demand for labour?
    a.  high price elasticity of demand for the final product
    b.  no good substitutes for the labour skill in question
    c.  high ratio of labour to total costs
    d.  a very long period of time after the wage change

7.  The supply of labour
    a.  to a perfect competitor is positively sloped.
    b.  for the entire industry is perfectly elastic.
    c.  is positively sloped for the industry.
    d.  depends on labour's marginal physical product.

8.  Which of the following will **NOT** lead to an increase in the demand for labour?
    a.  price of labour falls
    b.  increase in the productivity of labour
    c.  increase in the price of a labour substitute input
    d.  increase in the demand for the final product

9.  If firm B is a competitor in the labour market and a monopolist in the product market, then
    a.  its demand for labour is negatively sloped.
    b.  its supply of labour is positively sloped.
    c.  its selling price is a constant.
    d.  its wage rates rise as it hires more labour.

10. If firm B is a competitor in the labour market and a monopolist in the product market, then
    a.  its supply of labour curve is perfectly elastic at the going wage rate.
    b.  it hires labour up to the point where MRP of labour equals the going wage rate.
    c.  its MRP curve falls because the marginal product of labour falls and its selling price falls.
    d.  All of the above

11. The monopolist in the product market finds that its MRP for labour falls as it hires labour because
    a.  the MPP of labour falls and output price is constant.
    b.  the MPP of labour falls and output price falls.
    c.  the MPP of labour is constant and output price falls.
    d.  the MPP of labour rises but output price falls faster.

12. If a perfectly competitive market is suddenly monopolized, the amount of labour hired will
    a.  remain constant.
    b.  fall.
    c.  rise.
    d.  fall in the short run, rise in the long run.

13. If a firm hires two variable inputs, A and B, it is minimizing costs when
    a.  MPP of A/price of A = MPP of B/price of B.
    b.  MPP of A/price of B = MPP of B/price of A.
    c.  MRP of A/MPP of B = MRP of B/MPP of A.
    d.  MRP of A/price of B = MRP of B/price of A.

## MATCHING
Choose the item in column (2) that best matches an item in column (1).

|           (1)           |           (2)           |
| --- | --- |

a.  MPP
b.  MPP x MR
c.  MPP x price
d.  least cost combination
e.  derived demand

1.  insider-outsider theory
2.  MRP of competitive firm
3.  MRP of monopolistic firm
4.  labour demand curve
5.  change in output for a unit input change
6.  equate MPP/price of all factor inputs

## WORKING WITH GRAPHS

1.  Analyze the graphs below, then answer the questions that follow.  Assume that the minimum wage rate is $4.50 per hour.

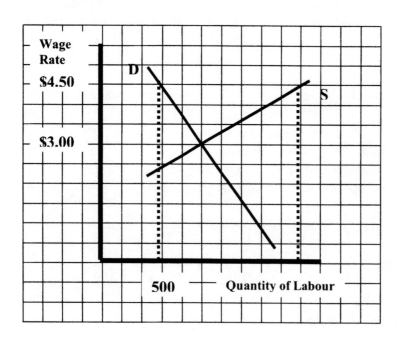

a.  What is the equilibrium wage rate in this market?

b.  What is the quantity supplied of labour at the minimum wage rate?

c.  What is the quantity demanded for labour at the minimum wage rate?

d.  What market situation exists at the minimum wage rate?


e.  How many workers were laid-off, due to the minimum wage rate?


f.  How many workers entered the labour force, seeking a job, due to the minimum wage rate?


g.  Are workers in this industry better off or worse off as a result of this minimum wage?


h.  Which workers are more likely to be laid off?


## PROBLEMS

1.  In the following table you are given information about a firm operating in a competitive market.  Consider all factors of production fixed at the moment, with the exception of labour services.  The other factors of production cost the firm $50 per day, which may be thought of as a fixed cost.  Assume the firm is a profit maximizer.

| Labour input (workers per day) | Total physical product (units per day) | Marginal physical product (units per day) | Marginal revenue product ($ per worker) |
|---|---|---|---|
| 0 | 0 | | |
| 1 | 22 | _____ | _____ |
| 2 | 40 | _____ | _____ |
| 3 | 56 | _____ | _____ |
| 4 | 70 | _____ | _____ |
| 5 | 82 | _____ | _____ |
| 6 | 92 | _____ | _____ |
| 7 | 100 | _____ | _____ |
| 8 | 106 | _____ | _____ |

a.  Assume that the firm sells its output at $3 per unit.  Complete the last two columns in the table above.

b.  If the going market wage is $36 per day, the firm will hire _____ workers per day and produce _____ units of output.

c.  Given your answer to part b, the firm will have total revenues of _____ per day and total costs of _____ per day.

d.  The above will result in a (profit, loss) of _____ per day.

2.  Suppose you work for a firm that sells its output in a monopoly market. Answer the following questions.

a.  If you hire an additional worker, output goes up by 50 units to 125 units per day. If you wish to sell the additional 50 units, you must lower your price from $3 per unit to $2 per unit. What is the maximum wage you would be willing to pay the additional worker?

b.  Assume you hired the worker from part a and output now stands at 125 units per day. If another worker is hired, output rises to 165 units per day. Given the demand curve for your product, you know that in order to sell the additional output, price will have to be dropped from $2 per unit to $1 per unit. What is the maximum wage you would be willing to pay this additional worker?

## BUSINESS SECTION

### Small Business/Management: Employing Multiple Resources to Maximize Profits

### Business Application Problem

Janet Joplin owns and manages a small private computer training business in a purely competitive market. Janet is in the process of deciding on the number of networking course sessions versus the number of database course sessions to offer in the next spring quarter . The only extra costs involved are the instructional (labour) costs involved in hiring instructors to teach these courses. Each instructor is hired to teach one course session. For each network course session offered, Janet must pay a network instructor $715. For each database course session offered Janet has to pay a database instructor $380.

Based on the attendance performance of the spring quarter in the previous year, Janet projects that the following marginal revenue product (MRP) amounts contributed by each instructor for each course. The reason that the marginal revenue product declines as more sessions of each course is put on is that enrolments tend to decline in late spring as the weather improves.

| Number of Course Sessions to Offer | Network Course | | Database Course | |
|---|---|---|---|---|
| | Marginal Revenue Product | MRP Per Instructional Dollar Spent | Marginal Revenue Product | MRP Per Instructional Dollar Spent |
| 1 | $3,000 | | $1,800 | |
| 2 | $2,700 | | $1,500 | |
| 3 | $2,400 | | $1,200 | |
| 4 | $2,100 | | $ 900 | |
| 5 | $1,800 | | $ 600 | |
| 6 | $1,500 | | $ 300 | |

1.  a.  Fill in the table above.

   b.  Assuming that Janet plans to spend a  maximum of $4,000 (in total) in hiring network and database instructors in the next spring quarter, how many network course sessions and how many database course sessions should she offer to maximize profits.  Keep all calculations in the table above to two decimals.

   c.  Based on your answer in part a. above, project the total contribution to profit (and fixed costs)  that will result from offering the two types of courses.

**ANSWERS TO CHAPTER 15**

**COMPLETION QUESTIONS**

1.  marginal physical product; price
2.  marginal physical product; diminishing returns
3.  wage; remains constant; taker
4.  MRP of labour; wage; total
5.  derived; right; negatively
6.  perfectly elastic; horizontal; positively
7.  marginal physical product of labour; MR; marginal physical product; diminishing returns; MR; price; MRP; the wage rate

**TRUE-FALSE QUESTIONS**

1.  F   The demand for labour curve is negatively sloped.
2.  T
3.  F   It declines due to the law of diminishing returns.
4.  F   If wage rates change, we move along a given labour demand curve.
5.  F   It will be lower.
6.  T
7.  T
8.  T

9.    F    Fewer workers will be hired, because output falls.
10.    T

## MULTIPLE CHOICE QUESTIONS

1.c; A perfect competitor is a price taker.
2.d; A perfect competitor will maximize total profits.
3.a; The firm will produce products that are expected to be sold at a profit.
4.a; The firm can hire all the workers they want at that rate.
5.d; Workers are desired only to produce products that can be sold at a profit.
6.b; The more substitutes, the higher the price elasticity of demand for labour.
7.c; As wages increase, quantity of labour increases.
8.a; All the others cause a shift in demand for labour.
9.a; The MPP decreases and price decreases as output increases.
10.d; The monopolist hires fewer workers than a perfectly competitive worker would.
11.b; The demand for labour is negatively sloped.
12.b; Monopolists hire fewer workers.
13.a; This is referred to as the least-cost combination of resources.

## MATCHING

a and 5;    b and 3;    c and 2;    d and 6;    e and 4.

## WORKING WITH GRAPHS

1.    a.    $3.00
      b.    800
      c.    300
      d.    surplus, or excess quantity supplied of labour
      e.    200
      f.    300
      g.    Those who kept their jobs are better off; those who became unemployed are worse off.  Group income fell from $1500 to $1350 because demand was (here) price elastic.
      h.    younger, lower income—lower productivity workers.

## PROBLEMS

1.    a.    MPP: 22, 18, 16, 14, 12, 10, 8, 6
            MRP: 66, 54, 48, 42, 36, 30, 24, 18
      b.    5, 82
      c.    $246, (5 x $36) + $50 = $230
      d.    profit, $16
2.    a.    $25 per day since MRP = $25
      b.    A negative wage, because the price decrease necessary to sell the additional output causes total revenues to decline (MR < 0), MRP for this worker is negative, and the firm must be paid to hire another unit of labour.

## BUSINESS SECTION

1.    a.    Network Course: MRP Per $:    $4.20    $3.78    $3.36    $2.94    $2.52    $2.10
            Database Course: MRP Per $:    $4.74    $3.95    $3.16    $2.37    $1.58    $.79
      b.    Four network course sessions and three database  course sessions will maximize the contribution to profit (and fixed costs).
      c.    Total contribution to profit (and fixed costs) =Total Revenue – Total Cost = (3000+2700+2400+2100+1800+1500+1200) –(4000) = 14,700 – 4000 = $10,700

**ANSWERS TO EXAMPLE QUESTIONS FOR CRITICAL ANALYSIS**

I    **POLICY EXAMPLE 15-1: Should the Minimum Wage be Raised to Help Young People?** (p. 353)
Younger people are likely to be most affected by increases in the minimum wage because they have the lowest MRP of any age group in the labour market. The reason is that they have the least education and training, and thus the lowest productivity (i.e. MPP). Therefore, given the prices of the product they produce, the MRP for them is lowest and an increase in the minimum wage reduces employment among them by the greatest amount.

II   **EXAMPLE 15-1: Does to Pay to Study?** (p. 355)
Identical twins have exactly the same genetic make-up. Therefore, they have the same physical appearance and abilities. They will normally have the same childhood influences from family. They may also have the same (or nearly the same) IQ. Thus any innate abilities and familial influences should be the same. The only real differences between them that would determine wage differences would be education, training, and experience, or all those factors that determine human capital differences.

III  **EXAMPLE 15-2: Cost Minimization and the Substitution of Software for Labour** (p. 360)
Yes, software could have an impact on doctors similar to the effect on lawyers and CGAs. Expert diagnostic programs could allow doctors' assistants or RNs to be able to diagnose many medical conditions. The demand for doctors would grow more slowly as a result.

# CHAPTER 16

# UNIONS AND LABOUR MARKET MONOPOLY POWER

## PUTTING THIS CHAPTER INTO PERSPECTIVE

Chapter 16 is the second chapter devoted to an analysis of the labour market; the next chapter is devoted to the other factors of production. It is important for you to keep a proper perspective about the labour market. Even though this chapter considers noncompetitive labour markets—monopoly supply and monopoly demand—the Canadian labour market is inherently very competitive. Our labourers traditionally have had both the freedom and the willingness to relocate; labour mobility, then, has certainly limited the economic power that any particular employer could exert on workers.

What does a competitive market imply? Because employers compete for workers, wage rates will be driven up to labour's true MRP. Similarly, because workers compete for jobs, wage rates will be driven down toward labour's true MRP. In short, competitive supply and demand set wage rates at market-clearing values and workers get paid (approximately) their MRP.

One major source of monopolistic power in the labour market is the government. Because employers know that their competition for labour will drive wage rates up toward labour's MRP, they have exerted time and effort to obtain special privilege from the government—usually in the form of exemption from antitrust action. Examples can be taken from professional sports. Also, witness the intercollegiate athletics monopsony considered in this chapter.

Monopoly power on the seller side of the labour market also is derived from government sources. As mentioned in Chapter 15, unions are exempted from antitrust action even though they act in restraint of trade. Similarly, the Canadian Medical Association and scores of other professional associations attempt to restrict the supply of labour into specific occupations through licensing; note how government sanction is necessary for such monopsonistic power to arise. Labourers know only too well that if they compete, their wage rates will be driven down to competitive levels.

Consider first a firm that is a perfect competitor in the product market, but a monopsonist in the labour market. Such a firm faces a downward sloping demand for labour curve; its MB for hiring labour is labour's MRP, which falls due to a declining marginal physical product of labour. That firm faces an upward sloping supply of labour curve, however, because it is the only buyer of labour. In order to obtain another worker it must pay a higher wage rate—to the new worker and to all the previously employed workers. Hence that firm's MC of hiring labour is the marginal factor cost (MFC) of labour, which exceeds the wage rate and rises as the firm hires more labour. The profit-maximizing quantity of labour to hire occurs where the decreasing MRP of labour curve intersects the rising marginal factor cost curve. That firm then sets the wage rate at a level consistent with obtaining that quantity of labour—as given by the industry supply of labour curve.

In the second model, consider a labour-hiring firm that is a monopolist in the product market and a monopsonist in the labour market. Its MB curve is labour's MRP curve, which falls due to decreasing marginal product of labour *and* a falling output price. Its MC curve is its MFC curve, which rises because it must pay higher wages (to new and old workers) as it hires more labour. The profit maximizing quantity of labour to hire occurs where the rising MFC of labour equals the declining MRP of labour; that is, at the point where the MC = MB of hiring labour, the firm maximizes total profits.

Also theoretically noteworthy in this chapter is the treatment of unions as a monopolistic seller of labour. The issue becomes: what do unions maximize? It is not clear what unions maximize; once this is decided, then it becomes easier to predict their behaviour. You should be aware that unions can set wage rates, or they can choose the quantity of labour employed; they cannot do both. In general, unions redistribute income to high-seniority workers (who keep their jobs when unions set wage rates above equilibrium) from low-seniority workers (who lose their jobs when unions so behave). Because low seniority job losers find work elsewhere—thereby increasing the supply of labour in other areas—unions don't raise *overall* wage rates. Union action causes wage rates to rise in some areas and to fall in other areas.

## LEARNING OBJECTIVES

After you have studied this chapter you should be able to

1.  define labour unions, craft unions, collective bargaining, industrial unions, featherbedding, monopsonist, monopsonistic exploitation, strikebreakers, and bilateral monopoly.

2.  identify the key provisions of major legislation dealing with unions.

3.  distinguish between craft unions and industrial unions.

4.  list three possible union goals and predict the quantity of labour that will be employed under each union strategy.

5.  show how unions can redistribute income from low seniority to high seniority workers.

6.    predict the quantity of labour hired and the wage rate that will result, given a market structure in which a firm is a perfect competitor in the product market and a monopsonist in the labour market.

7 .   predict the quantity of labour hired and the wage rate that will result, given a firm that is a  monopolist in the product market and a monopsonist in the labour market.

## CHAPTER OUTLINE

1.   Unions are workers' organizations that usually seek to secure economic improvements for their members.
     a.    The Canadian labour movement started with **craft unions**, which are composed of workers who engage in a particular skill or trade.
     b.    In 1883, the Trades and Labour Congress (TLC)formed as a meeting ground for **crafts unions** and the Knights of Labor, a U.S. based group.
     c.    During World War I, union membership grew but fell off in the prosperity of the 1920's. In response the All-Canadian Congress of Labour (ACCL) formed to rival TLC and divorce Canadian unionism from the United States.
     d.    The Great Depression brought a time of labour turmoil. The ACCL dropped the "A" and became the Canadian Congress of Labour (CCL).
     e.    In 1944 the federal government enfranchised the public section with the *Trade Union Act*.
     f.    In 1946, a Supreme Court decision gave unions the legal right to organize, to engage in **collective bargaining**, and to strike.
     g.    The "Rand formula" guaranteed the solvency of unions by ensuring a union check-off - a law stipulating that employees in a union shop must pay dues whether or not they choose to join the union.
     h.    In 1956, the TLC and the CCL merged into the Canadian Labour Congress (CLC) and today has over 2 million members.

2.   Unions can be analyzed as setters of minimum wages; the strike is the ultimate bargaining tool for unions.

3.   It is not clear what unions wish to maximize.  Unions can either set wage rates or select the quantity of its membership that will be employed; they can't do both.
     a.    To the extent that unions set wage rates above equilibrium, they create a surplus of labour, or a shortage of jobs that they ration.
     b.    If unions wish to employ all members, they must accept a relatively low wage rate.
     c.    If unions wish to maximize total wages, they set wage rates where the price elasticity of demand equals 1; some members will be unemployed.
     d.    If unions maximize wage rates for a given number of workers—presumably high-seniority workers—low-seniority workers will become unemployed because wage rates probably will be set above equilibrium.
     e.    One union strategy is to limit total union membership to the original quantity; over time, if demand increases, wage rates will rise.

f.  Unions can raise wage rates for members by (a) limiting membership, and (b) increasing the demand for union labour by increasing labour productivity and increasing the demand for union labour relative to nonunion labour.

4.  It is not apparent that unions have raised *overall* wage rates; on average, unions redistribute income within unions from low- to high-seniority workers.

5.  Recent studies indicate that unions can both (a) act as monopolies that redistribute income from low-seniority to high-seniority members and (b) increase labour productivity.

6.  Consider a firm that is a perfect competitor in the product market and a *monopsonist* in the labour market.
    a.  That firm faces an upward sloping supply of labour curve; before it can hire more labour it must raise wage rates for *all* of its employees.
    b.  As a consequence, the **marginal factor cost** of hiring labour to that firm exceeds the wage rate; the MFC curve is that firm's MC to hiring labour, and it rises as the firm hires more labour.
    c.  The marginal benefit to hiring labour to such a firm is its MRP curve, which falls (due to declining marginal product of labour) as it hires more labour.
    d.  The profit-maximizing employment level occurs where the decreasing MRP curve intersects the rising MFC curve; the wage rate is set on the supply curve, consistent with that quantity of labour.
    e.  In such a situation **monopsonistic exploitation** of labour results, because the wage rate is below the MRP of labour.

7.  A summary of monopoly, monopsony, and perfectly competitive situations is presented in Figure 16-8.

8.  In professional sports we have seen a movement from monopsony power to bilateral monopoly as owner power has diminished; both owners and players are subsidized by taxpayers who pay for new stadiums.

## KEY TERMS AND CONCEPTS

Labour unions
Craft unions
Industrial unions
Collective bargaining
Strikebreakers

Featherbedding
Monopsonist
Monopsonistic exploitation
Bilateral monopoly

## COMPLETION QUESTIONS
Fill in the blank or circle the correct term.

1.  The Canadian labour movement started with local _____ unions, which are comprised of workers in a particular (city, trade); the other major type of union is the

_____ union, which consists of workers from a particular (province, industry).

2.  In 1946, the Supreme Court gave unions the legal right to: organize; engage in _____ and _____ .

3.  The "_____" stipulates that employees in a union shop must pay (dues,   wages) whether or not they choose to join the union.

4.  The original craft unions were the (American, European) merchant guilds .

5.  The ultimate bargaining tool for the union is the _____.

6.  If a union sets wage rates above market-clearing levels, it creates a (shortage, surplus) of labour; viewed alternatively, it creates a (shortage, surplus) of jobs, which it must then ration to workers.

7.  If a union chooses to employ all of its members, it (must, need not) accept a relatively lower wage rate; if the union wants to maximize the value of total wages, it sets wage rates where the price elasticity of demand for labour equals the number (0, 1); if the union wants to set relatively high wages for its high-seniority members, its (low, medium) seniority members will be laid off.

8.  Assume that a firm is a perfect competitor in the product market and a monopsonist in the labour market. The marginal benefit to hiring labour for such a firm is its (MFC, MRP) of labour curve, which is (horizontal, negatively sloped, positively sloped), due to the law of _____; the marginal cost to hiring labour for such a firm is its (MFC, MRP) of labour curve, which is (horizontal, positively sloped, negatively sloped). The firm's MFC curve rises because as it hires more labour, wage rates (fall, rise, remain constant) because the industry supply of labour curve is _____ sloping; the firm's MFC is (equal to, greater than, less than) the wage rate.

9.  Assume a firm is a monopolist in the product market and a monopsonist in the labour market. The marginal benefit to hiring labour for that firm is its (MFC, MRP) of labour curve, which falls due to _____ and _____ as output increases. The marginal cost to hiring labour is that firm's (MFC, MRP) of labour curve, which rises because in order to hire more labour, that firm must _____ wage rates of _____ employees; this is because the firm's supply of labour curve is _____ sloping.

10.  A firm maximizes total profits by hiring labour up to the point where the (MB > MC, MB < MC, MB = MC) of doing so. Suppose Firm A is a perfect competitor in the product market and a monopsonist in the labour market. Firm A will hire labour up to the point where a downward sloping (MFC, MRP) of labour curve intersects an upward sloping (MFC, MRP) of labour curve; given that quantity of labour, the wage rate will be set at that level consistent with the (supply, demand) curve of labour.

11.  Firm B is a monopolist in the product market and a monopsonist in the labour market. If it wants to maximize total profits, it will hire labour up to the point where a downward sloping (MFC, MRP) of labour curve intersects an upward sloping (MFC, MRP) of labour curve.

12.  When a resource is paid less than its (ARP, MRP), monopsonistic exploitation exists.


## TRUE-FALSE QUESTIONS

Circle the T if the statement is true, the F if it is false. Explain to yourself why a statement is false.

T  F  1.  The growth rate of unions and the extent to which unions are effective has depended on government support.

T  F  2.  The Supreme Court gave unions the right to strike.

T  F  3.  Unions were tranquil during the Great Depression.

T  F  4.  In recent years, strikes have increased significantly.

T  F  5.  Unions tend to create a shortage of labour and a surplus of jobs.

T  F  6.  In Canada, unions can set wage rates or determine the quantity of labour hired, but they can't do both.

T  F  7.  If a union wants to maximize the value of total wages, it sets wage rates as high as it possibly can.

T  F  8.  If a union can restrict the total quantity of labourers to a fixed number, its members must earn higher wages in the future.

T  F  9.  Recent studies indicate that unions do not increase labour's productivity.

T  F  10.  A profit-maximizing firm that is a perfect competitor in the product market but a monopsonist in the labour market will hire labour up to the point where MRP of labour equals the going wage rate.

T  F  11.  A firm that is a monopolist in the product market and a monopsonist in the labour market maximizes total profit by hiring labour up to the point where the MRP of labour equals the MFC of labour.

T  F  12.  The NCAA qualifies as a cartel with monopsony power.

T  F  13.  Monopsonistic exploitation exists when workers receive a wage below their MRP.

**MULTIPLE CHOICE QUESTIONS**
Circle the letter that corresponds to the best answer.

1.  Which of the following is true about the union movement?
    a.  The growth and effectiveness of unions depends in part on the extent of government help.
    b.  Since 1967 union membership has risen.
    c.  Since the mid-1960's union membership has shifted into manufacturing away from the services sector.
    d.  All of the above

2.  Unions tend to
    a.  set minimum wages for members above the market clearing level.
    b.  create unemployment for low-seniority members.
    c.  create surpluses of labour and shortages of union jobs.
    d.  All of the above

3.  If a union sets wage rates above market clearing levels, then
    a.  jobs must be rationed among union members.
    b.  a surplus of jobs is created.
    c.  a shortage of labour is created.
    d.  high-seniority members will complain.

4.  Which of the following is inconsistent with the others?
    a.  surplus of labour
    b.  shortage of jobs
    c.  wage rate above market-clearing level
    d.  wage rate below market-clearing level

5.  If unions want to maximize the value of total wages, they set wage rates
    a.  as high as they can.
    b.  as low as they can.
    c.  where the price elasticity of demand for labour equals 1.
    d.  in the inelastic range of the product demand curve.

6.  If unions maximize the wage rate of high-seniority workers, then
    a.  low-seniority workers will become laid off.
    b.  all union members will remain employed.
    c.  they violate the Canadian Labour Congress Act.
    d.  they violate the Senitorial Act.

7.  Which of the following statements probably best describes the impact of unions on wage rates?
    a.  Unions have increased all wage rates in the economy.
    b.  Unions have increased all union worker wage rates.
    c.  Unions increase the wage rates of some workers at the expense of other workers.
    d.  Unions cannot raise wage rates for their members.

8.   Unions
     a.   can set wage rates, but not employment levels.
     b.   can set wage rates and employment levels.
     c.   can set neither wage rates nor employment levels.
     d.   can set either wage rates or employment levels, but not both.

9.   Unions, according to the Freeman-Medoff analysis,
     a.   on net, probably raise social efficiency.
     b.   reduce wage inequality.
     c.   create workplace practices valuable to workers and costless to management.
     d.   All of the above

10.  If Firm B is a monopsonist in the labour market and a perfect competitor in the product market, then
     a.   it faces a horizontal supply of labour curve.
     b.   it faces a horizontal demand for labour curve.
     c.   its wage rate equals its MFC.
     d.   its MB to hiring labour equals the MRP of labour.

11.  Firm B, in the previous question (No. 10), can maximize total profits by hiring labour up to the point where
     a.   a decreasing MRP of labour curve intersects a decreasing MFC of labour curve.
     b.   a decreasing MRP of labour curve intersects a rising MFC of labour curve.
     c.   a decreasing MRP of labour curve intersects a horizontal supply of labour curve, at the going wage rate.
     d.   a horizontal MRP of labour curve is intersected by a rising MFC of labour curve.

12.  Firm B, in questions 10 and 11, faces a(n)
     a.   rising MFC of labour.
     b.   declining labour MRP
     c.   upward sloping supply of labour curve.
     d.   All of the above

13.  If Firm A is a monopolist in the product market and a monopsonist in the labour market, then
     a.   it faces a horizontal labour supply and a horizontal labour demand curve.
     b.   it faces a downward sloping supply of labour curve.
     c.   its MB of hiring labour falls and its marginal cost to hiring labour rises.
     d.   its MB to hiring labour is constant and its marginal cost to hiring labour rises.

14.  Firm A, in the previous question (No. 13), can maximize total profits by hiring labour up to the point where
     a.   a downward sloping MRP of labour curve intersects an upward sloping MFC of labour curve.
     b.   an upward sloping MRP of labour equals a constant wage rate.
     c.   a constant MRP of labour curve equals a falling MFC of labour.
     d.   a horizontal MRP of labour curve is intersected by a rising supply of labour curve.

15.   Firm A in question 13
   a.   observes a MFC that exceeds the wage rate.
   b.   observes a selling price that exceeds the marginal revenue of an extra unit of output.
   c.   maximizes profits by hiring where MRP of labour = MFC of labour.
   d.   All of the above

16.   The NCAA
   a.   cannot regulate the number of athletes a university can "hire."
   b.   cannot enforce its regulations and rules.
   c.   sets the prices, wages, and conditions under which universities can "hire" student athletes.
   d.   sets the "wage rates" for student athletes at levels above their market value.

17.   Which of the following is probably an example of monopsony exploitation, as defined in this text?
   a.   A low-skilled labourer is paid $1 per hour in a competitive labour market.
   b.   A professional athlete gets paid $1 million per year but his MRP is $1.5 million per year.
   c.   Mr. Smith can earn $35,000 per year as a plumber but chooses to work as a high school teacher for $20,000 per year.
   d.   Mrs. Calvo has a Ph.D. in English, but only earns $10,000 per semester teaching university English because there are so many qualified teachers in that area.

18.   Monopsonistic exploitation equals
   a.   marginal physical product of labour minus the wage rate.
   b.   marginal revenue product of labour minus the wage rate.
   c.   marginal physical product of labour minus marginal revenue product of labour.
   d.   marginal factor cost of labour minus marginal physical product.

## WORKING WITH GRAPHS

1.  Suppose you are given the following graphical representation for a monopsonist selling its output in a competitive market.  Answer the following questions.

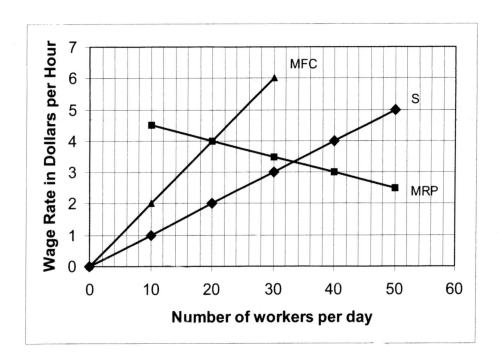

  a.  Given the market conditions that exist in the above graph, the monopsonist will hire _____ workers per day at a wage of _____ per hour.

  b.  Suppose that the government (or a labour union) initiates a minimum wage of $2.50 per hour in this particular market.  As a result, the monopsonist will (increase, decrease) its employment rate to _____ workers per day at a wage of _____ per hour.

2.  Use the graph below to answer the following questions.  Note:  define monopolistic exploitation as being equal to the difference between VMP (or price times the marginal product of labour) and MRP—as defined in the text.  (Note: VMP is not defined in your text, therefore this is a difficult question.  It is purely optional.)

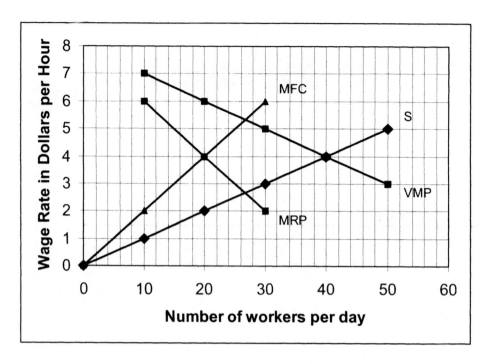

a.  This monopolist-monopsonist will hire _____ workers per day and pay a wage of _____ per hour.

b.  At this rate of employment, the value of marginal product of labour (VMP) is _____ per hour.

c.  With no outside intervention in this market, we will observe (monopsonistic, monopolistic, both monopsonistic and monopolistic) exploitation.

d.  The level of monopsonistic exploitation is _____ per hour, and the level of monopolistic exploitation is _____ per hour.

e.  The total level of exploitation is _____ per hour, represented by the difference between the _____ and _____.

## BUSINESS SECTION

### Accounting: Buying Power and Retail Markups

In the context of labour markets the text explains how monopsony power can enhance the firm's overall profit by keeping labour costs below the marginal revenue product. One can apply this same concept to illustrate how market power on the buyers side can enhance the levels of markup that a firm can achieve when purchasing merchandise for resale from a manufacturer. It is important to note that the firm with buying power can achieve a higher markup without having to raise the retail price to the consumer. Thus this type of market power is much more difficult to detect by less fortunate competitors.

Consider the following example. Audrey's Outerwear is a small independent retail store which specializes in selling stylish high quality trench coats. During 2000, Audrey's sold 1000 trench coats at the "manufacturer's suggested retail price" (MSR) of $300 per coat. Since Audrey's is not large enough to possess "buying power" the manufacturer provides a typical "markup structure of 45 points" which means a 45% markup based on the retail price. Assuming that operating expenses are 30% of sales, calculate the annual net profit achieved in 2000 by constructing a simple retail income statement.

| | | |
|---|---|---|
| Sales | (300 x 1000) | $300,000 |
| Cost of Goods Sold | (.55 x 300 x 1000) | $165,000 |
| Gross Margin | (.45 x 300 x 1000) | $135,000 |
| Operating Expenses | (.30 x 300 x 1000) | $ 90,000 |
| Net Profit | (135000 – 90000) | $ 45,000 |

## Business Application Problem

Global Rainwear is a large international retail chain. Global sells the same trench coat that Audrey's specializes in. However with 1200 retail stores worldwide, Global sells over a million of these trench coats each year. With this type of "buying clout" the manufacturer provides Global with a "markup structure of 65 points".

a.  Assuming that Global sells 1000 trench coats in each of its stores, and assuming that operating expenses are also 30% of sales, calculate the net profit for one of Global's typical stores.

b.  Is the higher level of profit enjoyed by Global, in each of its stores , based on its operating efficiency or is it based on its market power?

## ANSWERS TO CHAPTER 16

### COMPLETION QUESTIONS

1.  craft; trade; industrial; industry
2.  collective bargaining; strike
3.  Rand formula; dues
4.  European
5.  strike
6.  surplus; shortage
7.  must; 1; low-seniority
8.  MRP; negatively sloped; diminishing returns; MFC; positively sloped; rise; upward; greater than
9.  MRP; diminishing marginal physical product of labour; decreasing product price; MFC; raise; all; upward
10.  MB = MC; MRP; MFC; supply
11.  MRP; MFC
12.  marginal revenue product (MRP)

## TRUE-FALSE QUESTIONS

1.   T
2.   T
3.   F   Unions were in turmoil during the Great Depression.
4.   F   Strike have decreased in recent years.
5.   F   Unions create a surplus of labour and a shortage of jobs.
6.   T
7.   F   A union will set wage rates where the price elasticity of demand equals 1.
8.   F   Not necessarily; demand for workers may fall dramatically.
9.   F   Unions may increase productivity by creating a safer and securer environment.
10.  F   A profit-maximizing firm hires up to where MRP = MFC of labour
11.  T
12.  T
13.  T

## MULTIPLE CHOICE QUESTIONS

1.a; The policies of governments towards unions can impact the unions.
2.d; Unions do impact the labour market.
3.a; A surplus of workers is created.
4.d; A wage rate below market-clearing level would create a shortage of labour.
5.c; Some members will be unemployed.
6.a; The least senior workers can lose their jobs.
7.c; Usually long term workers win, short term workers lose.
8.d; Wage rates will impact employment levels.
9.d; Unions can reduce profits as well.
10.d; They will not hire when MPR is greater than MB.
11.b; MRP = MFC.
12.d; All of these choices are true.
13.c; This is a bilateral monopoly.
14.a; MPR = MFC.
15.d; All of these choices are true.
16.c; The NCAA operates as a cartel.
17.b; The athlete is paid less than their contribution.
18.b; Marginal revenues are higher than the wages.

## WORKING WITH GRAPHS

1.   a. 20, $2;   b. increase, 25, $2.50
2.   a. 20, $2;   b. $6;   c. both monopsonistic and monopolistic;   d. $2,$2;
     e. $4, VMP of $6 per hour, wage of $2 per hour

## BUSINESS SECTION

|   | | | |
|---|---|---|---|
| a. | Sales | (300 x 1000) | $300,000 |
|   | Cost of Goods Sold (.35 x 300 x 1000) | | $105,000 |
|   | Gross Margin | (.65 x 300 x 1000) | $195,000 |
|   | Operating Expenses (.30 x 300 x 1000) | | $ 90,000 |
|   | Net Profit | (135000 – 90000) | $105,000 |

b.   Global's higher profit level ($60,000 per store) is based solely on its ability to negotiate a lower cost per unit with the manufacturer as a result of "buying power".

**ANSWERS TO EXAMPLE QUESTIONS FOR CRITICAL ANALYSIS**

I   **INTERNATIONAL EXAMPLE 16-1: Europe's Management-Labour Councils** (p. 369)
Canadian unions are probably opposed to the idea of labour-management cooperation in the decision making process in the firm. This would violate the separation of labour and management as practiced in Canada, and blur the historical roles of unions and management. Also, quality circles could lead to a situation where unions might not be needed.

II  **EXAMPLE 16-1: Strike Activity in Canada** (p. 371)
A strike might help organized labour not only be in the area of wages, but in the area of benefits. Many strikes are not only about wages but also about working conditions, pensions, medical coverage and dental plans. Skilled workers are a lot harder to replace with strikebreakers then unskilled workers. Management will be more likely to offer profit sharing to their skilled workers. If workers know that they will share in any profits the firm achieves they are a lot less likely to strike.

III **INTERNATIONAL EXAMPLE 16-2: Monopsony in College Sports** (p. 377)
The major argument that college athletics is related to academics is that the players are also students. For many players, the athletic scholarship is what allows them to enroll in college. In many sports there are no large revenues to be earned for the average school (for example, track, soccer, golf, or tennis) and at the smaller colleges the athletics programs do not even pay for themselves through ticket sales, let alone through contracts with the media. The athletes are essentially supported by scholarships that allow them to attend college.

# CHAPTER 17

# RENT, INTEREST, AND PROFITS

## PUTTING THIS CHAPTER INTO PERSPECTIVE

Chapters 15 and 16 dealt with labour and its payment: wage rates. Chapter 17 analyzes land, capital, and entrepreneurship, and the (roughly) corresponding payments to those factors: rent, interest, and profits.

Probably the most important thing you can learn from this chapter is that rent, interest, and profits (and wage rates too) are *prices*. As such they perform an allocative function; in a market economy, land, capital, and labour flow to the highest (business) bidder. (Profits are a little more difficult to analyze; we deal with them later in this section.) In general, the highest bidders will be those firms that are the most profitable or have the best profit record in the past. Consequently, through the price system, resources flow from less profitable firms to more profitable firms; this means that resources (factors of production) flow from lower-valued to higher-valued uses, and economic efficiency prevails. To the extent that governmental price controls such as minimum wage laws exist, then economic efficiency suffers. Inefficiency results also when governments subsidize firms that are going bankrupt. Note, however, that just because government economic policies are inefficient does not mean that we *should not* permit such interferences; remember that questions of "should" are normative in nature. Economists can only present the results of their positive economic analysis to society; society can then determine whether or not other matters outweigh efficiency considerations.

Rent is typically regarded as a payment for land. Economists have extended the term *rent* to include the payment to any resource that is fixed in supply. More specifically, we define economic rent as the payment to any resource over and above what is necessary to keep the resource in supply at its current level. This extended concept of rent permits us to analyze economic rents involved with professional athletes and entertainers. Note again the point about price as an allocating, or rationing, device. Suppose Eddie Vedder would be *willing* to perform for $500 a night. At such a price he would be in great demand and a shortage of his services would exist. If a law were passed that limited his income to $500 a performance, his economic rents would disappear, but how would we ration his performances? That is, where would he entertain? In a market system, his shows might be bid up to $100,000 a night. Eddie Vedder sells his services to the highest bidder and earns economic rents, and economic efficiency obtains. Society maximizes the value of his services, because the highest bidders value his services most highly.

Interest is the cost of obtaining credit; it arises because most people prefer to consume in the present rather than in the future—due to the uncertainty of life. In order to induce people to save now, they are offered interest, which permits them to consume more in the future. Borrowers can reward lenders in the future if they use the funds (saving) so obtained to produce capital goods that increase output in the future. Hence we have a supply of credit by savers and a demand for credit by businesses, and the interest rate is thereby established. The interest rate is a price, and it allocates credit to the highest bidder; ultimately physical capital is being allocated because business-borrowers purchase capital goods with the money they borrow. Capital is allocated to its most profitable use and economic efficiency results.

Profits are less easy to analyze. The economic function of profit is to help society decide which industries, and which firms within an industry, are to expand and which are to contract. In the process, resources move from lower-valued to higher-valued uses.

## LEARNING OBJECTIVES

After you have studied this chapter you should be able to

1. define economic rent, interest, nominal rate of interest, real rate of interest, present value, rate of discount, and discounting.

2. understand the allocative function of economic rents.

3. distinguish between the nominal interest rate and the real interest rate.

4. calculate the (approximate) nominal interest rate, given the real interest rate and the anticipated rate of inflation.

5. list three things that account for variations in interest rates.

6. answer questions that require an understanding of the rationing function of rent, interest, and profits.

7. calculate the present value of an amount of money to be received at a future date.

## CHAPTER OUTLINE

1. **Economic rent** is a payment for the use of any resource that is in fixed supply.
   a. Land is often believed to be in fixed supply.
   b. Even if land is absolutely in fixed supply, rent payments help society to decide how land is to be used.
   c. **Economic rents** also accrue to factors of production other than land.
   d. Rents help society decide how to allocate a factor fixed in supply.

2.  The term **interest** is used to mean two things:  (1) the price paid by debtors to creditors for the use of loanable funds, and (2) the market return earned by capital as a factor of production.
    a.  **Interest** is the payment for obtaining credit.
    b.  **Interest** rates vary with the length of loan, risk, and handling charges.
    c.  The equilibrium rate of interest is found at the intersection of the downward sloping demand for loanable funds curve and the upward sloping supply of loanable funds curve.
    d.  The **nominal interest** rate is (approximately) equal to the sum of the **real interest rate** and the expected rate of inflation.
    e.  The **interest** rate, ultimately, allocates physical capital to various firms for investment projects.

3.  **Interest** rates link the present with the future.
    a.  A money value in the future can be expressed in today's value by a process referred to as **discounting** to present worth.
    b.  **Discounting** is the method by which the **present value** of a future sum, or a stream of future sums, is obtained.
    c.  The **rate of discount** is the interest rate used in the **discounting** to present worth equation.

4.  Profit is the reward to the entrepreneurial factor of production.
    a.  **Accounting profits** are the difference between total revenues and total explicit costs; **economic profits** equal the difference between total revenues and the opportunity cost of all factors of production.
    b.  Various explanations for profit exist.
        i.   **Economic profits** can be the result of barriers to entry.
        ii.  Some economists, notably Joseph Schumpeter, maintain that economic profits result from innovation.
        iii. Frank Knight believed that profit is the reward for assuming uninsurable risk.
    c.  The function of economic profit is to (a) spur innovation and investment and (b) allocate resources from lower-valued to higher-valued uses.

## KEY TERMS AND CONCEPTS

Economic rent
Interest
Nominal rate of interest
Real rate of interest
Present value

Discounting
Rate of discount
Economic profit
Accounting profit

## COMPLETION QUESTIONS
Fill in the blank or circle the correct term.

1. A payment for the use of any resource that is (fixed, variable) in supply is an economic rent.

2. Frank Knight believed that profit was the reward for assuming (insurable, uninsurable) risk.

3. Interest is the cost of obtaining (cash, credit).  Interest is used to mean two different things:  (1) _____, and (2) _____.

4. Interest rates vary due to _____, _____, and _____.

5. Interest rates are determined at the intersection of the demand for (loanable, non-loanable) funds curve and the supply of (loanable, non-loanable) funds curve.  The supply curve is positively sloped because as people save more, the marginal utility of *present* consumption (falls, rises, remains constant); therefore before people will save more, the interest rate must _____.

6. The three major sources of demand for loanable funds are _____, _____, and _____.

7. The consumer demand for loanable funds exists because people, typically, prefer to consume (earlier than later, later than earlier); businesses demand loanable funds for investments that increase _____.

8. The nominal interest rate equals the real interest rate plus the _____; ultimately the interest rate allocates (labour, physical capital) to various firms for investment projects.

9. If a factor is fixed in supply, society must decide who gets to use it; _____ plays this allocative role.

10. The process of finding the value today of a sum of money in the future is called _____; the interest rate used in that process is called the _____ rate.

## TRUE-FALSE QUESTIONS
Circle the T if the statement is true, the F if it is false.  Explain to yourself why a statement is false.

T  F    1.  Economic rent accrues only to the factor land.

T  F    2.  Economic rent is the price paid to a factor that is perfectly elastic in supply.

T  F    3.  If economic rent was totally taxed away, society would have to decide who gets to use the resource in question.

T  F    4.  For a factor fixed in supply, economic rent has no economic function.

T  F    5.  Economic rent occurs because specific resources have perfect substitutes.

T  F    6.  If a rock star prices tickets at a price way below equilibrium, that is an efficient way to help poor people.

T  F    7.  Other things being constant, the greater the risk of non-repayment, the higher the interest rate.

T  F    8.  At higher interest rates, businesses will find fewer investments in capital goods profitable, other things being constant.

T  F    9.  The nominal interest rate (approximately) equals the real rate of interest plus the expected interest rate.

T  F    10.  Ultimately, the interest rate allocates physical capital to *specific firms* and households.

T  F    11.  Discounting is the process of converting future money values to present worth.

T  F    12.  Profits serve no economic function.

T  F    13.  Accounting profits are less than economic profits.

T  F    14.  State lotteries understate the true value of their awards.

T  F    15.  If an inefficient firm goes bankrupt, that is socially efficient.

## MULTIPLE CHOICE QUESTIONS
Circle the letter that corresponds to the best answer.

1.  For a factor that earns economic rent,
    a.  its quantity varies only in the long run.
    b.  its supply is perfectly elastic.
    c.  its supply curve is perfectly inelastic.
    d.  no taxation is possible because no surplus exists.

2.    In David Ricardo's economic model,
      a.  land was fixed in supply.
      b.  wages and salaries were set by government.
      c.  land rent falls as industrialization occurs.
      d.  All of the above

3.    Economic rents
      a.  have no allocative function.
      b.  have no economic function.
      c.  do not bring forth a greater quantity of the resource.
      d.  exist only for land.

4.    Mr. Pulsinelli earns $800,000 per year as a tennis pro; he could earn, at best,
      $100,000 per year as an economist.  Which statement is the most accurate?
      a.  He should be a tennis pro.
      b.  He would earn economic rents as a tennis pro.
      c.  He would earn economic rents as an economist.
      d.  His comparative advantage is as an economist.

5.    Credit card interest rates are high because
      a.  such loans are unsecured.
      b.  of adverse selection.
      c.  risks are high to the issuers of credit cards.
      d.  All of the above

6.    Economic rents
      a.  accrue only to land.
      b.  accrue only to labour.
      c.  accrue only to entrepreneurs.
      d.  can accrue to any factor, in principle.

7.    Other things being constant, the interest rate varies with the
      a.  length of a loan.
      b.  risk of non-repayment.
      c.  handling charges.
      d.  All of the above

8.    Which of the following statements is **NOT** true?
      a.  As people save more, their marginal utility for present consumption falls.
      b.  In order to induce households to save more, the interest rate must rise.
      c.  The supply of loanable funds curve is positively sloped.
      d.  At higher interest rates people substitute future consumption for present
          consumption.

9.    Which of the following statements is **NOT** true?
      a.  Households demand loanable funds to purchase durable goods.
      b.  Governments demand loanable funds to finance surpluses.
      c.  Businesses demand loanable funds to purchase investment capital.
      d.  Households demand loanable funds to maintain consumption when income falls
          temporarily.

10.   The nominal interest rate approximately equals the real interest rate
      a.  minus the expected interest rate.
      b.  plus the expected interest rate.
      c.  plus the expected rate of inflation.
      d.  minus the expected inflation rate.

11.   Interest rates
      a.  have no economic function.
      b.  allocate money capital to less efficient firms.
      c.  allocate physical capital to firms in a random manner.
      d.  allocate physical capital to specific firms for investment projects.

12.   Discounting
      a.  converts future dollar values into present values.
      b.  connects the future with the present.
      c.  uses the interest rate.
      d.  All of the above

13.   If the interest rate is 5 per cent, the present value of $100 that is to be received one
      year from now is about
      a.  $90
      b.  $950
      c.  $95
      d.  $105

14.   Profits
      a.  perform no economic function.
      b.  move resources from lower-valued to higher-valued uses.
      c.  provide useful information, but losses do not.
      d.  lead to a misallocation of resources because producers produce for profit, not
          for consumer needs.

15.   When Miller won a $1,000,000 lottery in British Columbia, he found out that the
      money would be paid to him at the rate of $50,000 per year for the next twenty
      years.  Which of the following is probably true?
      a.  Miller will refuse the money, after he finds out what the lottery is really worth.
      b.  The lottery winnings are worth considerably less than $1 million.
      c.  Miller would *prefer* to receive his lottery winnings over twenty years, instead of
          all at once.
      d.  Miller would have preferred to receive $25,000 per year for 40 years.

## MATCHING
Choose the item in column (2) that best matches an item in column (1).

| (1) | (2) |
|---|---|

a. profit
b. real rate of interest
c. economic rent
d. present value calculation

1. inflationary expectation
2. nominal rate of interest
3. bearing uninsurable risk
4. payment for labour
5. discount rate
6. payment to resource fixed in supply

## WORKING WITH GRAPHS

1. Use the information given below to answer the questions that follow. The figures other than the rate of interest are given in thousands of dollars per month.

| Rate of interest | Quantity demanded of: | | Total loans | Supply of loanable funds |
|---|---|---|---|---|
| | Consumption loans | Investment loans | | |
| 16 | 10 | 30 | _____ | 300 |
| 14 | 20 | 40 | _____ | 250 |
| 12 | 30 | 60 | _____ | 200 |
| 10 | 40 | 100 | _____ | 140 |
| 8 | 50 | 140 | _____ | 90 |
| 6 | 60 | 180 | _____ | 50 |
| 4 | 70 | 210 | _____ | 30 |

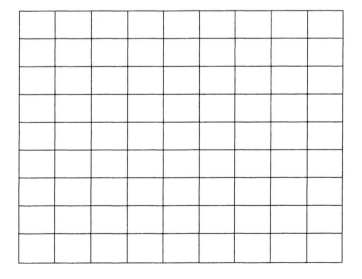

a. On the grid provided above, plot the demand curve for consumption loans and label it D (consumption), and plot the demand curve for investment loans and label it D (investment).

b. Complete the column for the total loans demanded in the above table.

c. On the above grid, plot the total demand curve for loanable funds and the supply curve for loanable funds.

d. The equilibrium rate of interest is _____, and the equilibrium quantity of loanable funds is _____ per month.

e. _____ per month will be lent for the purpose of consumption loans at equilibrium, and _____ will be lent for investment.

2. Use the following graphs to answer the questions that follow.

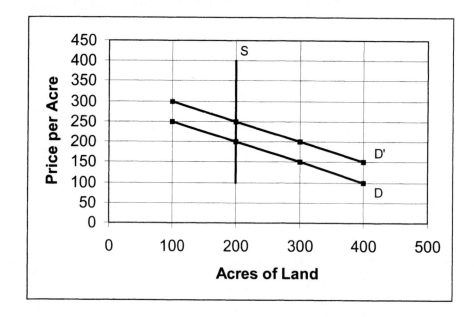

a. If the demand for land is represented by D, what is the total rent received by the owner of the 200 acres of land?

b. If the demand for land increases to D', what is the rent received by the landowner?

## PROBLEMS

1.  Suppose you win a lottery that offers the following payoff.  At the end of each year for the next 3 years you are to receive $1000.  At the end of each of the following 3 years you will receive $500, for a total of $4500 over the six-year period.  If the current going rate of interest is 8%, what is the present value of your winnings?  If someone offered you $3700 today for your lottery ticket, should you take it?

2.  Gladstone Gander just learned that a long-lost aunt has set up a trust for him, whereby he will receive $1 million exactly ten years from now.  Assume that the relevant interest rate is 10 percent.
    a.  Can Gladstone sell his inheritance, right now, for $1 million?  Why or why not?

    b.  What is the present value of Gladstone's inheritance?

3.  Suppose that you had used a discount rate of 20 percent in question (2) above.  How would you answer (a) and (b) now?

    a.  How are present value and the interest rate related?

## BUSINESS SECTION

### Small Business and Finance: Determining the Price of a Business

The text explains how one can use the interest rate to find the present value of a lump sum in the future.  The following example illustrates the use of the interest rate in determining the present value of an annuity, which is a series of equal payments made at periodic intervals in the future. Finding the present value of an annuity is one common way potential buyers of a business can determine the maximum price to pay for a business.

The following time line describes an annuity consisting of  N annual payments starting one year from now.

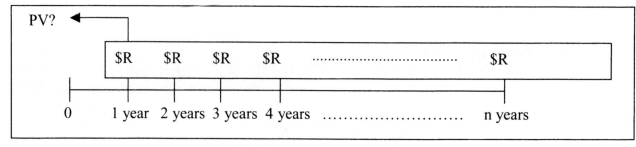

The present value of an annuity consisting of N annual payments starting one year from now is:

$$PV = \$R\left(\frac{1-(1+i)^{-n}}{i}\right)$$

## Business Application Problem

Bill Clinstone is thinking of purchasing The Cinammon Roll which is a franchise outlet located in a food court of a large suburban mall. Based on information sent by the franchiser, Bill projects that the business will last about 10 years and will yield an annual net profit (after taxes) of $38,000 per year starting one year from now. Bill does not plan to work in this small business. The funds to be used to pay for this business are currently invested in mutual funds, which earn an annual compound rate of return of 9%.

    a.   Calculate the maximum price that Bill should pay for The Cinammon Roll. Hint: Find the present value of the annuity consisting of the 10 annual profit payments of $38,000 each. Use 9% as the interest rate in the annuity formula.

    b.   If Bill pays the maximum price calculated in a. above, what amount of economic profit would he earn from the Cinammon Roll?

### ANSWERS TO CHAPTER 17

**COMPLETION QUESTIONS**

1.   fixed
2.   uninsurable
3.   credit; price paid by creditors to debtors, return to capital
4.   length of loan, risk of non-repayment, handling charges
5.   loanable funds, loanable funds; rises; rise
6.   households, businesses, governments
7.   earlier than later; profits or productivity
8.   expected inflation rate; physical capital
9.   economic rent
10.   discounting; discount

## TRUE-FALSE QUESTIONS

1.   F   Economic rent accrues to any factor fixed in supply.
2.   F   Economic rent is the price paid to a perfectly *in*elastic resource supply.
3.   T
4.   F   Economic rent allocates the fixed factor to its highest-valued use.
5.   F   Rent is earned by resources that cannot be replicated exactly.
6.   F   Giving poor people money income directly would be more efficient.
7.   T
8.   T
9.   F   Plus the expected *inflation (not expected interest)* rate.
10.  T
11.  T
12.  F   They help to allocate capital, and they help to decide which firms should grow and which should contract.
13.  F   They normally exceed economic profits because the latter takes into account the opportunity costs of factors of production; accounting profits do not.
14.  F   They overstate, because they don't tell the discounted value.
15.  T

## MULTIPLE CHOICE QUESTIONS

1.c; Supply of the resource is limited.
2.a; Society helps decide how land will be used.
3.c; Supply is fixed.
4.b; Economic rent is payment for a resource that is fixed.
5.d; All of these choices are true.
6.d; Economic rents are payments for the use of a resource that is in fixed supply
7.d; Interest varies with the length, risk and handling charges.
8.a; Their interest rate will also rise.
9.b; Governments need them to finance deficits.
10.c; Nominal means unadjusted for inflation while real means adjusted for inflation.
11.d; Interest rates allocate resources to more efficient firms.
12.d; In discounting the present value of a future sum is obtained.
13.c; $P = S(1 + I)^{-n}$ so, $100(1 + 5\%)^{-1} = 95$
14.b; Profits also spurs innovation and investment.
15.b; The present value is not $1,000,000.

## MATCHING

a and 3;   b and 1;   c and 6;   d and 5

## WORKING WITH GRAPHS

1.    a. See the graph below.

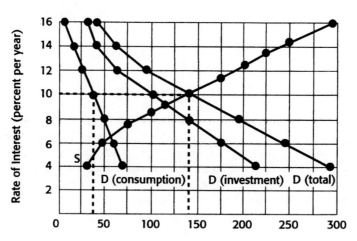

Loanable Funds per Month (in thousands of dollars)

   b. 40, 60, 90, 140, 190, 240, 280;
   c. See the graph above;
   d. 10 percent, $140,000;
   e. $40,000, $100,000
2.  a. $40,000;  b. $50,000

## PROBLEMS

1. From Table 17-2 on page 392 of your text we can see:

| Year | Present Value | (Found by) |
|------|---------------|------------|
| 1 | $ 926.00 | (.926 x 1000) |
| 2 | 857.00 | (.857 x 1000) |
| 3 | 794.00 | (.794 x 1000) |
| 4 | 367.50 | (.735 x 500) |
| 5 | 340.50 | (.681 x 500) |
| 6 | 315.00 | (.630 x 500) |
| Total | $3600.00 | |

  Yes, you would be $100 better off, as is seen by the present value calculation.
2. a. No, no one would give him $1 million right now because such a sum could be invested and earn interest for ten years, and at the end of that period it would be worth $1 million plus the accumulated interest.
  b. $\dfrac{\$1,000,000}{(1.1)^{10}} = \dfrac{\$1,000,000}{2.5937425} = \$385,543$
   Or from Table 17-2, use the discount factor of .385.
3. a. See (2) above
  b. $161,506.
  c. They are inversely related.

**BUSINESS SECTION**

a.   Maximum Price = PV = $38000\left(\dfrac{1-(1+9\%)^{-10}}{9\%}\right)= \$38000\left(\dfrac{1-(1.09)^{-10}}{.09}\right)=38000$ x

=$243,871

b.   If Bill pays the full $243,871 he will just earn an annual return of 9% which is equal to his next best alternative (mutual funds) so he will earn a normal profit. If Bill can purchase the franchise for less than $243,871 he will earn a rate of return in excess of 9% or a positive economic profit.

c.   government, with its taxing powers, is more able to pay back interest and principal to investors.

## ANSWERS TO EXAMPLE QUESTIONS FOR CRITICAL ANALYSIS

I    **INTERNATIONAL EXAMPLE 17-1: Do Entertainment Superstars Make Super Economic Rents?** (p. 393)
The forces that cause superstars to earn high incomes are all related to the demand for their talent. By definition there is only one Harrison Ford. Because his movies earn large amounts of money, producers seek his acting services. His problem is that the number of parts he is offered is more than he could possibly take on. He can thus limit the demand for his services (and the hassles by those who wish to employ him) by accepting only the highest offers, and be known to only accept very high offers.

II   **POLICY EXAMPLE 17-1: Should Rent-to-Own Stores Be Regulated?** (p. 396)
If cost-of-credit legislation is passed, the growth of rent-to-own stores should slow. The rent-to-own stores will not admit to charging interest. Consumers may refuse to pay the high interest but the rent-to-own stores serve a certain demand.

III  **INTERNATIONAL EXAMPLE 17-2: Combating Japanese Loan Sharks with "Instant Cash Loans"** (p. 397)
One of the factors would be the lack of competition in the banking industry in Japan. If customers have been  charged high rates of interest in the past, then even a small drop in the rate would be considered significant.  Inflation also would have an impact on interest rates. Government borrowing can cause crowding out, increasing the interest rates.

IV   **INTERNATIONAL EXAMPLE 17-3: *Viager*, or Betting on an Early Death (Someone Else's)** (p. 401)
Payments on a life insurance policy are based on the extended life of the policy holder. The present value of the policy, i.e. its face value, is the discounted stream of future payments to the insurance company during the policy period. The shorter that period, the greater will be the payment given policy face value. In a *viager* contract the same principal would apply. If a person was buying a house worth $100,000 now (i.e. its present value), then larger payments would be required by an older house owner as compared with a younger one, other things being equal. Since the discount rate would of necessity be the same on both contracts, the payments would have to be different to make the present value the same for any seller or buyer.

# CHAPTER 18

# INCOME AND POVERTY

## PUTTING THIS CHAPTER INTO PERSPECTIVE

To this point we have analyzed factor markets and learned how factors of production are evaluated and priced in competitive and noncompetitive markets. Ultimately, payments to factors of production represent income to the people who own those factors. Chapter 18 explores how those incomes are distributed across the population.

It might be helpful for you to think of a "natural" distribution of income that would result from a perfectly competitive economic system. Each person would be paid (approximately, subject to imperfect information limitations) his or her marginal revenue product—for labour and nonlabour resources. Such a distribution of income would doubtless be very uneven because we each have different talents and skills, and we each start out with different degrees of family connections, inherited property, and other variables that potentially affect income. Depending on the tastes of society, a good deal of inequality of income results from the amount of luck (or ill fortune) in the match between inherent physical and mental traits and consumer tastes. Then, of course, there are traits that we can acquire by training and/or hard work.

Although such an unequal distribution might be "natural" in some sense, it hardly follows that such a distribution is desirable. A "natural" distribution of income can theoretically be consistent with a very small number having extremely high incomes and a large number living at near-subsistence.

This brings us to a potential problem. A "natural" distribution does have some benefits: it is consistent with economic freedom and provides economic incentives for people to improve their marginal productivity through training, education, risk-taking, and old-fashioned hard work. In contrast, a natural distribution of income also reflects mere luck. One's income may be relatively low due to a failure to inherit traits and characteristics that the marketplace (which reflects society's tastes for goods and services) values, or to a failure to inherit wealth from one's ancestors.

Unfortunately, when we tax some to give to others we affect economic incentives and economic freedom. In short, there is a trade-off between income equality and economic efficiency. There is, therefore, an optimal amount of inequality, but such an optimum depends on one's particular value system. The optimal distribution of income cannot be derived through positive economics; once again economic analysis can provide only limited aid in solving a crucial societal problem.   Nevertheless, economic analysis can serve to remind us that there are costs, as well as benefits, to redistributing income through government tax and transfer programs.  Combating poverty has proven to be a difficult problem.

## LEARNING OBJECTIVES

After you have studied this chapter you should be able to

1.   define distribution of income, Lorenz curve, income in kind, comparable-worth doctrine, and age-earnings cycle.

2.   list criticisms of using the Lorenz curve as an indicator of the degree of income inequality in a country.

3.   distinguish between income and wealth.

4.   recognize facts concerning income distribution and poverty in Canada.

5.   list three determinants of income differences.

6.   list two normative standards of income distribution and distinguish between them.

7.   describe the situation of poverty in Canada.

8.   list ways poverty is reduced in Canada.

## CHAPTER OUTLINE

1.   This chapter attempts to define **distribution of income** and present theories of why income is unevenly distributed across the population.

2.   The **Lorenz curve** is a geometric representation of the **distribution of income**.
     a.   There are some criticisms of using the **Lorenz curve** to measure the degree of income inequality in a nation.
          i.    The curve does not take into account income in kind.
          ii.   It does not account for differences in family size and effort.
          iii.  It does not account for age differences.
          iv.   It measures pretax money income.
          v.    It does not measure underground economy earnings.
     b.   In 25 years the distribution of money income in Canada has not changed very much.
     c.   Since World War II, the share of total income, which includes **in-kind** benefits, going to the bottom 20 percent of households has probably more than doubled.

3.  Wealth and income arc not synonymous.
    a.  Wealth is a stock concept, and income is a flow concept.
    b.  A stock is evaluated at a given moment in time; a flow is evaluated during a period of time.
    c.  Each of us inherits a different endowment, including human attributes and nonhuman wealth, which strongly affects our ability to earn income in the marketplace.

4.  There are numerous determinants of income differences.
    a.  The **wage-earnings cycle** typically shows that at a young age income is low; it builds gradually to a peak at around age 50, and then gradually curves down until it approaches zero at retirement age.
    b.  In competitive markets, workers can expect to earn, approximately, their marginal revenue product (MRP).
    c.  Determinants of an individual's marginal productivity include innate abilities and attributes, education, experience, and training.

5.  Inheritance is also a determinant of income differences.

6.  Discrimination also contributes somewhat to income differences. White males, on average, hold jobs in the highest-paying occupations; the lowest-paying jobs are held by nonwhite males, and by white and nonwhite females.

7.  The **comparable-worth doctrine** contends that females (or minorities) should receive the same wages as males if the levels of skills and responsibility in their different jobs are equal.  Skill and responsibility levels, in practice, are difficult to define and arbitrariness inevitably results in setting such wage rates.

8.  Investment in human capital, on average, earns a rate of return on a par with the rate of return to investment in other areas.

9.  There are normative standards of income distribution:  equality and productivity.

10. Western nations have sustained enough economic growth over the last several hundred years so that mass poverty has disappeared.

11. If poverty is measured in absolute terms, it will be eliminated by economic growth.  If poverty is defined in relative terms, it will be mathematically impossible to eliminate it, unless everyone has the same income—an improbable event.

12. There are a variety of income-maintenance programs designed to help the poor; they include Employment Insurance, Canada Pension Plan , and  the Old Age Security Plan.

13. In spite of the numerous programs in existence, the poverty rate has shown no long run tendency decline.

14. More income equality reduces economic incentives to both the people who are taxed and the people who receive transfers, and economic freedoms are reduced if more income equality is enforced; hence a trade-off exists between efficiency and equality of income.

15. Although the relative lot of the poor measured by household income seems to have worsened, the after-tax gap between the richest 20 percent and the poorest 20 percent of households has been narrowing.

## KEY TERMS AND CONCEPTS

Distribution of income                        Age-earnings cycle
Lorenz curve                                  Comparable-worth doctrine
Income in kind

## COMPLETION QUESTIONS
Fill in the blank or circle the correct term.

1.  A Lorenz curve shows what portion of total money income is accounted for by different (classes, proportions) of a nation's households; if it is a 45 degree line, then (high, zero) income inequality exists.

2.  The Lorenz curve as a representation of income inequality has been criticized because it does not account for (hours worked, taxes).

3.  In 1994, the lowest 20 percent of the income distribution in Canada had a combined money income of (5, 25) percent of the total money income of the entire population; however, if income in kind is taken into account, income inequality has (decreased, increased) since then.

4.  (Wealth, Income) is a stock concept, while (wealth, income) is a flow concept.

5.  One determinant of income inequality is age; the age-earnings cycle indicates that teenagers' incomes are relatively (low, high), then incomes rise gradually to a peak at around age (50, 60) and then gradually fall toward zero as people approach (middle age, retirement). People earn different amounts over their lifetime because age is related to a worker's (productivity, stability).

6.  If a worker's MRP exceeds her wage rate, chances are that she will (change jobs, be laid off); if a worker's wage rate is greater than her MRP, then chances are she will (change jobs, be laid off). As long as it is costly to obtain information about a specific worker's MRP, there (will, will not) be some difference between a worker's wage and his or her MRP.

7.  Two theories of normative standards of income distribution are (equality, inequality) and (productivity, stability).

8.  (Absolute, Relative) poverty will automatically be eliminated by economic growth, but (absolute, relative) poverty can never be eliminated, in practice.

9.  In Canada there are several income-maintenance programs aimed at eliminating poverty.    Such as Old _____ Security, Canada _____ Plan, _____ Insurance.

10.  In Canada there (has, has not) been a long-run trend toward reduced officially defined poverty.

11.  Many economists believe that the major cost to increased income equality is less economic (efficiency, productivity); hence a trade-off exists.

**TRUE-FALSE QUESTIONS**
Circle the T if the statement is true, the F if it false.  Explain to yourself why a statement is false.

T   F   1.   In the real world, no country has a linear (straight-line) Lorenz curve.

T   F   2.   When in-kind transfers are considered, measured income inequality in Canada rises and poverty levels fall.

T   F   3.   Not considering income-in-kind, the bottom 20 percent of Canadian income earners earn about 5% of total Canadian income.

T   F   4.   Income and wealth are unrelated.

T   F   5.   The comparable-worth doctrine accepts the notion that workers should be paid their MRP, as determined by markets.

T   F   6.   In Canada, over time, income inequality has increased dramatically.

T   F   7.   An age-earnings cycle exists because age and marginal productivity are related.

T   F   8.   In a competitive economy, workers tend to get paid their marginal revenue product.

T   F   9.   In Canada inheritance and discrimination are more important determinants of income differences than are marginal productivity differences.

T  F  10.   In Canada the return to investment in human capital is significantly higher than it is for other investments.

T  F  11.   Mass poverty is still a problem for even the advanced Western economies.

T  F  12.   Economic growth will eventually eliminate relative poverty.

T  F  13.   Despite massive sums of money devoted to income redistribution programs in Canada, officially measured poverty has remained roughly unchanged.

T  F  14.   All economists agree that more income equality in Canada is desirable.


## MULTIPLE CHOICE QUESTIONS
Circle the letter that corresponds to the best answer.

1.   The Lorenz curve
    a.   gives a numerical measure of a nation's degree of income inequality.
    b.   is a straight line in modern, industrial societies.
    c.   is a straight line in socialist countries.
    d.   overstates the true degree of income inequality, as it is currently measured.

2.   Which of the following is **NOT** a correct statement about the Lorenz curve?
    a.   It does not adjust for age.
    b.   It does not consider income-in-kind transfers.
    c.   It considers income earned in the underground economy.
    d.   It considers pretax income.

3.   In 1994, in Canada, the lowest 20 percent of income earning families had a combined income of about _____ percent of the total money income of the entire population.
    a.   5
    b.   10
    c.   15
    d.   20

4.   Analogy:  Income is to flow as _____ is to stock.
    a.   wealth
    b.   poverty
    c.   consumption
    d.   investment

5.   Total economic wealth
    a.   is a flow concept.
    b.   includes human attributes.
    c.   excludes non-human wealth.
    d.   is zero for most people in Canada.

6.    In Canada the long-run trend shows
      a.  increased poverty.
      b.  increased income inequality.
      c.  little change in officially measured poverty.
      d.  increased poverty once income-in-kind adjustments are made.

7.    In Canada, over the age-earnings cycle,
      a.  productivity changes.
      b.  income peaks at about age 65.
      c.  income rises with age, throughout.
      d.  income first falls with age, then rises with age.

8.    In Canada an age-earnings cycle exists because
      a.  age is unrelated to income.
      b.  age and income are related by law.
      c.  productivity and age are related.
      d.  of minimum wage laws.

9.    Which of the following is probably the **MOST** important determinant of income
      differences in Canada?
      a.  differences in marginal productivity
      b.  inheritance of non-human wealth
      c.  discrimination
      d.  welfare programs

10.   Which is **LEAST** like the others, with respect to productivity?
      a.  innate abilities and attributes
      b.  experience
      c.  education and training
      d.  inheritance of non-human wealth

11.   Which of the following does **NOT** occur with economic growth?
      a.  elimination of absolute poverty
      b.  elimination of relative poverty
      c.  increasing living standards
      d.  increasing life expectancy

12.   Which of the following could explain increased  poverty levels?
      a.  effect of increased welfare programs
      b.  downturn in overall business activity
      c.  reduced incentives to work due to means tested maintenance
      d.  All of the above

13.  The optimal amount of income inequality
    a.  is zero.
    b.  is a positive economics concept.
    c.  is a normative economics concept.
    d.  is agreed to by all economists.

14.  In a nation in which complete income equality has been achieved,
    a.  economic incentives would be reduced dramatically.
    b.  economic freedom would be curtailed dramatically.
    c.  national output and national income would fall dramatically.
    d.  All of the above

**MATCHING**
Choose the item in column (2) that best matches an item in column (1).

| (1) | (2) |
|---|---|
| a.  Lorenz curve | 1.  graphic measure of income distribution |
| b.  comparable-worth doctrine | 2  age-earnings cycle |
| c.  determinant of income inequality | 3.  stock |
| d.  wealth | 4.  flow |
| e.  income | 5.  geometric measure of income distribution |
|  | 6.  inherited traits or MRP |
|  | 7.  equal pay for equal work |

## WORKING WITH GRAPHS

1.  Use the table below and the grid provided to construct a Lorenz curve.

| Cumulative percent of population | Cumulative percent of income |
|:---:|:---:|
| 20 | 5 |
| 40 | 10 |
| 60 | 30 |
| 80 | 70 |
| 100 | 100 |

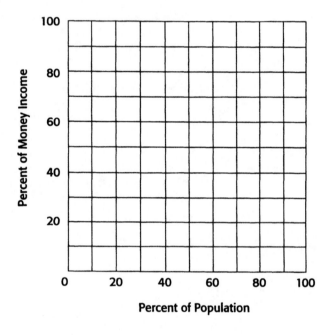

2.  Below are income figures for two countries.  Plot the Lorenz curve for both countries on the grid provided.

| Percent of population | Percent of Income Country A | Percent of Income Country B |
|---|---|---|
| 20 | 5 | 10 |
| 40 | 20 | 20 |
| 60 | 40 | 30 |
| 80 | 60 | 50 |
| 100 | 100 | 100 |

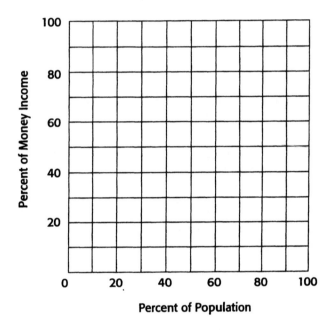

Which of the two countries has the more equal distribution?

**PROBLEM**

1.  In your text, you learned that income and wealth are different concepts.  But they can be related via the discounting technique that you learned in Chapter 17.  How?

# ANSWERS TO CHAPTER 18

## COMPLETION QUESTIONS

1.  proportions; zero
2.  taxes
3.  about 5; decreased
4.  Wealth; income
5.  low; 50; retirement; productivity
6.  change jobs; laid off; will
7.  equality; productivity
8.  Absolute; relative
9.  Social; minimum; dependent children
10. has not
11. efficiency
13. increased; older; increase; increased; little
14. ceiling; shortages

## TRUE-FALSE QUESTIONS

1.  T
2.  F    Income inequality falls.
3.  T
4.  F    The present value of income equals "human" wealth; see the problem section.
5.  F    The comparable-worth doctrine rejects MRP and substitutes an entirely different approach.
6.  F    Income inequality has remained constant, or fallen somewhat.
7.  T
8.  T
9.  F    Marginal productivity differences are the most important.
10. F    The rate of return is about the same.
11. F    Economic growth has eliminated mass poverty in advanced economies.
12. F    Relative poverty can never be eliminated.
13. T
14. F    Many believe income inequality is undesirable; almost all recognize its costs.

## MULTIPLE CHOICE QUESTIONS

1.  d;   The Lorenz curve does not adjust for family size, age, or underground earnings.
2.  c;   Underground income is difficult to track or eliminate.
3.  a;   Income in kind is not considered.
4.  a;   *TIP:* A stock is evaluated at a given moment in time.
5.  b;   Human attributes are not all equal.
6.  c;   Even with policies in place, there has been little change in poverty.
7.  a;   Earnings are low are a young age, peak at around 50, then gradually decrease.
8.  c;   Productivity increases with age, up to a certain point.
9.  a;   Differences in people due to talent, experience, and training determine the differences in marginal productivity.
10. d;   Inheritance is not a learned skill.
11. b;   Relative poverty can never be eliminated unless all earnings are equal.
12. d;   All of these answers could impact poverty levels.
13. c;   *TIP:* Productivity is also a normative economics concept.
14. d;   Complete income equality would leave no incentive to improve.

**MATCHING**

a and 5;    b and 7;    c and 6;    d and 3;    e and 4;

**WORKING WITH GRAPHS**

1.  See graphs below.

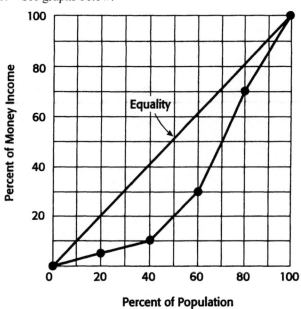

2.  See graphs below.  Country A has a more equal distribution of income.

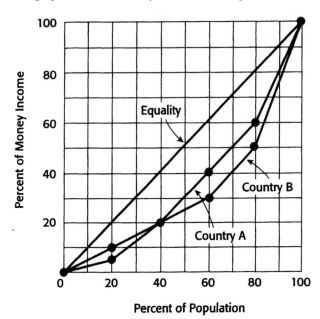

**PROBLEMS**

1.  The value of "human" wealth can be considered as being the present value of the (net) income stream
    that a person earns over his or her work life.

**ANSWERS TO EXAMPLE QUESTIONS FOR CRITICAL ANALYSIS**

**I    INTERNATIONAL EXAMPLE 18-1: Relative Income Inequality Throughout the Richest
Countries** (p. 412)

If the same group of individuals (or families) were getting the lowest 20 percent of income over a long
period of time with virtually no mobility between income groups, then there could be cause for
concern. In this case, it would be clear that opportunities for upward mobility were somehow being
prevented. If, on the other hand, a substantial number of families within each income group were
different each year, then one could conclude that income inequality was simply the outcome of relative
success in the economy. In this case, income inequality would not be as big an issue.

**II    EXAMPLE 18-1:  Are We Running to Stay in Place?** (p. 413)

Total compensation provides a person with a standard of living now and, when pension plans are
considered, in the future. Thus, employer provided health insurance allows a worker and that
individual's family to buy more nonmedical goods and services. Less must be saved for retirement if,
instead of higher wages, workers settle for part of their retirement program being paid by the employer,
and more can be used for current consumption. The point here is that compensation determines the
standard of living, regardless of whether it is in the form of take-home wages or divided up between
wage and nonwage benefits.

**III    EXAMPLE 18-2: Economists, Aging, and Productivity** (p. 416)

One of the major determinants of promotion, tenure, and raises in salary at most universities is an
economics professor's publication record. Younger economists will need to publish at the beginning of
their careers to gain tenure. Then promotion will depend in large part on the number of professional
publications. These are powerful incentives to publish for younger economists. Older economists will
most likely have become full professors. They cannot be promoted any higher and still remain in
teaching. They will have tenure in most cases. Thus there is considerably less incentive for such
professors to publish. Some publishing would still be predicted for older economists, however, since
annual raises are based in part on publication records at many universities.

**IV    INTERNATIONAL EXAMPLE 18-2: Poverty Rates in the European Union** (p. 420)

Comparing poverty rates across nations can be difficult because of all the factors that countries have to
take into consideration. Canada has no official poverty line although Statistics Canada does have a
low-income cutoff. This low-income cutoff includes such programs as, Employment Insurance,
Canada Pension Plan, scholarships and alimony payments. The question would then have to be asked,
do other nations have the same kinds of programs and are they included in their poverty measurements.
There is no agreement in Canada about what our poverty line is, so how can we expect to compare our
nations?

# CHAPTER 19

# ENVIRONMENTAL ECONOMICS

## PUTTING THIS CHAPTER INTO PERSPECTIVE

One of the most important concepts brought out in Chapter 19 is the notion of the socially optimum quantity of a good or service to produce.  The optimum quantity, from society's point of view, occurs where the MB to society equals the MC to society; at that quantity the opportunity cost to society of the last unit produced just equals the marginal benefit society derives from it.  By now you know that if the MB to society exceeds the MC to society, then society wants more; and if the MB to society is less than the MC to society, then society wants less.  In short, from society's point of view, if MB does not equal MC, then a misallocation of resources (or social inefficiency) exists.

In Part Three you learned that economic agents are rational when they attempt to maximize:  businesses maximize total profits and households maximize total utility.  In each case the economic agent pursues an activity—either buying or selling in a product or a factor market—up to the point where its private MB equals its private MC.  That is, an economic agent pursues its own self-interest and is not concerned (usually) with society's well-being.  A major lesson learned in Part Three is that if firms attempt to maximize total profits in perfectly competitive markets, then social efficiency results.  Stated differently, when economic agents pursue their private self-interest, social efficiency results—usually.

As Part Four indicates, however, if imperfect competition exists in either the product market or the factor market, then if economic agents pursue their own self-interest, social inefficiency results.  If a firm is not a perfect competitor, too little will be produced from society's—not the firm's—point of view.

In Chapter 19 you discover yet another instance in which social inefficiency results when individuals pursue their own self-interest:  externalities.  If society's MC exceeds private MC, then an externality (such as pollution) exists, and social inefficiency results because too much will be produced.  Individuals pursue their own self-interest, but in equilibrium the MC to society exceeds the MB to society.

In this chapter you also learn about the common property alternatives to pollution-causing resource use, and recycling.

## LEARNING OBJECTIVES

After you have studied this chapter you should be able to

1.  define private costs, social costs, externality, optimal quantity of pollution, private property rights, common property, transaction costs, and recycling.

2.  distinguish between private costs and social costs.

3.  recognize how common property and species extinction are related.

4.  list three choices that businesses must make if they are charged to pollute.

5.  determine the optimal quantity of pollution, when given sufficient information.

6.  distinguish between private property rights and common property, and predict how rational economic agents behave under each.

7.  list various ways to reduce pollution toward the optimal quantity.

8.  recognize how to test whether or not a resource is becoming scarcer.

9.  recognize how voluntary exchange can solve the externality problem.

## CHAPTER OUTLINE

1.  It is important to distinguish between **private costs** and **social costs**.
    a.  **Private costs** are those incurred by individuals when they use scarce resources.
    b.  **Social costs** include **private costs** plus the cost of actions borne by people other than those who commit those actions; **social costs** embody the full opportunity cost of a resource-using action.
    c.  When people use resources in production or consumption, pollution may be an unwanted by-product; if so, the **social costs** of consuming and producing will exceed the **private costs** of doing so.

2.  An **externality** exists when a **private cost** or benefit diverges from a social cost or benefit; if an **externality** exists, the costs or benefits of an action are not fully borne by the two parties engaged in an exchange, or by an individual using resources.

3.  In theory, it is possible to change the signals in an economy so that individuals can be forced to take into account all the costs of their actions.
    a.  If polluters are charged to pollute, they will (i) install pollution-abatement equipment, (ii) reduce pollution-causing activities, or (iii) pay the price to pollute.
    b.  In general, charging a uniform price to pollute is inefficient because a given physical quantity of pollution has different **social costs** in different places.

4.  Ultimately, the **optimal quantity of pollution** is a normative, not a positive, economics concept.
    a.  The waste-disposing capacity of our ecosystem is a scarce resource that can be analyzed like any other resource; the marginal benefit curve for a cleaner environment declines, and the marginal cost curve for a cleaner environment rises.
    b.  The optimal quantity of pollution occurs where the declining marginal benefit curve intersects the rising marginal cost curve; in general the optimal quantity of pollution will exceed zero.

5.  **Common property** is owned by everyone; hence **private property rights**, which allow the use, transfer, and exchange of property, do not exist for **common property**.
    a.  If a resource is scarce and it is **common property**, it will be wasted; certain species will become extinct if people value them but property rights do not exist.
    b.  A resource that is scarce, but is not **common property**, can be used efficiently under certain conditions.
    c.  **Externalities** can be internalized via voluntary contracting even when property rights do not exist:
        i.   if the **transaction costs** associated with making, reaching, and enforcing agreements are low relative to the expected benefits of reaching an agreement.
        ii.  if the number of individuals involved is small.
    d.  **Private property rights** can be assigned (through governments), so that an **externality** can be internalized.

6.  **Recycling** has the potential to save scarce resources and reduce pollution; unfortunately the existing state of the art is such that recycling processes are costly, and create pollution themselves.

7.  The fact that the price of landfills is falling implies that Canada is not "running out" of landfills; in fact, the prices of *most* resources have been falling, which means that, in general, the resource base is getting larger!

8.  Unfortunately, attempts to protect species often leads to costs imposed on land owners, producers, and consumers; trade-offs exist.


## KEY TERMS AND CONCEPTS

Private costs
Social costs
Externality
Optimal quantity of pollution

Common property
Transaction costs
Recycling
Private property rights

**COMPLETION QUESTIONS**
Fill in the blank or circle the correct term.

1. Costs incurred by individuals when they use scarce resources are called _____ costs; _____ costs include private costs and external costs and represent the full cost that society bears when a resource-using action occurs.

2. When we add external costs to internal costs, we get _____ costs; an externality exists if there is a divergence between _____ and _____.

3. In theory, decision makers can be made to take into account all of the costs of their actions if people who impose costs on others are (taxed, subsidized).

4. A uniform tax on polluters will not be economically efficient if a given physical quantity of pollution imposes different _____ costs in different places.

5. As more and more pollution is reduced, then the marginal benefit (falls, rises) and the marginal cost _____; the optimal quantity of pollution occurs where _____.

6. If at a zero price the quantity demanded of a resource (exceeds, equals) its quantity supplied, that resource is scarce; if a scarce resource is common property, it probably (will, will not) be wasted.

7. Sheep, cows, and other species are not in danger of extinction because they are valued and _____ rights exist; other species are becoming extinct because they are _____ property.

8. If a businessperson/environmentalist treats pollution voluntarily, he or she will be at a competitive (advantage, disadvantage) in the marketplace.

9. Externalities can be internalized if _____ costs are low and if the number of parties involved is (small, large).

10. Recycling in theory, can save scarce resources; however it is very (cheap, expensive) and itself creates (conflict, pollution).

11. Many people feel that the world is running out of resources; but the evidence is that the inflation-adjusted price of most resources has (fallen, increased) historically.

12. Attempts to protect a specific species usually involve a (law, trade-off).

**TRUE-FALSE QUESTIONS**
Circle the **T** if the statement is true, the **F** if it is false.  Explain to yourself why a statement is false.

T  F   1.   Social costs do not include private costs.

T  F   2.   Private costs do not include external costs.

T  F   3.   If social costs exceed private costs, too much of the good normally will be produced.

T  F   4.   Pollution is an example of a social cost.

T  F   5.   The optimal quantity of pollution is zero.

T  F   6.   Air pollution is a problem because air is common property.

T  F   7.   A given quantity of physical pollution causes the same amount of economic damage everywhere.

T  F   8.   If polluters are charged to pollute, we may end up with less pollution.

T  F   9.   If a specific firm pays to reduce its output of pollution, it may be at a competitive disadvantage.

T  F  10.   If private property rights don't exist, the private sector cannot internalize externalities.

T  F  11.   Externalities may be internalized if the government assigns private property rights.

T  F  12.   Private property rights to sheep exist; therefore they are not in danger of extinction.

T  F  13.   Attempts to protect one species may well impose costs on humans.

T  F  14.   Recycling is always a good idea.

T  F  15.   The inflation-adjusted price of most resources has fallen, historically.

**MULTIPLE CHOICE QUESTIONS**
Circle the letter that corresponds to the best answer.

1.  Social costs
    a.  exclude internal costs.
    b.  exclude external costs.
    c.  exclude both internal and external costs.
    d.  include both internal and external costs.

2.  Air pollution
    a.  is an internal cost to firms.
    b.  is an external cost to firms.
    c.  exists because air is a privately owned resource.
    d.  has the same costs to society everywhere.

3.  A misallocation of resources may result if
    a.  social costs exceed private costs.
    b.  social benefits exceed private benefits.
    c.  a scarce resource is communally owned.
    d.  All of the above

4.  If polluters are charged to pollute, then
    a.  pollution will disappear.
    b.  the environment will be damaged severely.
    c.  less pollution is a probable result.
    d.  less voluntary pollution abatement will result.

5.  Which of the following will **NOT** help to reduce the problem that exists if social costs exceed social benefits?
    a.  subsidize polluters
    b.  subsidize parties damaged by pollution
    c.  charge polluters to pollute
    d.  internalize external costs

6.  If polluters are charged to pollute, efficiency requires that
    a.  they be charged according to the economic damages they create.
    b.  they be charged the same amount.
    c.  they be charged according to the physical quantity of pollution they generate.
    d.  nonpolluters be charged also.

7.  The optimal quantity of pollution exists at that level of pollution at which, for pollution abatement, a
    a.  rising marginal benefit equals a falling marginal cost.
    b.  rising marginal cost equals a falling marginal benefit.
    c.  constant marginal cost equals a falling marginal benefit.
    d.  constant marginal benefit equals a rising marginal cost.

8.  Externalities can be internalized by the private sector if
    a.  transaction costs of doing so are low.
    b.  benefits of doing so are high.
    c.  the number of people involved is small.
    d.  All of the above

9.  Which statement is **NOT** true?
    a.  Recycling can be costly and can add to pollution.
    b.  Attempts to protect one species often harm landowners and consumers.
    c.  The evidence is that most natural resources are becoming scarcer.
    d.  The inflation-adjusted price of landfills has been falling in the U.S.

10.  Recycling
    a.  may save resources.
    b.  can be very costly.
    c.  can create its own pollution problems.
    d.  All of the above

**WORKING WITH GRAPHS**

1.  Use the graphs below to answer the questions that follow.  Note that S represents the industry supply curve and SS represents the marginal costs to society—which include marginal private costs and external costs.  Assume that no positive externalities exist.

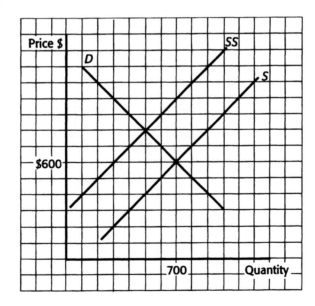

    a.  Which curve represents the marginal private costs of producing the good in question?

    b.  Which curve reflects the marginal social costs of producing this good?

c.  Which curve represents both the marginal private benefits and the marginal social benefits of this good?

d.  How many units of this good will be produced by the private sector?  What is the value of the marginal social cost of that quantity?  the value of the marginal social benefits?

e.  What is the optimal quantity of this good, from society's point of view?  Why?

2.  Suppose you are given the following graph for the demand and supply of fertilizer per week.  As a by-product of fertilizer production, the fertilizer plant dumps harmful chemicals into local streams.  A local agency has determined that if fertilizer production were limited to 2 tons per week, the local streams would be able to handle the by-products without harm.  The agency has decided to impose a tax on the fertilizer plant.  What tax per unit of output is necessary to achieve the agency's goal of no harm to the local streams?  Can we conclude that if the agency charges this tax that society is better off?  Why or why not?

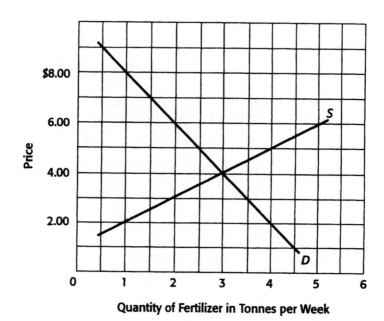

Quantity of Fertilizer in Tonnes per Week

## PROBLEMS

1.  Suppose you live in a small town with a privately owned solid-waste disposal facility (garbage dump) just west of town that services a larger city about 30 miles away.    Because of the prevailing westerly wind, your town suffers from an unpleasant odor generated at the dump.  The more garbage that arrives at the dump in a given week, the more unpleasant the odor.  A study is undertaken, and the results are partially summarized in the table that follows.

| (1)<br>Garbage<br>processed<br>in tonnes<br>per week | (2)<br>Dump's<br>marginal<br>cost | (3)<br>Consumers'<br>valuation<br>of disposal<br>services | (4)<br>External<br>costs<br>due to<br>odor | (5)<br>Marginal<br>social cost |
|---|---|---|---|---|
| 5 | $4.00 | $8.00 | $0.00 | $4.00 |
| 10 | 4.25 | 7.60 | 0.20 | 4.45 |
| 15 | 4.50 | 6.60 | 0.50 | 5.00 |
| 20 | 4.80 | 5.80 | 1.00 | _____ |
| 25 | 5.20 | 5.20 | 1.75 | _____ |
| 30 | 5.80 | 4.80 | 2.75 | _____ |

Column 1 represents the quantity of garbage disposed of at the dump in tonnes per week.

Column 2 is the private marginal cost of disposing of various quantities of garbage—the supply of disposal services.

Column 3 represents the demand (willingness to pay) for various quantities of garbage disposal by the consumers of the service in the city to the west.

Column 4 is the external costs that are imposed on residents in your town by the dumping of various quantities of garbage.

Column 5 is the marginal social cost of the dumping services, which includes both private and external costs.

a.  Under present conditions, with the disposal plant ignoring external cost, what is the equilibrium price and quantity of disposal services in the market?

b.  Complete column 5.

c.  Using your answers from a and b, can you tell what is happening in this market at the present?

d.  If the disposal plant were forced to internalize all the relevant costs of operation, what would be the equilibrium price and quantity in this market?

**ANSWERS TO CHAPTER 19**

**COMPLETION QUESTIONS**

1.  private; social
2.  social; social costs (social benefits); private costs (private benefits)
3.  taxed
4.  social
5.  falls; rises; MB = MC of pollution reduction
6.  exceeds; will
7.  private property; common
8.  disadvantage
9.  transaction; small
10. expensive; pollution
11. fallen
12. tradeoff (because property owners; producers; and consumers are harmed)

**TRUE-FALSE QUESTIONS**

1.  F  Social costs are the sum of private costs and negative externalities (if any).
2.  T
3.  T
4.  T
5.  F  It is a positive amount, because it costs society resources to have a cleaner environment.
6.  T
7.  F  The next unit of air pollution causes more economic damage in Toronto than it does in a small town in Saskatchewan.
8.  T
9.  T
10. F  The private sector, throughout history, has sometimes been able to do so, when transaction costs are low.
11. T
12. T
13. T
14. F  Sometimes recycling is too costly, or it creates pollution itself.
15. T

**MULTIPLE CHOICE QUESTIONS**

1.  d;  Social costs are the full opportunity cost of a resource using action.
2.  b;  Costs of the action are not fully borne by the firm.
3.  d;  All of the factors mentioned can misallocate resources.
4.  c;  The polluters will bear the cost of polluting.

5. a;  A subsidy would encourage polluters, not discourage them.
6. a;  Pollution has different social costs in different places.
7. b;  The optimal quantity of pollution will exceed zero.
8. d;  All of the choices would have an impact.
9. c;  The evidence does not seem to support this statement.
10. d;  Recycling has the potential to save scarce resources and reduce pollution.

## WORKING WITH GRAPHS

1. a. curve S
   b. curve SS
   c. curve D
   d. 700; $1000; $600
   e. 500; that is where the MB to society equals the MC to society
2. $3 per tonne of fertilizer; no.  We are given no information about how much society values unharmed streams in the area, so we are not justified in concluding that the tax has made society better off.

## PROBLEMS

1. a. $5.20, 25 tons per week
   b. Marginal social cost:  $5.80, $6.95, $8.55
   c. With the external costs being ignored, the disposal plants' marginal cost at the equilibrium level is below the true marginal social cost
   d. 5.80, 20 tons per week

## ANSWERS TO EXAMPLE QUESTIONS FOR CRITICAL ANALYSIS

I  **INTERNATIONAL EXAMPLE 19-1: The Black Sea Becomes the Dead Sea: The Results of Externalities** (p. 433)
One country could control the degradation if that body of water were completely within its borders because it could use the force of the law to monitor and reduce the amount of pollution being put into it. That country and its citizens would clearly benefit from such an environmental improvement program. With many countries involved, it would be difficult for any one of them to capture the benefits of reducing wastes if the others did not go along. It is unlikely that there could be a single agency to enforce pollution abatement efforts in different countries. Also the free rider problem becomes an issue because each country knows that if all of the others do significantly reduce pollution, then the entire Black Sea will not be badly degraded by its own, relatively minor, pollution. Thus it can avoid the costs of cleaning up pollution.

II  **INTERNATIONAL POLICY EXAMPLE 19-1: Dead Dogs in the Hills of Italy** (p. 436)
You have now changed the land from common property to private property and therefore all the laws that govern private property will exist. You can now allow the use, transfer and exchange of your property. Transaction costs involved would be such items as guards to protect the land, fencing, labour, and training. It might be difficult to enforce any agreements or contracts that you make with individuals. Government might step in to resolve the issue of who gets to harvest the crop each year. The problem of dead dogs will not necessarily go away just because the land is now privately owned.

III  **INTERNATIONAL POLICY EXAMPLE 19-2: Privatizing the Right to Pollute** (p. 438)
The rich countries in the world would be prepared to pay the excess pollution rights up to the point that the payment was less than the cost of reducing the emissions covered by the rights. Once emission reduction is cheaper than paying for more rights, countries will reduce emissions instead.

**IV  INTERNATIONAL EXAMPLE 19-2: Preventing Overfishing by Trading Quotas**
(p. 439)

The market for quotas makes it less likely that a black market for fish or any other agricultural product such as milk and eggs will exist. It makes it more likely that the farmers will feed the excess to the animals than to try to sell the product in a black market. Fish would be considered common property until the quota system was implemented. The quota itself now becomes a valuable product to be sold to the highest bidder.

**V  INTERNATIONAL EXAMPLE 19-3: Can Citizens Recycle Too Much? The Case of Germany**
(p. 441)

"Too much" recycling occurs when the marginal of the last unit of garbage recycled is greater than the price that can be obtained for it in the market. Resources could be moved out of recycling and into other economic activities, and the total value produced in the economy would increase.

# CHAPTER 20

# CYBERNOMICS

## PUTTING THIS CHAPTER INTO PERSPECTIVE

Chapter 20 can be considered a capstone chapter for your text. It deals with how the new world of cyberspace affects economics and vise versa. Of course we are talking about the Internet, as well as its major component, the World Wide Web. Along with the explosion in Internet use and worldwide communications is the growing information technology (IT) sector, not only in the United States, but in the world. The Canadian computing and telecommunications industry has been growing at a prodigious rate, now exceeding $116.4 billion a year. While business use of the Internet has been going on for some time, household use is increasing even more dramatically. Between 100 and 200 million global citizens are connected via the Net and that number is certain to expand.

You can think of the Internet and the World Wide Web as reducers of transaction costs. Ecommerce is extensive between businesses. Retail electronic commerce is in its infancy, but is growing, too. When more Canadians are certain that their credit cards cannot be "stolen from thin air," e-'tailing will increase, too. The use of intelligent shopping agents over the Web is certain to reduce differentials in prices per constant-quality unit for any good or service. Because the Net does not allow customers to touch and feel goods, brand names will become even more important. Marketing and advertising on the Net will become more important, also.

The pricing of software that can be distributed on the Net poses a problem. The marginal cost for disseminating one more unit of any given software program is effectively close to zero. Therefore, marginal cost pricing would generate no revenues for traditional software developers. The law of diminishing marginal returns as far as this particular example goes, does not quite work. Software producers must develop additional ways to raise revenues if they are worried that their software will be distributed for free.

A major issue because of the Internet has to do with the protection of intellectual property, in particular CDs, the written word, and computer programs. How this issue will be handled in the future remains to be seen.

## LEARNING OBJECTIVES

After you have studied this chapter, you should be able to

1.    understand how technological change affects the demand for labour.

2.    understand the relationship between increased usage of the Internet and increased economic efficiency.

3.    explain the different ways that the Internet can be used for reducing transaction costs.

4.    understand the increasing importance of brand names because of Internet retailing.

5.    discuss the issue of pricing and the law of diminishing marginal returns for the dissemination of software products on the Internet.

## CHAPTER OUTLINE

1.    One way that extensive use of the Web will lead to greater efficiency is through a reduction in transaction costs.

2.    Most e-commerce is between businesses today.

3.    Retail business will expand as better encryption methods are used for capturing credit-card numbers.

4.    Internet retailing requires no inventory costs, for Web "malls" that simply send orders to other companies for fulfillment.

5.    As more Internet retailing occurs, the demand for traditional retail space will decrease over time.

6.    Brands can be established on the Web itself, such as Amazon.com, a now major retailer of books and other merchandise available only on their website.

7.    The Internet allows for a better way of reaching more finely tuned groups of potential customers. In this way, it is cheaper and may be more effective than traditional direct-mail marketing methods.

8.    Pricing decisions for software products that can be downloaded off of the Internet are difficult. After all, the marginal cost becomes zero, but a product given away doesn't yield revenues to pay for its development.

9.    Some firms have succeeded by giving away their programs, but charging for upgrades and updated versions.

10.    The Internet is leading to lower costs of entry, especially in retailing.

## KEY TERMS AND CONCEPTS

Protocol                           e-commerce
Cybernomics                        Intelligent shopping agents

## COMPLETION QUESTIONS
Circle the correct term or fill in the blank.

1. Technological change often reduces the demand for (temporary, traditional) labour services, but it usually increases the demand for (old, new) types of labour services.

2. The greatest use of the Internet is (e-commerce, e-mail)

3. One way to look at the Internet and the World Wide Web is that the new system is simply a(n) (increaser, reducer) of transaction costs.

4. Electronic retailing can eventually lead to a reduction in the demand for (retail space, brand names).

5. Anybody who puts up a Web home page can sell ad space, but faces a(n) (high cost, opportunity cost) problem for use of this space.

6. The marginal cost of one more unit of a software program distributed on the Net is close to (the production costs, zero).

## TRUE-FALSE QUESTIONS
Circle the T if the statement is true, the F if it is false. Explain to yourself why a statement is false.

T  F  1. Electronic retailing will lead to an increase in mass merchandising.

T  F  2. On-line trading has lead to less efficiency in the securities industries.

T  F  3. Every bootlegged CD or computer program constitutes a one-for-one reduction in the revenues of firms selling those products.

T  F  4. As Internet shopping becomes more extensive, brand names will become more even important.

T  F  5. Technology displaces workers, permanently destroying jobs.

T  F  6. Surfing the Net is the most extensive use of the Internet.

## MULTIPLE CHOICE QUESTIONS
Circle the letter that corresponds to the best answer.

1. The Internet reduces transaction costs by
   a. making shopping more fun.
   b. increasing the cost of information.
   c. reducing the cost of information.
   d. All of the above.

2.    Better encryption will increase e-commerce because
    a.    software programmers will have more work.
    b.    retailers will be able to spend more to set up electronic commerce sites.
    c.    more consumers will understand what encryption means.
    d.    more consumers will feel safer about using credit cards on-line.

3.    Brand names may become more important because of electronic shopping
    a.    because sales people will not be able to explain differences in different manufactures' products.
    b.    because the Internet cannot handle a large number of brands.
    c.    because it takes longer to download longer brand names.
    d.    All of the above

4.    There is an opportunity cost to offering space ads on a home page because
    a.    each screen has a limited amount of space.
    b.    it takes time to load ads and more screens, and consumers value their time when they are on the Web.
    c.    there is always an alternative use of the "real estate" on a home page.
    d.    All of the above.

5.    The sale of an additional unit of a software program on the Net is
    a.    equal to the cost of producing the diskettes for the software program.
    b.    equal to the cost of producing the software program in the first place.
    c.    equal to the cost of developing the next version of that program.
    d.    effectively equal to zero for Net distribution.

6.    Often organizations calculate the cost to record companies of bootlegged compact disks.
    These cost estimates usually grossly overstate lost revenues because
    a.    no one can accurately estimate how many bootlegged copies exist.
    b.    no revenues are ever lost.
    c.    some users of bootlegged copies would not have bought a new copy at the full retail price.
    d.    None of the above

## MATCHING

Choose the item in column (2) that best matches an item in column (1).

| (1) | (2) |
|---|---|
| a. e-commerce | 1. shopping over the Net |
| b. encryption | 2. decreased transaction costs |
| c. intelligent shopping agents | 3. increased security on the Net |
| | 4. electronic mail |
| | 5. cyber chatting |

**ANSWERS TO CHAPTER 21**

**COMPLETION QUESTIONS**

1.  traditional, new
2.  electronic mail
3.  reducer
4.  retail space
5.  opportunity cost
6.  zero

**TRUE-FALSE QUESTIONS**

1.  F   More commerce on the Net will reduce the use of mass merchandisers.
2.  F   Commissions have dropped dramatically since on-line trading started.
3.  F   Because of the law of demand, not everyone would buy the same CD or software program if the full price had to be paid.
4.  T
5.  F   At least in Canada , technology has simply meant different jobs are demanded— employment has increased steadily over the years.
6.  F   The most extensive use is for e-mail

**MULTIPLE CHOICE QUESTIONS**

1.  c;  The Internet reduces transaction costs because you can get the information quicker and at no cost.
2.  d;  With better encryption comes security to consumers therefore credit card orders.
3.  a;  People will have faith in the brand name of the product.
4.  d;  The opportunity cost is that you can lose the customers interest.
5.  d;  The cost does not increase with the number of copies because the intellectual works has been done.
6.  c;  If people can't get bootlegged copies of software, they probably would  purchase used software.

**MATCHING**

A and 1;  b and 3; c and 2

**ANSWERS TO EXAMPLE QUESTIONS FOR CRITICAL ANALYSIS**

I   **INTERNATIONAL EXAMPLE 20-1: Luddites Unite Against Automated Textile Machinery** (p. 449)
The development of computer controlled robots has replaced large numbers of assembly line workers in the automobile industry. Scanners that can read magnetic ink greatly increased the speed with which cheques can be processed, thus reducing the need for bank workers who previously sorted and cleared cheques by hand. The personal computer and word processing software have significantly reduced the demand for clerk typists and secretarial workers.

II  **CYBERSPACE EXAMPLE 20-1: Buying a Car on the Net** (p. 452)
It may matter to the dealers themselves since they will lose some degree of control over the price they can charge. This would occur because of a decrease in product differentiation associated with customer preferences for individual dealerships.

**III  CYBERSPACE EXAMPLE 20-2: Not Just Brand Loyalty, Also Country Loyalty** (p. 454)

Small Canadian businesses can take advantage of Canadian loyalty by making sure that Canadians can find them on the Web. For the low cost of setting up a website, smaller Canadian businesses will be able to compete with larger companies, who have much higher advertising budgets.

**IV  CYBERSPACE EXAMPLE 20-3: The Cost of Entry is Low, the Cost of Not Succeeding is High** (p. 457)

Amazon.com had lots of venture capital as backing for their website. This allowed them to make it through the critical first few years. Amazon.com also keeps no inventory and only orders an item when it has been sold, reducing their costs. Venture capital allows companies with viable ideas to get a start. This has been true for the most part, but if confidence in the stock of the company declines the venture capital quickly disappears.

# MICROECONOMICS GLOSSARY

**Absolute advantage**   The ability to produce a good or service at an "absolutely" lower cost, usually measured in units of labour or resource input required to produce one unit of the good or service.

**Accounting profit**   Total revenues minus total explicit costs.

**Adverse selection**   The circumstance that arises in financial markets when borrowers who are the worst credit risks are the ones most likely to seek loans.

**Age-earnings cycle**   The regular earnings profile of an individual throughout his or her lifetime.  The age-earnings cycle usually starts with a low income, builds gradually to a peak at around age 50, and then gradually curves down until it approaches zero at retirement.

**Aggregates**    Total amounts or quantities; aggregate demand, for example, is total planned expenditures throughout a nation.

**Allocative efficiency**   Producing the mix of goods and services most wanted by society.

**Anti-combines legislation**   Laws that restrict the formation of monopolies and regulate certain anti-competitive business practices.

**Asymmetric information**   Information possessed by one side of a transaction but not the other. The side with more information will be at an advantage.

**Average cost pricing**   The monopoly firm is forced to set a price equal to average total cost.

**Average fixed costs**   Total fixed costs divided by the number of units produced.

**Average physical product**   Total product divided by the variable input.

**Average tax rate**   The total tax payment divided by total income.  It is the proportion of total income paid in taxes.

**Average total costs**   Total costs divided by the number of units produced; sometimes called *average per-unit total costs*.

**Average variable costs**   Total variable costs divided by the number of units produced.


**Best response function**   The manner in which  one oligopolist reacts to a change in price, output, or quality made by another oligopolist in the industry.

**Bilateral monopoly**   A market structure consisting of a monopolist and a monopsonist.

**Black market**   A market in which goods are traded at prices above their legal maximum prices or in which illegal goods are sold.

**Bond**   A legal claim against a firm, usually entitling the owner of the bond to receive a fixed annual coupon payment, plus a lump sum payment at the bond's maturity date. Bonds are issued in return for funds lent to the firm.

**Budget constraint**   All of the possible combinations of goods that can be purchased (at fixed prices) with a specific budget.

**Bureaucracy**   An administrative system run by a large staff following rules and procedures set down by government.

**Bureaucrats**    Non-elected government officials who are responsible for the day-to-day operation of the government and the observance of its regulations and laws.


**Capital gain**   The positive difference between the purchase price and the sale price of an asset.  If a share of stock is bought for $5 and then sold for $15, the capital gain is $10.

**Capital loss**   The negative difference between the purchase price and the sale price of an asset.

**Capture hypothesis**   A theory of regulatory behaviour that predicts that the regulators will eventually be captured by the special interests of the industry being regulated.

**Cartel**   An association of suppliers in an industry that agrees to set common prices and output quotas to prevent competition.

**Ceteris paribus assumption**   The assumption that nothing changes except the factor or factors being studied; "other things constant," or "other things equal."

**Collateral**   An asset pledged to guarantee the repayment of a loan.

**Collective bargaining**   Bargaining between management of a company or of a group of companies and the management of a union or a group of unions for the purpose of setting a mutually agreeable contract on wages, fringe benefits, and working conditions for all employees in all the unions involved.

**Collective decision making**   How voters, politicians and other interested parties act and how these actions influence non-market decisions.

**Common property** Property that is owned by everyone and therefore by no one. Air and water are examples of common property resources.

**Comparable-worth doctrine**   The belief that women should receive the same wages as men if the levels of skill and responsibility in their jobs are equivalent.

**Comparative advantage**   The ability to produce a good or service at a lower opportunity cost compared to other producers.

**Complements**   Two goods are complements if both are used together for consumption or enjoyment.  The more you buy of one, the more you buy of the other.  For complements, a change in the price of one causes an opposite shift in the demand for the other.

**Concentration ratio**   The percentage of total industry sales contributed by the four largest firms; sometimes called the *industry concentration ratio*.

**Conglomerate merger**   The joining of two firms from unrelated industries.

**Constant returns to scale** No change in long-run average costs when output increases.

**Constant-cost industry**   An industry whose total output can be increased without an increase in long-run per-unit costs; an industry whose long-run supply curve is horizontal.

**Consumer optimum**   A choice of a set of goods and services that maximizes the level of satisfaction for each consumer, subject to limited income.

**Consumption**   The use of goods and services for personal satisfaction.

**Cooperative game**   A game in which the players explicitly collude to make themselves better off.  As applied to firms, it involves companies colluding in order to make higher than competitive rates of return.

**Corporation**   A legal entity that may conduct business in its own name just as an individual does; the owners of a corporation, called shareholders, own shares of the firm's profits and enjoy the protection of limited liability.

**Cost-of-service regulation** Regulation based on allowing prices to reflect only the actual cost of production and no monopoly profits.

**Craft unions**   Labour unions composed of workers who engage in a particular trade or skill, such as shoemaking, printing or baking.

**Creative response** Behaviour on the part of the firm that allows it to comply with the letter of the law but violate the spirit, significantly lessening the law's effects.

**Cross elasticity of demand**   The percentage change in the demand for one good (holding its price constant) divided by the percentage change in the price of a related good.

**Cybernomics** The application of economic analysis to human and technological activities related to the use of the Internet in all of its forms.

**Decreasing-cost industry**   An industry in which an increase in output leads to a reduction in long-run per-unit costs, such that the long-run industry supply curve slopes downward.

**Demand**  A schedule of how much of a good or service people will purchase at any price during a specified time period, other things being equal.

**Demand curve**  A graphical representation of the demand schedule; a negatively sloped line showing the inverse relationship between the price and the quantity demanded (other things being equal).

**Demerit good**   A good that has been deemed socially undesirable through the political process. Cigarettes are an example.

**Deregulation**   The elimination or phasing out of regulations on economic activity.

**Derived demand**  Input factor demand derived from demand for the final product being produced.

**Diminishing marginal utility**   The principle that as more of any good or service is consumed, its extra benefit declines.  Otherwise stated, increases in total utility from the consumption of a good or service become smaller and smaller as more is consumed during a given time period.

**Discounting**   The method by which the present value of a future sum or a future stream of sums is obtained.

**Diseconomies of scale**  Increases in long-run average costs that occur as output increases.

**Distribution of income**   The way income is allocated among the population.

**Dividends**  Portion of a corporation's profits paid to its owners (shareholders).

**Division of labour**   The segregation of a resource into different specific tasks; for example, one automobile worker puts on bumpers, another doors, and so on.

**Dominant strategies**  Strategies that always yield the highest benefit. Regardless of what other players do, a dominant strategy will yield the most benefit for the player using it.

**E-commerce** The use of the Internet in any manner that allows buyers and sellers to find each other. It can involve business selling directly to other businesses, or business selling to retail customers. Both goods and services are involved in e-commerce.

**Economic goods**   Goods that are scarce.

**Economic profit**   The difference between total revenues and the opportunity cost of all factors of production.

**Economic profits**   Total revenues minus total opportunity cost of all inputs used, or the total of all implicit and explicit costs.

**Economic rent**   A payment for the use of any resource over and above its opportunity cost.

**Economic system**   The institutional means through which resources are used to satisfy human wants.

**Economics**    A social science that studies how people allocate limited resources to satisfy unlimited wants.

**Economies of scale** Decreases in long-run average costs resulting from increases in output.

**Effluent fee** A charge to a polluter that gives the right to discharge into the air or water a certain amount of pollution. Also called a pollution tax.

**Elastic demand** A demand relationship in which a given percentage change in price will result in a larger percentage change in quantity demanded. Total expenditures and price changes are inversely related in the elastic region of the demand curve.

**Empirical** Relying on real-world data in evaluating the usefulness of a model.

**Entrepreneurship** The factor of production involving human resources that performs the functions of raising capital, organizing, managing, assembling other factors of production, and making strategic business policy decisions. The entrepreneur is a risk taker.

**Entry-deterrence strategy** Any strategy undertaken by firms in an industry, either individually or together, with the intent or effect of raising the cost of entry into the industry by a new firm.

**Equilibrium** The situation when quantity supplied equals quantity demanded at a particular price.

**Exclusion principle** The principle that no one can be excluded from the benefits of a public good, even if the person hasn't paid for it.

**Explicit costs** Costs that business managers must take account of because they must be paid; examples are wages, taxes, and rent.

**Externality** A situation in which a private cost diverges from a social cost; a situation in which the costs of an action are not fully borne by the two parties engaged in exchange or by an individual engaging in a scarce-resource-using activity. (Also applies to benefits.)

**Featherbedding** Any practice that forces employers to use more labour than they would otherwise or to use existing labour in an inefficient manner.

**Financial capital** Money used to purchase capital goods such as buildings and equipment.

**Firm** A business organization that employs resources to produce goods or services for a profit. A firm normally owns and operates at least one plant in order to produce.

**Fixed costs** Costs that do not vary with output. Fixed costs include such things as rent on a building. These costs are fixed for a certain period of time; in the long run, they are variable.

**Free-rider problem** A problem that arises when individuals presume that others will pay for the public goods, so that, individually, they can escape paying for their portion without a reduction in production.

**Game theory** A way of describing the various possible outcomes in any situation involving two or more interacting individuals when those individuals are aware of the interactive nature of their situation and plan accordingly. The plans made by these individuals are known as *game strategies*.

**Goods** All things from which individuals derive satisfaction or happiness.

**Government, or political, goods** Goods (and services) provided by the public sector; they can be either private or public goods.

**Horizontal merger** The joining of firms that are producing or selling a similar product.
**Human capital** The accumulated training and education of workers.

**Implicit costs** Expenses that managers do not have to pay out of pocket and hence do not normally explicitly calculate, such as the opportunity cost of factors of production that are owned; examples are owner-provided capital and owner-provided labour.
**Import quota** A physical supply restriction on imports of a particular good, such as sugar. Foreign exporters are unable to sell in Canada more than the quantity specified in the import quota.
**Incentive structure** The system of rewards and punishments individuals face with respect to their own actions.
**Incentive-compatible contract** A loan contract under which a significant amount of the borrower's assets are at risk, providing an incentive for the borrower to look after the lender's interests.
**Incentives** Potential rewards available if a particular activity is undertaken.
**Income elasticity of demand** The percentage change in demand for any good, holding its price constant, divided by the percentage change in income; the responsiveness of demand to changes in income, holding the goods relative price constant.
**Income in kind** Income received in the form of goods and services, such as health care; to be contrasted with money income, which is simply income in dollars, or general purchasing power, that can be used to buy any goods and services.
**Income-consumption curve** The set of optimum consumption points that would occur if income were increased, relative prices remaining constant.
**Increasing-cost industry** An industry in which an increase in industry output is accompanied by an increase in long-run per-unit cost, such that the long-run industry supply curve slopes upward.
**Indifference curve** A curve composed of a set of consumption alternatives, each which yields the same total amount of satisfaction.
**Industrial organization** studies how the industry environment affects the behaviour and performance of the firm.
**Industrial unions** Labour unions that consist of workers from a particular industry, such as automobile manufacturing or steel manufacturing.
**Industry supply curve** The locus of points showing the minimum prices at which given quantities will be forthcoming; also called the *market supply curve.*
**Inefficient point** Any point below the production possibilities curve at which resources are being used inefficiently.
**Inelastic demand** A demand relationship in which a given percentage change in price will result in a less-than-proportionate percentage change in the quantity demanded. Total expenditures and price are directly related in the inelastic region of the demand curve.
**Inferior good** Goods for which demand falls as income rises.
**Inside information** Information that is not available to the general public about what is happening in a corporation.
**Intelligent shopping agents** Computer programs that an individual or business user of the Internet can instruct to carry out a specific task such as looking for the lowest priced car of a particular make and model. The agent then searches the Internet (usually just the World Wide Web) and may even purchase the product when the best price has been found.

**Interest**  The payment for current rather than future command over resources; the cost of obtaining credit.  Also the return paid to owners of capital.

**Labour**  Productive contributions of humans who work, involving both mental and physical activities.

**Labour market signalling**  The process by which a potential worker's acquisition of credentials, such as a degree, is used by the employer to predicate future productivity.

**Labour unions**  Worker organizations that seek to secure economic improvements for their members; they also seek to improve the safety, health, and other benefits (such as job security) of their members.

**Laissez faire**  French for "leave [it] alone." This term is used to describe the limited government feature of pure capitalism.

**Land**  The natural resources that are available from nature.  Land as a resource includes location, original fertility and mineral deposits, topography, climate, water, and vegetation.

**Law of demand**  The observation that there is a negative, or inverse, relationship between the price of any good or service and the quantity demanded, holding other factors constant.

**Law of diminishing (marginal) returns**  The observation that after some point, successive equal-sized increases in a variable factor of production, such as labour, added to fixed factors of production, will result in smaller increases in output.

**Law of increasing relative costs**  The observation that the opportunity cost of additional units of a good generally increases as society attempts to produce more of that good. This accounts for the bowed-out shape of the production possibilities curve.

**Law of supply**  The observation that the higher the price of a good, the more of that good sellers will make available over a specified time period, other things being equal.

**Limited liability**  A legal concept whereby the responsibility, or liability, of the owners of a corporation is limited to the value of the shares in the firm that they own.

**Limit-pricing model**  A model that hypothesizes that a group of colluding sellers will set the highest common price that they believe they can charge without new firms seeking to enter that industry in search of relatively high profits.

**Long run**  The time period in which all factors of production can be varied.

**Long-run average cost curve (LAC)**  The locus of points representing the minimum unit cost of producing any given rate of output, given current technology and resource prices.

**Long-run industry supply curve**  A market supply curve showing the relationship between price and quantities forthcoming after firms have been allowed the time to enter into or exit from an industry, depending on whether there have been positive or negative economic profits.

**Lorenz curve**  A geometric representation of the distribution of income.  A Lorenz curve that is perfectly straight represents complete income equality.  The more bowed a Lorenz curve, the more unequally income is distributed.

**Macroeconomics**  The study of the behavior of the economy as a whole, including such economy-wide phenomena as changes in unemployment, the general price level, and national income.

**Majority rule**   A collective decision making system in which group decisions are made on the basis of 50.1 percent of the vote.  In other words whatever more than half of the electorate votes for, the entire electorate has to accept.

**Marginal cost pricing**   A system of pricing in which the price charged is equal to the opportunity cost to society of producing one more unit of the good or service in question. The opportunity cost is the marginal cost to society.

**Marginal costs**   The change in total costs due to a one-unit change in production rate.

**Marginal factor cost (MFC)**   The cost of using an additional unit of an input.  For example, if a firm can hire all the workers it wants at the going wage rate, the marginal factor cost of labour is the wage rate.

**Marginal physical product**   The physical output that is due to the addition of one more unit of a variable factor of production; the change in total product occurring when a variable input is increased and all other inputs are held constant; also called *marginal productivity* or *marginal return* .

**Marginal physical product (MPP) of labour**   The change in output resulting from the addition of one more worker.  The MPP of the worker equals the change in total output accounted for by hiring the worker, holding all other factors of production constant.

**Marginal revenue**   The change in total revenues resulting from a change in output (and sale) of one unit of the product in question.

**Marginal revenue product (MRP)**   The marginal physical product (MPP) times marginal revenue.  The MRP gives the additional revenue obtained from a one-unit change in labour input.

**Marginal tax rate**   The change in the tax payment divided by the change in income, or the percentage of additional dollars that must be paid in taxes.  The marginal tax rate is applied to the highest  tax bracket of taxable income reached.

**Marginal utility**   The change in total utility due to a one-unit change in the quantity of a good or service consumed.

**Market**   All of the arrangements that individuals have for exchanging with one another. Thus we speak of the labour market, the automobile market, and the credit market.

**Market clearing, or equilibrium, price**   The price that clears the market, at which quantity demanded equals quantity supplied; the price at which the demand curve intersects the supply curve.

**Market demand**   The demand of all consumers in the marketplace for a particular good or service. The summing at each price of the quantity demanded by each individual.

**Market failure**   A situation in which an unrestrained market economy  leads to too few or too many resources going to a specific economic activity.

**Market structure**   refers to key characteristics of an industry.

**Marketing boards**   A policy which allows producers to band together to restrict total quantity supplied by using quotas.

**Merit good**   A good that has been deemed socially desirable via the political process. Museums would be an example.

**Microeconomics**   The study of decision making undertaken by individuals (or households) and by firms.

**Minimum efficient scale (MES)**   The lowest rate of output per unit of time at which long-run average costs for a particular firm are at a minimum.

314

**Minimum wage**   A wage floor, legislated by government, setting the lowest hourly rate that firms may legally pay workers.

**Mixed economy**   An economic system in which decisions about how resources should be used are made partly by the private sector and partly by the government or the public sector.

**Models, or theories**   Simplified representations of the real world used as the basis for predictions or explanations.

**Money price**   The actual price that you pay in dollars and cents.   Also called the *absolute, nominal,* or *current* price.

**Monopolist**   A single supplier that comprises the entire industry for a good or service for which there is no close substitute.

**Monopolistic competition**   A market situation where a large number of firms produce similar but not identical products.   Entry into the industry is relatively easy.

**Monopoly**   A firm that has great control over the price of a good.   In the extreme case, a monopoly is the only seller of a good or service.

**Monopsonist**   A single buyer.

**Monopsonistic exploitation**   Exploitation due to monopsony power. It leads to a price for the variable input that is less than its marginal revenue product. Monopsonistic exploitation is the difference between marginal revenue product and the wage rate.

**Moral hazard**   A problem that occurs because of asymmetric information *after* a transaction occurs.   In financial markets, a person to whom money has been lent may indulge in more risky behavior, thereby increasing the probability of default on the debt.

**Natural monopoly**   A monopoly that arises from the peculiar production characteristics of an industry. It usually arises when there are large economies of scale relative to the industry's demand such that one firm can produce at a lower average cost than can be achieved by multiple firms.

**Negative-sum game**   A game in which players as a group lose at the end of the game.

**Nominal rate of interest**   The market rate of interest expressed in today's dollars.

**Non-cooperative game**   A game in which the players neither negotiate nor collude in any way.   As applied to firms in an industry, this is the common situation in which there are relatively few firms and each has some ability to change price.

**Non-price rationing devices**   All methods used to ration scarce goods that are price controlled.   Whenever the price system is not allowed to work, non-price rationing devices, such as "first-come, first-serve" with queuing, result.

**Normal good**   Goods for which demand rises as income rises.   Most goods are considered normal.

**Normal rate of return**   The amount that must be paid to an investor to induce investment in a business; also known as the *opportunity cost of capital*.

**Normative economics**   Analysis involving value judgments about economic policies; relates to whether things are good or bad.   It involves statements of *what ought to be*.

**Offer to purchase policy**   A price floor policy reinforced by the purchase of surplus output by the government.

**Oligopoly**   A market situation in which there are very few sellers.   Each seller knows that the other sellers will react to its changes in prices and quantities.

**Opportunistic behavior** Actions that ignore possible long-run benefits of cooperation and focus solely on short-run gains.

**Opportunity cost** The highest-valued, next-best alternative that must be sacrificed to attain something or to satisfy a want.

**Opportunity cost of capital** The normal rate of return or the available return on the next-best alternative investment. Economists consider this a cost of production, and it is included in our cost examples.

**Optimal quantity of pollution** That level of pollution for which the marginal benefit of one additional unit of clean air just equals the marginal cost of that one additional unit of clean air.

**Partnership** A business owned by two or more co-owners, or partners, who share the responsibilities and profits of the firm and are individually liable for all of the debts of the partnership.

**Payoff matrix** A matrix of outcomes, or consequences, of the strategies available to the players in a game.

**Perfect competition** A market structure in which the decisions of individual buyers and sellers have no effect on market price.

**Perfectly competitive firm** A firm that is such a small part of the total industry that it cannot affect the price of the product it sells.

**Perfectly elastic demand** A demand that has the characteristic that even the slightest increase in price will lead to a zero quantity demanded.

**Perfectly elastic supply** A supply characterized by a reduction in quantity supplied to zero when there is the slightest decrease in price.

**Perfectly inelastic demand** A demand that exhibits zero responsiveness to price changes; no matter what the price is, the quantity demanded remains the same.

**Perfectly inelastic supply** A supply for which quantity supplied remains constant, no matter what happens to price.

**Physical capital** All manufactured resources, including buildings, equipment, machines, and improvements to land that is used for production.

**Planning curve** The long-run average cost curve.

**Planning horizon** The long-run, during which all inputs are variable.

**Plant size** Physical size of factories that a firm owns and operates to produce its output. Plant size can be defined by floor area, by maximum physical capacity, and by other physical measures.

**Positive economics** Analysis that is strictly limited to making either purely descriptive statements or scientific predictions; for example, *If A, then B*. A statement of *what is*.

**Positive-sum game** A game in which players as a group are better off at the end of the game.

**Present value** The value of a future amount expressed in today's dollars; the most that someone would pay today to receive a certain sum at some point in the future.

**Price ceiling** A legal maximum price that may be charged for a particular good or service.

**Price controls** Government mandated minimum or maximum prices that can be charged for goods and services.

316

**Price differentiation**   Establishing different prices for similar products to reflect differences in marginal cost in providing those commodities to different groups of buyers.

**Price discrimination**   Selling a given product at more than one price, with the price difference being unrelated to differences in cost.

**Price elasticity of demand**   The responsiveness of the quantity demanded of a commodity to changes in its price.  The price elasticity of demand is defined as the percentage change in quantity demanded divided by the percentage change in price.

**Price elasticity of supply**   The responsiveness of the quantity supplied of a commodity to a change in its price; the percentage change in quantity supplied divided by the percentage change in price.

**Price floor**   A legal minimum price below which a good or service may not be sold. Legal minimum wages are an example.

**Price leadership**   A practice in many oligopolistic industries in which the largest firm publishes its price list ahead of its competitors, who then match those announced prices. Also called *parallel pricing*.

**Price searcher**   A firm that must determine the price-output combination that maximizes profit because it faces a downward sloping demand curve.

**Price support policies**   A set of government policies aimed at increasing the price that suppliers such as farmers receive for the goods they supply.

**Price system**   An economic system in which relative prices are constantly changing to reflect changes in supply and demand for different commodities.  The prices of those commodities are signals to everyone within the system about what is relatively scarce and what is relatively abundant.

**Price taker** A competitive firm that must take the price of its product as given because the firm cannot influence its price.

**Price war**   A situation where competing firms respond to a rival's price cut with even larger price cuts.

**Price-consumption curve**   The set of consumer optimum combinations of two goods that the consumer would choose as the price of one good changes, while money income and the price of the other good remain constant.

**Primary market**   A financial market in which newly issued securities are bought and sold.

**Principal-agent problem** The conflict of interest that occurs when agents—managers of firms—pursue their own objectives to the detriment of the goals of the firms' principals, or owners.

**Principle of rival consumption**   The recognition that individuals are rivals in consuming private goods because one person's consumption reduces the amount available for others to consume.

**Prisoner's dilemma** A famous strategic game in which two prisoners have a choice between confessing and not confessing to a crime.  If neither confesses, they serve a minimum sentence.  If both confess, they serve a maximum sentence.  If one confesses and the other doesn't, the one who confesses goes free.  The dominant strategy is always to confess.

**Private costs** Costs borne solely by the individuals who incur them.

**Private goods** Goods that can only be consumed by one individual at a time. Private goods are subject to the principle of rival consumption.

**Private property rights** Exclusive rights of ownership that allow the use, transfer, and exchange of property.

**Privatization** The sale or transfer of state-owned property and businesses to the private sector, in part or in whole. Also refers to *contracting out* - letting private business take over government-provided services such as trash collection.

**Product differentiation** The distinguishing of products by physical attributes, bundling of services, location and accessibility, sales promotion and advertising, and other qualities, real or imagined.

**Production** Any activity that results in the conversion of resources into products that can be used in consumption.

**Production function** The relationship between inputs and output. A production function is a technological, not an economic, relationship.

**Production possibilities curve (PPC)** A curve representing all possible combinations of total output that could be produced assuming (1) a fixed amount of productive resources of a given quality and (2) the efficient use of those resources.

**Productive efficiency** The case in which a given level of inputs is used to produce the maximum output possible. Alternatively, the situation in which a given output is produced at minimum cost.

**Profit-maximizing rate of production** That rate of production that maximizes total profits, or the difference between total revenues and total costs; also, the rate of production at which marginal revenue equals marginal cost.

**Progressive taxation** A tax system in which, as income increases, a higher percentage of the additional income is taxed. The marginal tax rate exceeds the average tax rate as income rises.

**Property rights** The right of an owner to use and to exchange property.

**Proportional rule** A decision making system in which actions are based on the proportion of the "votes" cast and are in proportion to them. In a market system, if 10 percent of the dollar votes are cast for blue cars, 10 percent of the output will be blue cars.

**Proportional taxation** A tax system in which, regardless of an individual's income, the tax bill comprises exactly the same proportion. Also called a *flat rate tax*.

**Protocol** The data formatting system that permits computers access each other and communicate.

**Public goods** Goods for which the principle of rival consumption does not apply; they can be jointly consumed by many individuals simultaneously at no additional cost and with no reduction in the quality or quantity.

**Pure capitalist economy** An economic system characterized by private ownership of all property resources. Households and firms interacting through a system of markets answer the three basic economic questions in a decentralized manner. This is also called a market economy or the price system.

**Pure command economy** An economic system characterized by public ownership of property resources. The three basic economic questions are answered in a centralized manner by government

**Random walk theory**  The theory that there are no predictable trends in security prices that can be used to "get rich quick."

**Rate of discount**  The rate of interest used to discount future sums back to present value.

**Rate-of-return regulation**  Regulation that seeks to keep the rate of return in the industry at a competitive level by not allowing excessive prices to be charged.

**Rationality assumption**  The assumption that people do not intentionally make decisions that would leave them worse off.

**Real rate of interest**  The nominal rate of interest minus the anticipated rate of inflation.

**Recycling**  The reuse of raw materials derived from manufactured products.

**Regressive taxation**  A tax system in which, as more dollars are earned, the percentage of tax paid on them falls.  The marginal tax rate is less than the average tax rate as income rises.

**Reinvestment**  Profits (or depreciation reserves) used to purchase new capital equipment.

**Relative price**  The price of a commodity expressed in terms of another commodity.

**Rent control**  The placement of price ceilings on rents in particular cities.

**Resource allocation**  The assignment of resources to specific uses by determining what will be produced, how it will be produced, and for whom it will be produced.

**Resources**  Items used to produce goods and services.

**Retained earnings**  Earnings that a corporation saves or retains for investment in other productive activities; earnings that are not distributed to shareholders.

**Scarcity**  A situation in which the ingredients for producing the things that people desire are insufficient to satisfy all wants.

**Secondary market**  A financial market in which previously issued securities are bought and sold.

**Separation of ownership and control**  The situation that exists in corporations in which the owners (shareholders) are not the people who control the operation of the corporation (managers).  The goals of these two groups are often different.

**Services**  Mental or physical labour or help purchased by consumers.  Examples are the assistance of  doctors, lawyers, dentists, repair personnel, house cleaners, educators, retailers, and wholesalers: things purchased or used by consumers that do not have physical characteristics.

**Share of stock**  A legal claim to a share of a corporation's future profits; if it is *common* stock, it incorporates certain voting rights regarding major policy decisions of the corporation; if it is *preferred* stock, its owners are accorded preferential treatment in the payment of dividends.

**Share the gains/share the pains theory**  A theory of regulatory behaviour in which the regulators must take account of the demands of three groups:  legislators, who established and who oversee the regulatory agency; members of the regulated industry; and consumers of the regulated industry's products and services.

**Short run**  The time period when at least one input, such as plant size, cannot be changed.

**Shortage**  A situation in which quantity demanded is greater than quantity supplied at a price below the market–clearing price.

**Short-run break-even price** The price at which a firm's total revenues equal its total costs. At the break-even price, the firm is just making a normal rate of return on its capital investment. (It is covering its explicit and implicit costs.)

**Short-run shutdown price** The price that just covers average variable costs. It occurs just below the intersection of the marginal cost curve and the average variable cost curve.

**Signals** Compact ways of conveying to economic decision makers information needed to make decisions. A true signal not only conveys information but also provides the incentive to react appropriately. Economic profits and economic losses are such signals.

**Social costs** The full costs borne by society whenever a resource use occurs. Social costs can be measured by adding private, or internal, costs to external costs.

**Sole proprietorship** A business owned by one individual who makes the business decisions, receives all of the profits, and is legally responsible for all of the debts of the firm.

**Specialization** The division of productive activities among persons and regions so that no one individual or one area is totally self-sufficient. An individual may specialize, for example, in law or medicine. A nation may specialize in the production of lobsters, computers, or cameras.

**Strategic dependence** A situation in which one firm's actions with respect to price, quality, advertising, and related changes may be strategically countered by the reactions of one or more other firms in the industry. Such dependence can exist only when there are a limited number of major firms in an industry.

**Strategy** Any rule that is used to make a choice, such as "Always pick heads"; any potential choice that can be made by players in a game.

**Strikebreakers** Temporary or permanent workers hired by a company to replace union members who are striking.

**Subsidy** Negative tax; payment to producers or consumers of a good or service. One way of encouraging merit goods is through a government subsidy.

**Substitutes** Two goods are substitutes when either one can be used for consumption to satisfy a similar want - for example, coffee and tea. The more you buy of one, the less you buy of the other. For substitutes, the change in the price of one causes a shift in demand for the other in the same direction as the price change.

**Supply** A schedule showing the relationship between price and quantity supplied for a specified period of time, other things being equal.

**Supply curve** The graphical representation of the supply schedule; a line (curve) showing the supply schedule, which generally slopes upward (has a positive slope), other things being equal.

**Surplus** A situation in which quantity supplied is greater than quantity demanded at a price above the market-clearing price.

**Tariffs** Taxes on imported goods.

**Tax bracket** A specified interval of income to which a specific and unique marginal tax is applied.

**Tax incidence** The distribution of tax burdens among various groups in society.

**Technology** Society's pool of applied knowledge concerning how goods and services can be produced.

**Terms of exchange** The terms under which trading takes place. Usually the terms of exchange are given by the price at which a good is traded.

**Theory of contestable markets** A hypothesis concerning pricing behaviour that holds that even though there are only a few in the industry, they are forced to price their products more or less competitively because of the ease of entry by outsiders. The key aspect of a contestable market is relatively costless entry into and exit from the industry.

**Theory of public choice** The study of collective decision making.

**Third parties** Parties other than the buyer and seller of the product.

**Three P's** Private property, profits, and prices inherent in capitalism.

**Tit-for-tat** A strategy in which a firm cheats in the current period if the rival firm cheated in the previous period, but cooperates in the current period if the rival firm cooperated in the previous period.

**Total costs** The sum of total fixed costs and total variable costs.

**Total revenues** The price per unit times the total quantity sold.

**Transaction costs** All of the costs associated with exchanging, including the informational costs of finding out price and quality, service record, durability, etc., of a product, plus the cost of contracting and enforcing that contract.

**Transfer payments** Money payments made by governments to individuals for which no services or goods are concurrently rendered. Examples are welfare, old age security payments, and Employment Insurance benefits.

**Transfers in kind** Payments that are in the form of actual goods and services, such as public education, low-cost public housing, and health care, and for which no goods or services are rendered concurrently in return.

**Unit elasticity of demand** A demand relationship in which the quantity demanded changes exactly in proportion to the change in price. Total expenditures are invariant to price changes in the unit-elastic region of the demand curve.

**Unlimited liability** A legal concept whereby the personal assets of the owner of a firm can be seized to pay off the firm's debts.

**Util** A representative unit by which utility is measured.

**Utility** The want-satisfying power of a good or service.

**Utility analysis** The analysis of consumer decision making based on utility maximization.

**Variable costs** Costs that vary with the rate of production. They include wages paid to workers and purchases of materials.

**Vertical merger** The joining of a firm with another to which it sells an output or from which it buys an input.

**Voluntary exchange** The act of trading, usually done on a voluntary basis in which both parties to the trade are subjectively better off after the exchange.

**Wants** The goods and services that people would buy if their incomes were unlimited.

**Zero-sum game** A game in which any gains within the group are exactly offset by equal losses by the end of the game.